VOICES-19

Their Legacies Live On

Stories Collected by

Brenda E. Cortez

Voices-19

Their Legacies Live On

Contributing Editor: Brenda E. Cortez

Associate Editors: Jean Sime, Shannon Phillips, Griffin Mill

Proofreaders: Judy Busalacchi, Lyda Rose Haerle

Contributing Authors: Jean Sime, Bari Himes, Jocelyn Himes, Sherry Horowitz Stein, Kim Letizi, Rosie Davis, Raenell Worrells, David Stedman, Patty Mazzola, Fiana Garza Tulip, Bert Foreman, John Lancos, Annette Allen, Mary Cabanillas, Marla Sarrel, Gina Sirico, Konstantina Dina Kess, Ira Richardson, Hannah Ernst, Amber Carter

Cover Design: Tabassum Hashmi
Front Cover Photo: Fiana Garza Tulip
Interior Layout: Michael Nicloy

All images have been provided by the individual contributors.

ISBN: 979-8-9853960-4-1

Published by BC Books, LLC, Franklin, Wisconsin
Quantity order requests may be emailed to the Publisher:
brenda@bcbooksllc.com

Printed in The United States of America

Donna,

Thank you for your support as we continue to help others, and let our loved ones memories live on.

♡

Brenda E. Cortez

Donna,

Thank you for writing our testimonial for our book. We are truely honored + love your work. Thank you for supporting our project + message for our lost loved ones. Their voices need to be heard! We look forward to deeping our relationship with you. Continued success to you! Regards — Jean ♡

Chapter #1 is my sister VIVIAN

DEDICATION

This book is dedicated to all those who have been impacted by COVID-19. We have all been affected in one way or another, but for those people who lost a loved one to the virus, life will never be the same. This book is dedicated to you and your families. My most heartfelt sympathies go out to all of you.

To all the essential workers, and frontline healthcare workers, who didn't get to stay safe inside their homes during the pandemic; many working tirelessly, risking their lives to help others. This book is dedicated to you.

To Jean Sime, who lost her sister Vivian early on in the pandemic. I mourned with you and I witnessed your pain, but I couldn't take it away. The only thing I could do was listen and help you keep Vivian's memory alive. This book is my way of doing that for you, and for all the others who have suffered such a tremendous loss. This book is for you, Jean, and for Viv.

To the courageous chapter authors who poured their hearts out, and shed many tears within these pages. Your loved ones are so proud of you. Thank you for entrusting me with the stories of your precious loved ones. I hope I've given them the proper respect they all deserve in creating this book to keep their legacies alive. It humbles me to be a part of this tribute, and it has been a true blessing to get to know your loved ones and celebrate the memories with you.

TABLE OF CONTENTS

INTRODUCTION

A CELEBRATION OF LIFE

As we rang in the 2020 new year, visions of a fresh start, full of dreams coming true, were on many of our minds, or at least that's what most of us were anticipating. No one could have ever imagined the devastation that was about to unfold in front of our very eyes. Something unfathomable. Something out of the history books. People had no idea what was coming. Like a runaway train, COVID-19 crashed into our lives. We were all targets, and no one was safe. People around the world hunkered down to try and stay safe, while others didn't have that option as they headed to the front lines, working endless hours, risking their lives daily. Our precious family members, who were supposed to be protected in the facilities they were living in, were not safe from the virus. Sadly, many lives were lost, and the losses continue even two years later.

As families locked down in the safety of their homes, many enjoyed reuniting with each other during the down time. It was a time of virtual teaching, never-ending Zoom meetings, game nights, and quality time at the dinner table. Paper products were in short supply, and necessities were rationed. Masks were required outside of the home, although they were difficult to obtain. Our essential workers, including healthcare workers, became heroes risking their lives to save others, often without the proper PPE they needed for their own safety. You will read about a few of these heroes in this book. We learned how truly precious life is, and that our lives can be changed or taken in an instant. COVID-19 has touched everyone in some way or another. It may have made a brief stop at your doorstep, but for many, it has turned their lives completely upside down, forever.

This book is a tribute to all of our lost loved ones and their families. It is a celebration of the life of the beautiful souls you will get to know in this book, but it is also a celebration of ALL the lives lost during the pandemic. We are mourning our dear loved ones, but we are also honoring who they were and what they meant to those who loved them. Through these courageous human beings, we give Covid a face. They are not just a number, and they will never be forgotten.

To all those who have lost a loved one during the pandemic, we send our heartfelt sympathy and condolences to you and your family. You are not alone. If you are grieving due to the loss of a loved one to COVID-19 and are in need of emotional support, please connect with our chapter authors, or find a support group (if you haven't already) to help you navigate through the pain. Please also consider professional counseling. Be sure to read the section at the end of this book, written by Rachelle Coffey, a psychotherapist and trauma-informed care specialist, for ways to cope with your grief and toxic stress.

Please join me as we *say their names* and allow their legacies to live on through all of us.

~ Brenda E. Cortez

Vivian's Story

HEAVEN NEEDED A HERO

By Jean Sime

"Click your heels together three times and say 'There's no place like home,' and you will be there" is one of the most famous lines from *The Wizard of Oz.*

On April 16th, 2020, my sister, Vivian Meitzler, went home to be with our mom, dad, babcia (grandma), and the rest of our angel family. This day changed my life forever as my only sister was taken away from us, suddenly, and without warning. My life shattered the night I received the call telling me she passed, and my heart is forever broken. I am sharing Viv's life, her story, so the world will never forget the legacy she leaves behind; the kind, caring, intelligent, witty, determined person with a heart of gold who lived every minute of her life as if it were her last. She was taken too soon, as were millions of other lives, robbed by this virus. Vivian was not just a number, nor will she ever be forgotten. She was a wife, a mother, a daughter, a sister, an aunt, and she was my best friend.

This is for you, Viv. This is your story… It needs to be told…

THE NIGHTMARE

March 2020 was the beginning of the pandemic nightmare that took so many innocent lives, including that of my loving sister. As we hunkered down in our own bubbles, we were in "lockdown" and unable to be with anyone other than our household members. Despite the risk, Vivian continued to go to work at her job as a Patient Access Representative in the emergency department of a local hospital. She reported to work every day, never knowing what disaster awaited her when she would enter the hospital's rotating doors. She knew the patients needed her, and she would not let them down. I could hear the anger in her voice as she cursed the awful beast called COVID-19. "What do you mean we can't see each other in person? I need to see my son, my 87-year-old dad, and my only sister." Viv wasn't a fan of change, or of being told what she could or could not do. But with her family, she understood this sacrifice was necessary to keep us "safe."

None of us truly understood this new virus. "It's a war zone in the hospital," Viv told me. "Patients are lined up in the hallways because there are no rooms for them." PPE (personal protective equipment) was in scarce supply and was not available to most hospital staff during this time. I gave her some of my KN95 masks, which I always have on hand. I'm a kidney transplant recipient and am no stranger to wearing masks. I said to myself, *If the hospital and the government won't protect my sister, then I will.* Sadly, no one, not even me, could keep her safe from this virus.

April 2020 began with Viv not feeling well. Her first symptoms were back pain and a high fever. Over the weekend, she tried everything to break her fever, but on Monday, April 6th, 2020, she called in sick and said she was going to the ER to get checked out. They advised her to stay home because they would turn her away unless she was having difficulty breathing. She went anyway, was tested for Covid, and they determined she had slight pneumonia. They gave Viv medication and sent her home to quarantine and await her results. During this time, she was brave, never mentioning to me that she had developed a cough and was having trouble breathing. I felt helpless. Darkness was looming, and there was nothing I could do to change it. No one knew how to stop this hostile intruder called COVID-19.

I visited Viv's doorstep daily, dropping off Vitamin C and D, Tylenol, Zinc, chicken soup, Gatorade, or any food she desired. She lost her sense of taste and smell, so nothing seemed appealing to her. The last time I saw her, she was standing behind the porch window screen, holding her cat, telling me not to worry. I felt her courage when she told me that she would be ok, but deep down, I knew it wasn't good. My soul was crushed; I sat in my car, tears running down my face. I don't know what possessed me to take a picture of her at that moment, but I did. I never imagined that this would be the last time I would see my sister, my best friend, alive.

On Wednesday, Viv's test results came back positive. The dreaded news pierced my heart. Her symptoms got worse, and she became more panicked. Viv asked her husband, Tim, to take her back to the ER the next day on Thursday, April 9th. I knew it wasn't good when she wanted him to drive, instead of her driving herself.

I never spoke with Viv on the phone while she was in the hospital. We only texted. They started her off with supplemental oxygen at first. Knowing this, I didn't want her to waste her breath talking to me on the phone. Oh, how I regret not calling her and hearing her voice. To this day, I still can't bring myself to look at our text message exchanges that remain on my phone. The pain is still too raw.

While Viv was hospitalized on Thursday, my family appointed me as the spokesperson to communicate with the doctors daily and relay any updates. That emotional roller coaster was full of hope and anguish. At first, they allowed me to call the nurse twice per day for an update, but then they asked me to only call once in the evening. Complications from the virus included kidney failure, which resulted in kidney dialysis, and very low blood pressure. Along with the breathing issues, all of this led to the one thing that no one ever wants: to be placed on a ventilator.

Vivian passed away on Thursday, April 16th, 2020, just one week after they admitted her to the hospital. That day my world stopped. A beautiful, amazing woman was gone, just like that. My sister, my best friend, left this world. I will never forget the moment the phone rang. *Tell me this isn't happening.* Numb and in shock, I had to ask the nurse (this courtesy was not offered) if he would FaceTime my family, so we could say our goodbyes. We could not be with Viv in person at the hospital because of the no-visitor restriction. She lay peacefully in the hospital bed as we said our goodbyes, outside of her house, in the middle of the night, socially distanced from each other. Masked up for protection, we could not even hug each other for comfort. It was too risky. COVID-19 was not only claiming lives, but it also stole how we grieve. Because of this, my family and so many others who lost a loved one at the beginning of the pandemic, especially during lockdown, still suffer from PTSD and PGD (Prolonged Grief Disorder).

We were one of the fortunate families allowed to have a thirty-minute funeral viewing with ten of our "closest" family members. How do you choose "your closest" family and friends? We buried Viv in one of her favorite outfits, in a purple casket. She had made her wishes clear to us; when it was her time, she wanted her casket to be purple since it was her favorite color. More specifically, she requested an open casket so she could see those who came to pay their respects. Unfortunately, it was only her immediate family she was able to see that day. As our seven cars followed her hearse to the cemetery, I kept thinking about how angry Viv must be at this horrific virus for taking the celebration of her life away from her friends and family. The dagger was pushed deeper into our wounds when we found out only one person could witness her burial. Who do you choose? My nephew, Steven, Viv's son, was brave and represented our family at her gravesite while we waited in separate cars outside the cemetery. I'm so sorry, my sweet sister. You deserved so much more. This pain and regret are forever ingrained into our souls.

THE DASH

May 1959 – April 2020

Each time I visit Viv's gravestone, the tears roll down my face. I ask God why he took her so soon. Why did she have to die this way? Alone, suffering, and in pain? A sharp pain rips through me each time I imagine how scared she must have been. What thoughts were running through her head? Did she know she was going to die? Viv was supposed to be the one looking at my headstone, not me looking at hers.

But if you knew Viv, you knew she wouldn't want us to cry for her. "Ok, guys, enough already. Get over it and move on," is probably what she'd say. For someone else looking at the dates on her headstone, they might focus on her birthdate, or the date she passed, and think, *How sad. She was so young. She must have had underlying conditions.* Rather than look at the dates, Viv would want you to focus on the DASH in between, which represented her life… It's all about the DASH. Live life to the fullest like she did. Viv wasn't financially rich, but everything she had, she valued. She had a wonderful family with lots of love. I swear, "fun" should have been her middle name. She made life fun for all of us. Even a routine trip to the grocery store turned into an adventure, as we would be laughing for no reason while strolling through the frozen food section. I sure miss those times, but Covid has taken those silly sister moments away from me. Live the life you love; love the life you live. That was my sister, Vivian Meitzler. Big or little… just enjoy the ride.

Vivian was born in Jersey City, New Jersey, to Mary and Kazimierz Luszcz. She was the middle child, between our older brother, Charlie, and me. We were blessed with loving parents from Italian and Polish heritage. Vivian moved to the beat of her own drum, always shining, dancing, and smiling. Maybe it was the middle child within her that gave her extra flair and passion to shine bright.

Sitting still to learn in school was a challenge for Viv. She learned from doing and participating. As kids, we asked her if she had "ants in her pants," because she was always moving, never idle. Little did we know back then, it was because her mind was always racing with ideas and things she would rather be doing. Even as an adult, she lived for days off from work, so she could be out and on the go. I can still hear Viv calling me on her day off, asking me "What's up for today? What do you want to do because I'm not staying home?" What I wouldn't do to hear her voice one more time! Even though school was not her thing, ironically, as an adult, she was the first one to pick up a book to read or do research in a medical or legal journal. Her desire to learn new things and stay informed came from the flame burning deep inside her soul. Never afraid to give her opinion or question things, one night she was with her husband at the doctor's office, chiming in, giving the doctor her opinion on the situation. He leaned over and asked her, "Are you the doctor, or am I?"

Growing up, Viv enjoyed every minute she could. As a young teenager, she loved watching Donny Osmond every Friday night. I can still envision her sitting on our living room floor, smack dab in front of our console TV, wearing her purple socks (purple was Donny's favorite color too), crying at the top of her lungs as he sang.

The song was "Puppy Love," and her heart beat out of her chest, feeling as if Donny were singing it just for her. Even as an adult, Viv still crushed on Donny Osmond. She enjoyed most of the 70s shows, including *The Partridge Family, The Brady Bunch*, and *The Love Boat*, especially. Cruising was her passion, and she loved to go with her family. We always knew where to find her… hanging out at the pool, spraying "Sun-In" in her hair, working on her glistening tan. As Viv got older, and the disco years came along, she lived for going to the club and dancing the night away with her girlfriends. Although Viv and I were seven years apart, I remember admiring her through a small crack in the door's opening, watching her get all dolled up for her Saturday night clubbing adventure. Her makeup was perfect, and her Danskin outfit or Jordache jeans fit her just right. I watched in envy, wishing with all my might that I were old enough to join her. With her head held high, she headed out, ready for the time of her life. *Saturday Night Fever* was all the rage back then, and until the day she passed, it remained one of her all-time favorite movies. John Travolta was her other celebrity crush.

After Viv graduated high school, she knew college was not for her. She began her successful career at the Prudential Law Library, where she worked for 31 years. After they forced her to leave by taking "early retirement" at age 48, she found work at a local hospital in their medical library and then transferred several years later to the emergency department, which, sadly, would lead to the demise of her life. Viv thrived in the healthcare industry, and even though she was not a registered nurse, she just wanted to help people, especially children. She educated herself by reading medical journals, articles published by doctors, and by doing research for the medical staff. Her supervisors, patients, and coworkers all adored her. With kindness and compassion, Viv would do anything to help anyone. If you met her, she probably touched your soul with her sparkle. Her light shined so bright here on Earth since she lived her life to the fullest. "It's all about the dash!"

MY WIFE

by Timothy Meitzler

I was only 17, and Viv was 19 when we met. I told her on our first date that I was going to marry her because I knew right away. After five years of dating, Viv's mom told me to "poop or get off the pot!" "You are taking too long!" she said, and she was right, so on August 21st, 1982, I married Vivian, the love of my life! At first, we struggled financially, as most newlyweds do. Rent was high, and Viv worked two jobs to help us make ends meet. She didn't sweat the small stuff, as she trusted things would always work out. We enjoyed our life together as husband and wife. She taught me how to cook and always told me I could do anything. Viv believed in me, even when I doubted myself. We had plans to grow old together, but now, because of this virus, I must grow old by myself.

On May 31st, 1987, we received our greatest blessing: the birth of our only son, Steven. He brought so much joy to our family, and Viv beamed with pride as a new mom. She always supported and helped at Steven's school whenever she could. Carnivals, sporting events, fundraisers, school bingo… Viv was there. She and Steven shared a love of horror movies, and they couldn't wait until the next one premiered in the theaters so they could see it together. With all her heart, Viv supported Steven's dream of becoming a film director one day, and I know she's still supporting him from up above.

Even after 38 years of marriage, I cherished every moment we had together and every wonderful memory we made. I miss EVERYTHING about her! Covid took the love of my life away from me, from all of us, and our lives will never be the same. How can I "live" without her? All I can do now is cherish what we had through memories and photos. Memories I hope will never fade, memories of family vacations, traveling, and going out on Friday nights for a special dinner. Friday nights used to be very special for us, but now they are the hardest for me as I still wait for her to walk through the door asking, "Where are we going to eat tonight?"

Our travels took us to many fun places; Ocean City, Maryland, Hershey Park, Pennsylavania, Seaside Heights, New Jersey; and our quick weekend getaways to Atlantic City. Slots and crab legs at the buffet were pure delight for Viv. She LOVED Atlantic City. All her stress and worries disappeared the moment we entered the hotel and casino. What I wouldn't do to take her there just one more time.

All of Vivian's feline friends enjoyed her compassion throughout the years. She adored animals, especially her previous cats Jerry and Hershey, and her most recent kitty, Becker. The poor guy was only a baby when Viv passed. She only had a few months to love him, but I will tell you Viv's spirit definitely lives on through Becker. He is always so curious, running around the house and literally climbing walls. Sometimes, he cries and stares at the ceiling or the loveseat that Viv would rest on. They say animals can sense the presence of spirits, and he definitely senses hers! To honor her love for animals, Viv was a huge supporter of the ASPCA and PETA.

Viv was famous in our family for her apple "pit" pie and her delicious meatballs. Besides crab legs, she loved a great dish of shrimp scampi, chicken franchise, or a nice slice of Jersey pizza. She loved frogs, dolphins, and penguins, and she collected rubber duckies of all shapes and sizes. They made her happy. Viv had to have her morning tea, Lipton or green tea only. If she didn't start her day off with her tea, she was not a happy camper. My sister-in-law, Jean, even buried Viv with her favorite tea bags since we weren't sure heaven had the ones she liked.

If you had ears to listen, then Viv was talking. She had the gift of gab. Her family and I joked, if you are ever going on a long car ride, take Viv with you because she will keep you awake for the entire journey. Whether a stranger or a friend, she could talk to anyone about anything. Sadly, Covid has silenced her voice forever. I still have an answering machine at home, and I cannot bring myself to erase her voice recording. I never want to forget how she sounded.

Smart and witty, Viv knew how to motivate people. She was a born leader, not a follower. She treated everyone with respect, expecting nothing in return. What Vivian gave to others is exactly what you'd want in a best friend. She was my best friend and always will be. It took very little to make her happy because she wasn't materialistic. She just wanted to be with her family. Family came first, and she loved us with all of her heart and soul. Viv would call her dad and her sister every day just to share her day with them.

Vivian Meitzler, you will always be the love and light of my life. Until we meet again, my love…

MY MOTHER

By Steven Meitzler

My mom was a great person, and I miss her every day. As I smile and think of what I would like to share with the world about her, I will say the only way I can really express or explain how she touched my life is by sharing a few of my favorite stories about her.

CLEM KADIDDLEHOPPER SOCKS

Every year, my elementary school hosted a back-to-school dance in the fall. I was excited at first but then disliked going to the dances because many other students in my class would make fun of me for going. Ironic, since many of them also went. Looking back, I think they made fun of me, not because I went to the dances, but because my mom was the chaperone most of the time. One year, I didn't want to go, but my mother insisted I go because some of my friends would be there, and I would have fun. That night, I got dressed in a nice shirt and pants and wore black dress shoes. My mom was rushing me so I wouldn't be late because she was a chaperone. I quickly put on a pair of socks, laced up my shoes, and got into her car. We only got as far as a stoplight around the corner, when she looked over at me and asked what socks I was wearing. I pulled my pant leg up a little and said "white." Suddenly, she blurted out, "Take those Clem Kadiddlehopper socks off! You can't go to the dance wearing white socks with black dress shoes and pants!" The funny thing is, I don't even know if the "Clem" person she was referring to is real or not. To this day, I smile and think of my mom every time I put my white sweat socks on.

SWIMMING LESSONS AND A DATE

Friday nights were for swimming. When I was around four or five, my mother took me to a gym in town that gave swimming lessons a few times a week. Our day was on Friday. Along with swimming lessons, Friday was also "date night" for my mother and me. She worked a lot, so Friday nights were our night to spend quality mother and son time together. Next door, literally within a stone's throw, was and still is a McDonald's. After the swimming lesson, we would go next door, and she would treat me to a Happy Meal. Mostly chicken nuggets. I swear I could live off them if it wouldn't kill my cholesterol. We sat, ate, and talked. Since I was so young at the time, I don't remember what we spoke about, but I always remember getting to spend time alone with her. How I wish I could share some nuggets with her today.

BASKETBALL GAMES

Out of all the basketball team mothers, my mother was the biggest basketball fan. I played basketball from fifth through eighth grade. She drove me to every game and watched from the sidelines. I could hear her shouting encouraging words, and sometimes a few questionable ones if an opposing team had done something wrong during the game. I remember a specific game where she kept me going. It was against St. Rose. I don't recall the exact location, but I remember that the floor was finished in a professional design, the court was regulation NBA size, and the players were way taller than we were. They were a tough team. In the beginning of the fourth and final quarter, we were winning by a few points, but they turned it around and started crushing us. Near the last minute or two of the game, I was very upset and felt very discouraged. I wanted to foul myself out because the game was pretty much over. At that moment, I looked up from the sideline at the audience and saw my mom staring at me. The referee blew the whistle to let us know the timeout was over. I took my position on the court, and when the referee blew the whistle for the second time to signal that the game was back on, my mother immediately went into full "Rudy" mode. She began chanting and cheering (as they did in the movie Rudy). I knew I couldn't give up, so I kept playing until the final buzzer sounded. We lost, but with dignity. At the end of the game, I went over to my mother and soaked up all of her praise. She said she was so proud of me for giving it my all and for playing a great game. She always believed in me, which gave me confidence and pride in myself.

These are only a few of the many, many stories I have to tell about her. My mother was a fair person. She worked hard and sacrificed for the family. I know she loved me and was so proud of me. I could do no wrong in her eyes. My mom made a house into a home. For all these reasons and so many more, I will always love her.

I hope you are still proud of me, mom, as you look down from heaven! I will be forever proud of you. Thank you for being my mother.

MY SISTER AND BEST FRIEND

By Jean Sime

My sister Vivian was my life, my soul, and I still have to catch my breath when I think about how she is gone. From the day I was born, she was my biggest fan, and she believed in me no matter how crazy of an idea I had. Viv was my protector, my shield, my rock, and she would do anything for me. When I was recovering from my many surgeries, she was there with me, for me, researching options. She was my voice when I could not speak. During my kidney transplant journey, she was my number one advocate. I can only imagine how upset she is, knowing that because she passed from Covid, she could not be an organ donor as was her last wish. Viv was there, literally holding my hand when life got tough, and she always told me that, no matter what, we would get through it together. How am I going to "get through" life without her? Viv was my best friend, and we loved spending our time together, whether it was at the beach and the boardwalk, the mall, or just riding in my car, listening to my show tunes (which she despised). How do you fill such a void? A loss so painful, losing your only sister, your big sister, your best friend?

Death and tragedy bring people together. I have been blessed to have met so many other mourning families in the Covid community. They have helped me cope with the loss of Viv, a pain that only those who have lost a loved one to Covid could truly understand. They are part of my family now.

To honor Viv, I vow to keep her legacy alive. Our family dedicated boards on the Seaside Heights Boardwalk in Viv's memory. Seaside had been "our place" since we were little, so it was only fitting to place a permanent memorial for Vivian and my dad there. He passed away only four months after Viv passed. I'm convinced he died of a broken heart from losing her. How do you bury your own child?

There are many Covid memorials being created, not only across the U.S. but globally as well. Viv has been honored as far as London, England, Ireland, and Poland. She loved to travel but never had the chance to experience all these amazing places in her earthly life. My goal in carrying on Viv's legacy is for her to be honored in every state across the United States. I hope she will be honored some day in Australia, South Africa, and Greece; they are places we both dreamed of visiting together. Spread your angel wings, my dear sister, and keep flying high.

I know Vivian is still with me as she walks beside me every day. I promise to live my "dash" in her honor, living my best life as she did and would want me to. Thank you, Viv, for sending me earth angels to support me and love me in your absence. Your legacy lives on forever through me, your family, all who loved you, and in this book, a beautiful tribute honoring our lost loved ones. Thank you for not only being my sister, but for being my best friend and my hero! You will always be with me like a handprint on my heart. You're a doll, Viv! I love you and always will. Forever in my heart, forever my sister ♥.

ABOUT JEAN

Jean Sime lives in the northwestern part of New Jersey with Eric, her husband of 28 years. She is a graduate from Rutgers University with a degree in Business Management and Finance. Jean was a vice president for a large retail bank for 31 years. In March of 2020, her career shifted due to the pandemic. She is currently an editor and proofreader for several publishers. She enjoys spending time with her family and friends, time at the Jersey Shore, music, and traveling.

In June of 2019, Jean received a kidney from a living donor. She is a coauthor in the book, *Because of Organ Donation*, where she shares her transplant journey. Jean is active in the transplant community. She not only volunteers, but is also a mentor with The Transplant Journey, Inc.

Jean is an active member in the Covid community. She belongs to several support groups and keeps Vivian's memory alive by honoring her in the many memorials being created. Jean is honored to share her sister Vivian's story in this beautiful tribute, and she continues to keep her legacy alive.

You can connect with Jean through email at jeansime23@gmail.com, Facebook, or LinkedIn: Jean Sime.

Vivian at 3 1/2 years old.

A great memory from our childhood. Vivian with her baby sister Jeanie and her brother Charlie.

Vivian with her mom and dad on her wedding day, August 21, 1982.

Vivian, her husband, Tim, and their son, Steven, enjoying a family cruise together.

Vivian with her brother-in-law, Eric, her sister, Jean, her husband, Tim, her son, Steven, and her dad on a cruise.

Vivian and her husband Timothy enjoying their vacation at Ocean City, Maryland.

Vivian with her dad and sister, Jean, celebrating his birthday in Atlantic City, New Jersey. Vivian loved escaping to Atlantic City!

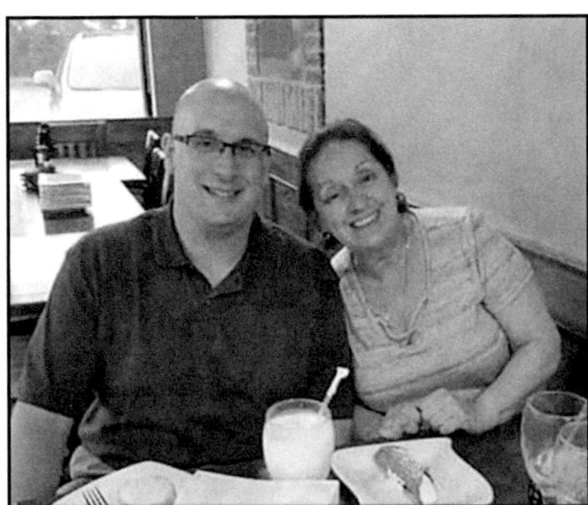

Vivian and her son, Steven, celebrating his birthday.

Vivian really enjoyed eating crab legs. She is also wearing the shirt that her memory bear is made from.

Vivian, with her sister, Jean, celebrating her 60th birthday. We never imagined it would be Viv's last birthday with us.

Rose's Story

A SURVIVOR'S TALE

By Bari Himes & Jocelyn Himes

The same song at different points in our life can evoke different raw emotions. The song "Seasons of Love," from the Broadway show *Rent*, always moved me. Prior to my mom passing, I would sing along with the cast and enjoy the composition for the pure beauty of the show. Now, when I hear it, the lyrics move me to tears.

How do you measure the life of someone? Is my mom to be remembered for her contributions to this world – my life, that of her granddaughter, the hearts she let in, or solely the way she died?

My mom, Rose Phillips, was the daughter of Sol and Bessie Kravitz. Both her parents came to America in search of a better life after fleeing the pogroms in Eastern Europe. They overcame the hardships of having to leave family in Russia and watching family members get killed, right before their eyes, for their beliefs. As a child, I remember listening to the stories of how my bubby and poppop (my grandparents) came to America, and how poppop fled to three different countries until he was safely on the shores. As a young girl, Bubby hid in a wagon with others, pitchforks poking at them while they were hiding in the hay. In their only child, they had instilled the values of survival and putting family first.

My mother grew up hearing these survival stories and recounting the stories of how other family members came to America. As time went on, my mother became known as the family historian. She told tales of how family members came through Ellis Island, and the hardships they had faced to get there. Memories of hearing these stories over cups of coffee – hers black with Sweet'N Low, sharing bagels over a smoked fish platter, my mom reminding me to "Vatch de baner" (Watch the bones) – are forever etched in my mind. We often said that, at some point, we would need to record these stories.

We never had the opportunity.

My mother was the epitome of what it means to be a strong woman. When I was younger, we used to watch the soap opera *All My Children* together, and she compared us to the Kane women – resilient. My mother was an only child, and I am an only child. She would curse me, saying I should have a child just like me.

My mom was very superstitious, and she had a superstition for just about everything, or so it seemed. If you drop a fork, step on it before you pick it up. "Don't ask me why. Just do it," she would say. If someone sneezes while talking about someone who has passed on, the person who sneezes has to pull their right ear up. I swear my right ear is longer because of following this practice over the years. A couple of years later, when we took my parents out to dinner to tell them I was expecting, I saw my mother get faklempt (choked up with emotion), her eyes welling with tears. It was one of the few times in my life I saw her cry.

Throughout my teenage years, my father was ill. My mother worked for an insurance company, but she had left that job to help him run his travel agency. She kept the house, took him to doctor appointments, and then later dialysis. When I was 18, my father passed away from complications of diabetes. My mom and I were in the room with him. I held his hand as he passed, and my mom had me switch spots with her. "I don't want you to feel him go cold," she said as she held his hand and I held hers. My mom was always my protector, sometimes to a fault. Often, I was unsure of her motive, but looking back, she thought she was shielding me.

Nineteen years after my dad died, my mom felt a lump in her armpit and didn't say anything or go to the doctor. It wasn't until it became quite enlarged that she made an appointment with her doctor. He sent her directly to the emergency room, and they diagnosed her with stage four metastatic breast cancer. In her perpetual pattern of resilience, my mother was not going to tell me about her diagnosis, but a nurse who thought I already knew accidentally informed me. When I went to see my mother in the hospital, her pride took over, and she told me everything was fine. I sat and talked with her until she finally sensed that I knew. Reluctantly, she shared her secret but followed it with the boisterous declaration that she was not doing treatment, and that was that. Like it was no big deal, she asked me for her cigarettes. I went into her pocketbook, took her cigarettes and lighter, and told her she had just quit. She was less than pleased with me but never had another cigarette. My grandmother-in-law, Lena, called her later that day and demanded she do the treatment. No way was she going to do that to her granddaughter! Setting her pride aside once again, my mom called to tell me she would do the treatment. When I asked her what had changed, she said Lena told her she had to and then hung up. If it weren't for Lena, I would not have had the next ten years with my mom.

While I was pregnant, my mom would tell me, "I take the curse back," and then laugh. The first time she saw her only grandchild was another one of the few times I saw her eyes swell with tears. My daughter became a beacon of love in my mom's hardened soul. A light that had been dim for so long began to shine again.

My mom and I had a complicated relationship. Growing up, we were not close. Our strong personalities created a rift between us. She was busy taking care of things that needed day-to-day tending, physical things, but emotionally, she was distant. When my father became ill and had surgeries, the responsibility of caring for him at home fell on me as a teenager. By the time my mom was diagnosed with stage four metastatic breast cancer, I was no stranger to the role of caregiver. She was at stage four for ten years, and I always thought it would be her demise. For ten years, I expected the inevitable. Then, one Monday morning, she called me while I was at work, and panic punched me in the gut; I had immediately thought something was wrong. Instead, my mother informed me she was in remission. *She's lying,* I thought. *Another heroic attempt on her part to protect me.* I told her I didn't believe her. "Call the oncologist yourself if you don't believe me," she said. I dialed him right up, and he told me even he had been taken aback and had to take her results home over the weekend to review. He had no explanation. I was dumbfounded; at the same time, my heart was doing a dance inside my chest. How was this possible? Did we finally have our reprieve, our miracle? Six months later, the results were the same; they had found no tumors.

My mom was a typical Jewish mother. She always made sure I brought a jacket when the temperature dropped so "I shouldn't get cold." Yiddish was spoken between her and my bubby, and I learned to understand some. Yiddish was used to describe things that, according to her, just couldn't be translated. When I didn't feel well, of course, matzah ball soup was the cure-all. My mom wasn't much of a cook, so my soup came from a restaurant, but it was the thought. When I had knee surgery, I got matzah ball soup. Matzah ball soup fixes everything.

We didn't go to synagogue, and I didn't have a bat mitzvah when I was 13. My mom gave me the choice, so I opted out. Later, as an adult, I changed my mind and had my bat mitzvah when I was seven months pregnant.

My mom kept her circle relatively small. For over 60 years, she had a best friend who lived in Florida, and she had had another friend for over 40 years; I had grown up with their children. They were like family. Jason was one of my best friends; for almost 40 years, he was almost like a brother as well. He later became like a son to my mom. The mom I knew growing up was not one to socialize. After my father passed, she was more content to stay home. Her spirits lifted, however, when she started working for the IRS as a tax examiner. She began to crawl out of her shell, and she made several friends at work.

My daughter gave my mom the name "Ba-bo" since she could not pronounce "Bubby" when she was little. Ba-bo thought the world of her granddaughter. I knew my mom loved me, but her granddaughter was her entire existence. My daughter adored her Ba-bo just the same. They shared a secret for many years, which I only recently found out about. When my mom watched my daughter, she secretly took her out to fast-food restaurants (knowing I didn't want my daughter to eat fast food). My daughter was cautiously instructed, "Don't tell your mother," so she kept the secret from me for many years.

Over the years, the lymphedema and the side effects of her cancer treatment had affected my mom's body, and she had several falls in her apartment. Thankfully, we had moved her into an apartment near my work, which made drop-ins more convenient. At one point, she went to the hospital three times in the same week because of her falls. While she was there, I met with the social worker to discuss getting her help at home. I fought through unbelievable red tape as they perpetuated an innocent-until-proven-guilty policy. Social Services wanted me to send her home without in-home services for 30 days to prove she was a fall risk and in need of support. I called Harrisburg, which is our state-level facility, and urged them to provide support, but none was given. My only choice was to place her in a nursing home because they would not pay for someone to come and provide assistance in her home. My mom stayed in the skilled nursing facility, and then, when insurance no longer covered her stay, they expected her to transition home without help. Not on my watch! I knew what would happen. There was only one option, and it was one of the hardest conversations I had ever had with my mother. I remember it vividly. In order to protect her as she had me, living in a nursing home was the only option. I watched my mom, who rarely showed emotion, sit and cry as she perceived her new, dreaded world. "Promise me you will put me in a nice place like this one. Don't throw me away," she pleaded.

After more hoop-jumping with the social worker, my mother had her new home. She retired from the IRS and lived in the nursing home for the next two years. While living there, my once reclusive mother came out of her darkness. She joined a committee and a jewelry-making group, and she ate dinner with friends almost every night.

Every Friday night, I called to wish her a Shabbat Shalom. Most of those nights, we would meet for dinner. For the next two years, my mom and I became best friends. I finally had the mother I had always wanted. We laughed, talked about my daughter and my job, shared stories, pictures, and drank bloody marys. It became our Friday night ritual. My daughter would share blintzes with her, and no meal was complete until my mom had asked for Moose Tracks ice cream. She delighted purely in a bowl of Moose Tracks. If they didn't have her ice cream in the bistro, my mom would boldly say, "I know the third floor has some. You can get it there." They let her know the third floor was also out of Moose Tracks. "But I just had it at lunch," she would insist. "Oh, then get me a coffee ice cream." It was almost predictable and always laughable. Afterward, my mom and daughter would head to the chessboard, even though neither one of them knew how to play chess. They invented their own game called "Checkerchess." Their game had rules only the two of them knew, and they would sit and play for at least an hour. "Checkerchess" was followed by a trip to my mom's room where my daughter would style her Ba-bo's hair or do her makeup. Afterward, we would watch TV, and the two of them would argue over what shows to watch.

In 2020, people were talking about a new virus called "Covid" and began wearing masks. At the beginning of March, I visited my mom, and a nurse brought her pills while my mom and I were discussing Covid. The nurse was not wearing PPE (personal protective equipment). She smiled as we continued our conversation about the seriousness of Covid. Apparently, I was the only one who thought it was serious then. My mom told me, "You are just sensitive because of where you work." (I work with students with special needs.)

"No, Mom, it's serious. People are dying from it," I told her.

"Eh, Covid Shmovid," she said, brushing it off.

I rolled my eyes and sighed. The conversation was dropped.

Two weeks later, the nursing home closed to visitors. Although we talked daily, I couldn't visit my mom. Our special dinners had to wait. "Checkerchess" was on pause. Passover came, and my mom, who was never one to use technology, took part in our Seder (Passover meal and prayers) the first night through Zoom. The nursing home staff respectfully helped her several times when she would accidentally log off.

Then Wednesday, April 15th, 2020, came. I wasn't able to reach my mom for two days. I called the nursing home and requested the supervisor. They told me my mom had been belligerent the night before. It had taken several individuals to get her in bed, and they put her on five liters of oxygen. My mom didn't use oxygen. Why wasn't I called? No one could answer me. I received a call from a staff member who was close to my mom. She was concerned because my mom hadn't recognized her. If she could get permission, she asked me if I would come there. Absolutely! Permission granted. They checked my temperature (I was already wearing a mask), and I sprinted to my mom's room. She lay on the bed, looking pale, nothing like the woman I knew as my mom. Half a bagel and a Styrofoam cup of water were next to her. She could not hold the bagel to take a bite. I broke off small pieces and fed them to her while watching her chew without purpose. I asked if she wanted water, and she nodded. Unable to hold the Styrofoam cup, she dumped some of the water on herself, so I held the cup and straw as she tried to sip. Lacking energy, she couldn't pull the water to her lips. I asked if she wanted to go to the hospital. My mother, who was never at a loss for words, said, "I no go." She had told the nurse the same thing earlier. "That's not my mom," I told her.

She was not making sense. Briefly, I left the room to grab a cup of coffee. When I returned, she looked confused. "You don't remember me being here giving you bites of bagel?" I asked her. She shook her head no. "You don't remember me giving you sips of water?" Again, she shook her head. I told the nurse to make the call. "You want me to call the doctor?" she asked. I replied, "No. Call 911. She's leaving."

The first responders showed up in hazmat suits and had me put a mask on my mom. One of the EMTs took her temperature and looked at the other. Her temperature was 101. I asked if I could ride with her, but the answer was a firm "no." In my car, I followed them to the hospital, even though I knew I would not be allowed in. After she arrived, I walked into the ER to explain that I was her POA and that they needed to let me know what was happening. They asked for my cell number and brushed me off to the parking lot. It was the longest 20 minutes of my life.

After a bit, I called and found out they were still assessing her. I called again, and they had me go home since I didn't live far. They gave me a diagnosis: sepsis, pneumonia, and Covid. They were keeping her in the ER because they had no rooms available. I called every couple of hours for updates. Two days later, on Friday, my mom finally got a room and called me. She told me she was coming home, but I told her I had spoken to the doctors and she had to stay. "No, they told me I am fine. I can come home."

"No, Mom," I insisted. "You have sepsis, Covid, and pneumonia. You have to stay."

"Oh, you are going to leave me here like you left me in the home?" she said and hung up.

Saturday and Sunday, we talked again, and she had no recollection of having talked to me on Friday. I was still calling the staff every couple of hours for updates. Monday, I received a phone call from the doctor, telling me to hurry up and get there. I panicked and thought, *This is it*. My "brother" Jason and I ran to the hospital. There were 112 people on what used to be a cardiac floor; it had been converted into a "Covid" floor. My mom was one of three people not on a ventilator. Two doors from my mom, I passed by a man, and our eyes locked for a few seconds. I will never forget his face for the rest of my life. He stared at me, pleading, fear in his eyes. My soul quivered. I will never know what happened to him, and it haunts me.

They told me I couldn't go in my mom's room, so I had to look at her through a small window and make a decision regarding her end of life. I refused. I needed to be with her. After debate, they dressed me in full PPE, and I went into my mom's room. She asked me, "What the f...k are you doing here?" Yep, that's my mom. We talked, but she was more concerned that she was contagious, and I was in the room. I told her why I was there, and she made me promise no morphine, and no ventilator. "You know my wishes," she stated. She said she wasn't in pain. "Well, my leg hurts a little from the lymphedema, but I'm fine." She didn't have trouble breathing. "How's the baby?" she asked. I had her FaceTime with my daughter, my dogs, and my mother-in-law. The conversation was perfectly normal. As I was leaving, I told her I loved her. "Yeah," she said. I said it again. "Yeah, I love you too," she replied. According to the family doctor I called after my visit, her stats were normal. The next day, her stats were the same. I called every couple of hours, and they remained the same.

On Wednesday, April 22nd, 2020, while on a video call at work, I got a phone call. I told the teacher I was on the chat with to hold on, since it was probably just the hospital giving me an update to adjust my mom's meds. That teacher, Dana, who would later become one of my best friends and the merchandise mastermind of the group I would soon create, watched as I took the phone call notifying me my mom had passed. I yelled at the doctor to take it back. "Stop saying that!"

"Bari, your mom passed away," he said again.

"I told you to stop saying that. Take it back," I demanded. I then asked the doctor to tell me she didn't die alone. He could not; he wasn't at the hospital. In the blink of an eye, my world turned dark. The piercing pain was like no other. I immediately left work and drove to the hospital. I really do not know how I got there. Outside of my mom's room, I met an "angel." She told me she was with my mom when she passed and prayed over her. I thanked the nurse "angel" and shared with her that all I wanted to know was that she didn't die alone.

"I hope you're not upset, but I'm Catholic and prayed for her. I know..."

Before she could finish her sentence, I told her God is God, and I thanked her. I asked if I could hug her, and we embraced, PPE to PPE. As we pulled away, I could see the tears in her eyes. There really are angels on Earth.

As I entered my mom's room, I took a mental picture of everything – the small window I had peered through, the blanket sitting on a windowsill, the white board with my info, the extra bedding and blue cloths sitting near the bed for use, along with a box of gloves. I didn't want to forget anything. I grabbed a blanket from under the window they had wanted me to view her from, and I covered her, not wanting her to be cold. She would have done the same for me. I stroked her hair, held her hand, and told her I loved her. She still felt warm. How could this be real? I had just seen her less than two days ago. Jason was in the room with me, and we prayed. I felt myself dropping to my knees. How could I have no parents left? I wanted to scream. This had to be a nightmare! *Someone, please wake me up.*

When I got home, my daughter asked how Ba-bo was doing. The pit in my stomach ached even more when I told her I had something to tell her. She thought I wanted her to talk to my mom, and she motioned for my phone. I shook my head no and said, "I just came from the hospital. Ba-bo died." I couldn't believe those words came out of my mouth. My daughter ran upstairs and let out the most gut-wrenching scream. I felt it deep in my soul. I ran upstairs to console her, but she asked to be alone. If I couldn't comprehend what had just happened, how could I expect a 10 year old to make sense of it?

Trying to plan for my mother's funeral, the next couple of days were a blur. The woman who loved to feel pretty could not have her hair or makeup done, as she had been deemed too contagious. We didn't get to pick out her favorite outfit because she had to be buried in her hospital nightgown. I begged the funeral home to let me come there to change her and do her makeup, but they wouldn't allow it. Had I known this, I would have done her hair and makeup when I was with her in the hospital. After much debate, they allowed an outfit of hers to be placed in the casket. Only ten people were allowed to attend my mother's funeral (the entire service had to be at the cemetery). Can you imagine trying to pick the ten most important people to pay homage to a life? The funeral director and I counted as part of the ten, as did my daughter and the rabbi. The rabbi graciously decided to attend virtually so there would be one more spot for a loved one. People paid their respects virtually. At the end of the service, in our tradition, it is the greatest honor to help bury your loved one. There was a small hand shovel for everyone to place earth on the casket. I looked for the large shovel for me to bury my mother out of respect. The funeral director informed me that I could not fulfill this honor, since even in death she could possibly contaminate the soil. They had to have a backhoe fill in the hole with dirt and then put a cement liner on top. My best friend Tiffany, the only one who got away with calling my mom Aunt Rose (even though she had hated the title), stayed and waited for two hours for them to fill the hole. No one came to fill the hole. My mom did not get the dignity she deserved in death.

Shiva is a period of time where friends and family come to the home of the deceased to pay respect. Prayers are said each night, food is brought in, and people share stories of the departed. Of course, this was virtual, and I had to call friends to join us for prayers where normally I would have had a full house of people. Again, another dignity stripped.

When my mom passed, I did not know anyone else who had lost a loved one to Covid, but I had connected with several people on Survivor Corps when my mom was diagnosed. It is a support group on Facebook for those who have contracted Covid. Almost 600 total strangers had prayed for my mom to recover. When she passed, there were continued prayers. Several of the people who I met through the group had also lost loved ones to Covid. In May of 2020, because of my pain and grief, I created a Facebook support group called "Inlovingmemory19." My daughter designed the logo, which is a yellow rose (yellow for Covid and a rose for my mom's name). The group has members internationally and has become a small, but mighty, community. We are truly a family. Everyone supports one another through our rough emotional moments, such as birthdays, "angel-versaries," and those times when our loved ones would normally have been there for us.

My daughter, Jocelyn, and I will never forget my mom. She was such a huge part of our lives. Together, we make hamantaschen every year for the holiday of Purim, and we make a special plate of just mohn (poppyseed) for my mom, since it was her favorite flavor.

I have found a voice I never knew I had. I was never one to be quiet; I am my mother's daughter, but her death has made me become an advocate. I have spoken at the Pennsylvania COVID-19 Remembrance, on radio and podcasts, took part in memorials, and have been honored to support other groups, as we are all here for the same purpose. We are working to bring awareness to the truth that this did not have to happen, and it does not have to continue to happen. My mother did not have the opportunity to get vaccinated, but now that opportunity exists. We can save lives. Losing one more life is one too many. Families like mine are hurting; we will never have closure. We need to remember the names, the voices, the people behind the numbers.

Do you look at the impact of the pandemic solely as a number, or do you look at the impact each human being who has been lost to Covid has made? How do you measure each life?

We are in this together ♥♥

ABOUT BARI

Bari Himes was born and raised in Philadelphia, Pennsylvania. She currently resides in a suburb of Philadelphia where she is an administrator at a school for students with special needs. Bari has volunteered as a chaplain at a nursing home for the past 10 years. She spends her free time watching mixed martial arts (MMA), boxing, and enjoying those she holds close to her heart.

Bari started the Facebook group Inlovingmemory19 so that those who've lost loved ones to Covid can connect. It was one of the first Covid loss support groups.

Bari is the proud mother to her daughter, and only child, Jocelyn.

Jocelyn Himes is a 12-year-old middle school student. She will be a Bat Mitzvah this year, something her Ba-bo wanted to live long enough to see. Jocelyn created the logo for Inlovingmemory19 in honor of her Ba-bo.

Jocelyn can be found weekly participating in karate, boxing, or horseback riding. Her dream job is to be a farrier. Jocelyn loves her four guinea pigs, her dog, and her family and friends.

You can connect with Bari through social media:
Facebook: Inlovingmemory19
Instagram: _Inlovingmemory19 and alwaysinlovingmemory19
Twitter: Lovingmemory19
Website: Inlovingmemory19.org

Ballerina Rose at approximately 4 years old. My grandparents loved the picture so much they had an oil painting of it in their living room.

Rose Phillips, a graduate of Northeast High School, Philadelphia, Pennsylvania, June 1964.

Rose Kravitz wed Jeffery Phillips October 17, 1971.

Mom, dad, and me celebrating the holidays together. They are both gone now. I miss them terribly. I never thought I would be an "orphan" at 46.

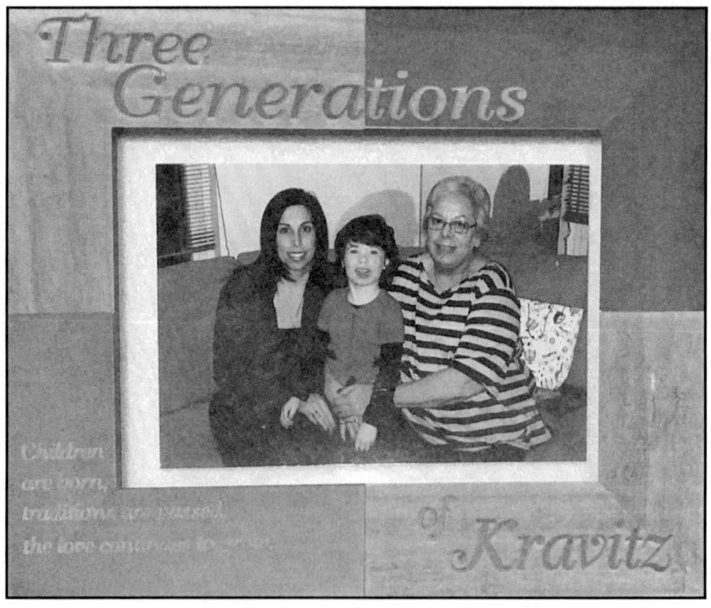

"You should only have one just like you." Three generations of strong women, each an only child. Each one who has survived their fair share and has found the strength and courage to keep going. Three generations that not even the loss to Covid will break.

My mom holding her one and only grandchild for the first time. Look at the joy in her eyes, the raw emotion. This is the epitome of "faklempt."

My mom, the coffee drinker, could be found the sole adult playing dress up as she enjoyed high tea with her granddaughter. The three of us would enjoy sharing finger sandwiches and scones. It became one of our favorite places to go and relax for lunch.

"Scrambled eggs well, bacon well, rye toast light." My mom knew what she liked. I love how she is admiring my daughter in this picture. I always knew my mother loved me, but my daughter was/is her world.

A game of Checkerchess was always the perfect end to a night. Only Jocelyn and my mom know the rules. They would not teach anyone else. The two of them would play and laugh.

Three generations together for Mother's Day 2019. Who knew it would be our last Mother's Day together? As much as my mother adored Jocelyn, my daughter equally loved her Ba-bo. There is a hole left in our heart where the matriarch should be. We miss you. We love you.

Hal's Story

THE MAN WITH THE GOLDEN SMILE

By Sherry Horowitz Stein

Harold "Hal" Austin Stein, the love of my life… taken too soon!

Looking back, February 1986 was a pivotal time in my life. When I first met Hal, I wasn't aware that I was meeting a very special man; the man I was going to fall deeply and forever in love with, a man who would feel the same love towards me. I never imagined that forever, in our case, would be cut short.

As a small business owner, I ran a little telephone and accessory retail booth in a large marketplace. Weekends were bustling with customers in search of the best deals and booth owners hoping their products would be chosen. Hal was working there on Saturday, February 15th, doing a remote broadcast with the radio station he worked for. He needed a new answering machine, so he made his way down to my booth. The owner of the marketplace knew Hal, and he had asked her which booth would be the best to make this purchase. She told me to expect him and that he was single, and then she winked at me. I was also single. Who knew that a transaction in my booth would lead to dinner, falling in love, and our wedding day exactly one year after we first met, February 15th, 1987.

Hal and I each had two children from our previous marriages. My son, Jason, was 17 years old when we met, and my daughter, Dawn, was 13 years old. Hal had two sons, Haddon and Adrian, both in their early twenties. Together, we were the perfect match for a "blended" family.

Hal was born and raised in Manhattan, New York City, in the area known as Washington Heights. He loved growing up in that part of the city. Hal had one younger brother, but he also had a cousin, Herbert, who lived in the same apartment building. Since he and his cousin were only two months apart, they became very close and loved spending time together. They went to ballgames, watched movies, and listened to music, especially classical music, Hal's favorite. Herbert loved singing and entertaining; he was trying to make it big in show business. During this time, Hal was his sidekick, so he would always go with Herbert to various clubs he performed at in Harlem, Hell's kitchen, and throughout New Jersey. Herbert, whose stage name was "Tiny Tim," was finally discovered, and he became best known for singing "Tiptoe Through the Tulips" in the falsetto voice that was to become his trademark. Once Tiny became a popular personality, he traveled quite a bit, and they didn't get to see each other very often.

Hal was an excellent student who took his education seriously. He was accepted into Stuyvesant High and continued his education at NYU in the hopes of becoming a screenwriter. Upon graduating from NYU, Hal then entered the Army. This was during the Korean War, in 1953. He loved our country and was proud to serve. Part of his time spent in the war was as a photographer. He enjoyed having an office and taking pictures of the men and the unbelievable sights. Hal's memories, however, were not all pleasant, and some were downright heartbreaking. He never wanted to discuss what he had seen, so I had to read between the lines most of the time. Upon his return home from the war, he went to California and attended Stanford University to earn his master's degree in writing and communication.

Screenwriting was not an easy gig to get into since you had to know the right people, so Hal went in a different direction and began a career in radio, a career that would serve him well. He started as the Marketing Director and Special Promotions for a radio station in Princeton, New Jersey, in the 1960s. It was an AM station called WHWH 1350AM, and when they added WPST 97.5 FM, he started working for both.

Hal loved his job. He was dedicated, sometimes working seven days a week. He worked many nights and spent a lot of time out in the field, but he never complained because it was his passion. He loved to work! When Hal worked with the AM station, he would be with the morning DJ, asking listeners questions about Hollywood trivia. The listeners would then call back in the afternoon with their answers. Most of the questions were about movies, movie stars, music, and musicians. Whoever gave the first correct answer would receive a prize. It was a very popular radio show and listeners looked forward to their daily dose of "Hollywood Hal." This became his nickname since he was so knowledgeable about Hollywood trivia. At work or at home, everyone called him that. He was proud of his new identity, and we always had fun with it.

As the Marketing Director, Hal set up remote broadcasts for the DJs. Since he also produced these shows, it was necessary for him to be on site, regardless of the location. Prior to me meeting Hal, he had traveled to London for a remote broadcast from Harrods Department Store. I loved it when I could accompany him on his work trips, and sometimes I would work with Hal to help him produce the show. It was a lot of work, but getting to be with him was what mattered. Many times, we were able to take advantage of other tourist activities, so it wasn't just all work. We were fortunate to do broadcasts from various locations in Jamaica five times! Another amazing remote broadcast was from Disney World in Florida. A new ride was opening, and Hal was helping promote it. These are all such fond and beautiful memories of Hal and me together.

Eventually, the radio station was purchased by a big corporation, which put an end to the large remote broadcasts. They still did small, local remote broadcasts, but since Hal had gotten involved with other projects, they did not require him to manage those broadcasts. He really didn't have time for traveling.

Hal took pride in the charity work he was involved with. It took much of his time, but he didn't mind. He became a Rotary member in Princeton, New Jersey, and he never missed his Friday afternoon meetings at the Hyatt Regency Hotel. There was always something going on through Rotary, such as the "Black Tie" and the "White Tie" balls. Sometimes, we attended a couple per month. The main ballroom at the hotel was always breathtaking, and when we entered, I would stand in awe of its beauty. The same people attended these balls, so I had to have a new dress every time. This was more of a chore for me since I wasn't into dressing to impress. Most of the women wore designer gowns they had had made in New York. Despite the dress investment, these events were so much fun, and we really felt blessed to be able to support a wonderful cause.

Hal did so much for the Rotary club that they tried to make him president a few times, but he didn't have enough time to devote to it. They gave him the Paul Harris Fellow award, one of the highest awards you can receive. My Hal was a humble man. He didn't like to be the center of attention, but we were both proud of this accomplishment. Besides Rotary, Hal was on the Board of Directors and Steering Committee for the Eden School in Princeton, New Jersey, a school for autistic children and adults. Once again, he was both humbled and proud to be involved with this school.

Hal never sat down for a minute; he was always on the go and with a smile on his face. Full of love and laughter, he enjoyed life and everything it offered. Hal changed my world in so many ways. I was happy because this man made the world a happy place for me and everyone he encountered. People would smile in his presence as his love for life radiated in all directions. In this crazy world we live in, Hal made a difference for all those whose paths he crossed.

I am so grateful for how active we were, living life to the fullest. One of my favorite events we ever attended was the hot air balloon races. Hal helped organize this event. He would get about 20 to 25 balloons, and they would all go up at the same time. It was a spectacular sight to behold. There was also the Catch a Rising Star Comedy Club at the Hyatt Regency Hotel on the weekends. The headlining comedian would come to the station Thursday before their weekend at the club for an on-air interview. If it was someone Hal thought would be good, we would go to the show. He had a good nose for comedy. Besides movies, that was the only entertainment he thought was worth seeing. I always enjoyed going to the movies, but once I met Hal, I could see films through entirely new eyes. I learned to enjoy films I would have never enjoyed before, especially foreign films with subtitles. After the film ended, we would discuss it, and he would point out certain parts to make sure I hadn't missed anything. If something didn't interest me at first, Hal made it interesting by sharing his perspective on it. I sure miss watching movies with him.

Hal received many awards for his community service and for distinguished service at the radio station. He had so many awards that we literally ran out of shelves to place them on in our home!

At the radio station, they honored Hal at a beautiful Christmas party for his years of service. His entire family was invited to attend. Aside from a splendid party with almost one hundred people in attendance, he was presented with the trip of a lifetime, two weeks anywhere he wished to go! We decided on Italy, and it was truly magical. The memories made on our trip to Italy will forever be embedded in my heart and soul. Thank you, Hal.

The following year, it was time for "Hollywood Hal" to hang up his hat and retire at 75. Once again, another beautiful party was thrown, honoring Hal and all he stood for. Choked up a bit, Hal gave an emotional speech and, once again, they presented him with a trip anywhere we wanted to go. This time, Hal picked the trip, a 16-day cruise to Australia and New Zealand. He had a motive for wanting to go there, aside from wanting to see all the sights. Hal's cousin Tiny Tim had been a sensation in Australia for many years. Many tributes, books, and stories had been written about him there. Hal had worked with an author, one who was friends with Tiny, on a book for a long time. They had communicated via phone and computer so often that they became friends, so Hal wanted to meet him desperately. He was a world-renowned music director who helped turn Tiny Tim into the sensation he had become, along with many other well-known singers. He couldn't wait to finally meet Tiny's family, so it was no surprise we were treated like royalty on this trip. I will never forget the look of happiness on Hal's face.

Hal enjoyed retirement in the beginning. No more waking up at 5:30 am, and no more long weekend hours running around. He could catch up on movies, casually do his crossword puzzles that he enjoyed so much, and go for walks when the weather was nice. The only thing he missed was me as I was still working, but a year later, I finally retired, which made him quite happy. We blissfully took day trips, went to various malls and just walked around together, went out for lunch and dinner, just simply enjoying life. We were together, and that was all that mattered. Hal had a way of making even the simple things fun. We always laughed, and he always had a smile on his face. Anytime, anywhere, I could count on his beautiful smile to warm my heart.

Then one day, something seemed off. Hal had been forgetting things, having some difficulty walking, and becoming moody. This was not the same pleasant, even-tempered man I knew. What was happening to my Hal? This went on for a few months, as I became more and more aware of this change happening in front of me. My heart ached as it was painful to watch. I prayed for change, but inevitably, after a year, it was time to see a doctor. I was in denial, but deep inside, I already knew what was wrong.

Hal was sent for tests, and they confirmed my beautiful, loving, wonderful husband had dementia. In my heart, I had known because I had experienced this with my mother. I recognized the patterns but had been hoping I was wrong. It was so cruel that such an intelligent man, who was capable of reading and understanding everything, may soon not understand anything. How was I going to deal with this and how would I deal with him? I thought it would be no problem. Sure, life would be different, but I would help him as best as I could. Fortunately, in the beginning, it was not too bad. He continued to get worse, and occasionally, he needed help with some things, but he was my husband, and it honored me to help him. How could I not help him? In sickness and in health, they say…

I took care of Hal for close to four years until he became violent, and my sweet, wonderful husband was someone I no longer knew anymore. Another man was living in our house, and he scared me. Hal would fall, and I could not pick him up. How many times can you call 911 in the middle of the night? Even our children told me he had to be placed somewhere because I could not care for him at home anymore. This was the hardest decision I ever made in my life, and I will never forget it. The morning he moved into the VA home, his new residence, he and I cried like babies for over an hour. He told me how much he loved me, and he understood why I had to do this. He said as long as I came to see him, he would be OK.

Hal was not thrilled living where he was, but he made the best of it. They treated him with respect and dignity. I visited him often during the three years he lived there, and so did our children, family, friends, and numerous co-workers. Every time I arrived, he was waiting for me, sitting in his wheelchair with a big smile on his face.

Then, along came the beast who would steal the hopes and dreams of so many. Sadly, on May 1st, 2020, Hal and many of the other residents tested positive for COVID-19. How did this happen? He was supposed to be protected within those walls. They put the facility on lockdown on March 6th, as they had had no cases until then. March 6th was the last day I saw him in person, the last time I was able to hold his hand or give him a kiss. After lockdown began, we spoke every day and sometimes twice a day. In the beginning, it was not so bad; it was almost like we were dating again. The VA staff set up Skype, so we could see each other. Hal loved that he could see me again, and I was able to see his wonderful smile.

Around the third week of May, I could see he was tiring. He looked good, no aches, pains, or problems, but he was asking more often when I was coming to see him. All I could do was put on my best smile and tell him as soon as they opened the front door, I would be the first person through it. My heart was aching, just as much as his, for us to be together in person so we could touch. Thinking back on it and reliving it brings me to tears.

Thursday, May 14th was the first day Hal had a fever of 100.6°F. I wasn't too concerned because the very next day it was normal, but then his oxygen level dropped, and they had to give him more oxygen for the first time. This was a pivotal moment, and we all knew. His nurses and I discussed his condition, but reality told us it was close to the end for my Hal.

My brother had just passed from COVID-19 on May 10th, so we were all dealing with the heartbreak of his untimely death. It was a tough time for our family, and all I could think was "this cannot be happening." On that Friday, while burying my brother, I was receiving messages concerning Hal's condition from the VA facility. Things were getting worse. We drove to the facility, and we were able to see him only through a window. He seemed to know we were there, but he had no reaction. He did, however, look at each of us, one by one. We were thankful we could see him, and he was able to see us.

My husband, lover, and best friend lay dying from a monster unfamiliar to us all, and there was nothing I could do about it. Hundreds of thousands of people were dying as we all watched in absolute horror and helplessness. For me, the sadness took over. I knew this was the end, and no one could be with him to hear his last breaths or hold his hand or kiss him. Aside from a nurse, he had no one by his side, which was what tore my heart to pieces. On May16th, 2020, my beloved husband, Harold Austin Stein, better known as "Hollywood Hal," passed away from COVID-19. He was 87 years old.

Despite this tragedy, I find comfort reliving all the good times we shared. Before Hal became sick, he told me he had the best life anyone could have ever had, and it was because he loved me, and he was loved by so many. He said, "I am a very lucky man to have all this love." The truth is, I was the very lucky one… we were the lucky ones!

Without the deep love and support of my children, I could not have written this, so I want to thank them with all my love. I dedicate this chapter to Hal, for showing me what true happiness really is. Because of Hal, I know what it is like to feel genuine love, and for that, I am forever grateful.

Hal, I will love and miss you every day that I breathe!!

ABOUT SHERRY

Sherry Stein was born and raised in Philadelphia, Pennsylvania. She graduated from South Philadelphia High School in 1961, and married her first husband in 1966. Together, they had two children: Jason and Dawn.

Sherry had an exciting career as an assistant to the owner of a custom drapery workroom for the interior design trade for 25 years. She met Harold (Hal) Stein in 1986, and they wed in 1987. Sherry became a stepmother to Hal's two sons: Haddon and Adrian. Sherry retired in 2000.

Hal visiting with his son, Haddon, on Veteran's Day 2019 at the Delaware Valley Veterans Home.

Sherry, Hal, Alyssa, Kait, Ryan, Jason and Haddon celebrating Thanksgiving at DVVH.

Sherry and Hal at Toga party in Jamaica during the week of the WPST Broadcast Circa early-mid 1990s.

Hal and Sherry Wedding photo February 15, 1987; a beautiful day.

Hal and his cousin, Tiny Tim (Herbert Khaury) – in their mid-teens.

Hal & co-worker, Dave Hoeffel, in Jamaica, WPST remote broadcast.

Hal's Army picture (Korean War); Circa 1953.

Hal's trip to Italy (with Sherry) 2006.

"Hal Caught By Surprise." Birthday Dinner 2017.

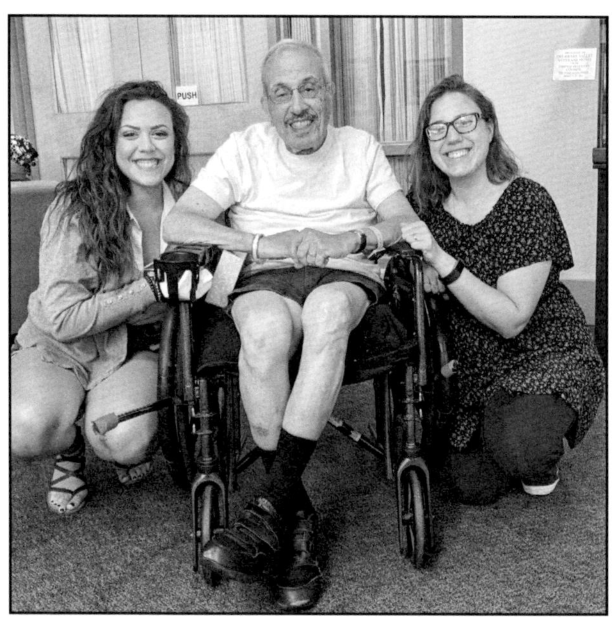

Hal and Granddaughters, Kait and Alyssa - Father's Day, 2018 at DVVH.

Paul's Story

MAKE IT A GREAT DAY

By Kim Letizi

INTRODUCTION

We are a close family, and I can't remember a time my dad wasn't there. We celebrated with a family gathering for every birthday, holiday, and occasion. My mom would often call me while they were on their way to our house: "Dad and I are coming to spend the weekend with you guys." I looked forward to our time spent together.

I dedicate this chapter to my dad, Paul Anthony Letizi, who lost his courageous fight with COVID-19 on October 29th, 2020, at the age of 67. Born and raised in Nanticoke, PA, my dad was one of three children. He loved his parents and adored his younger sister, Marian, and his best friend and older brother, David. My dad was a loving husband, father, grandfather, son, brother, uncle, cousin, and friend. I will always remember him for his warm smile and kind heart. Dad had a way of making those he met feel special by always offering a kind word and giving the biggest hugs.

A BROTHER AND BEST FRIEND

I will always remember the great times I had with my brother, Paul. He was my best friend and cruising buddy. We were always going somewhere, either to Pocono Downs for the horse races, or to the surrounding areas for walks and such. Paul was a gamer. He never complained, and I'll always admire him for that. My brother was a loyal husband, a devoted father, an adoring nonno (grandfather), a loving uncle, a supportive brother, and a friend to all. I miss him greatly.

Life changes radically, but memories… they don't, and for that I am totally grateful for having had a brother like Paul. – his brother, David

A LOVING BROTHER AND IDOL

I honestly cannot believe I am writing this in memory of my brother. It seems unfathomable to me that this virus could take someone you love in the blink of an eye before you can properly say goodbye. Paul was the sweetest, kindest man ever. Because of the kind of person he was and how he lived his life, I know he went straight to heaven (although much too soon).

Some of the fondest memories I have of Paul are riding in his gold Chevy Nova, watching Saturday morning cartoons together, and him allowing me and my friends to come to his house and borrow his car when our mother said I couldn't have the family car. I remember our childhood pet poodle, Mitzi, getting so excited when Paul would come to visit. He would just sit in the hall and pet her with genuine affection for hours. Paul enjoyed singing along at the George Thorogood and the Destroyers concert we went to, and he loved the *Three Stooges*. I remember many holidays, family gatherings, and vacations spent together laughing, especially down the shore. No one can ever take those memories away.

When I went back to school to be a registered nurse, they gave us an assignment to talk about a special person in our life, someone I admired or who had inspired me. While there were many people I could pick from, I chose my brother Paul. He was always there for me and reminded me a lot of my dad; he was also a kind, sweet man whom I adored.

Paul had a speech stuttering disability from early childhood, but with determination, he persevered. People could be cruel in life, but Paul never allowed that to hinder him. He graduated from school, married, and worked his entire life until retirement. He and his wife, Linda, raised a beautiful family. I am blessed to have had Paul as a brother.

The morning Paul went to the hospital, we talked on the phone. He told me he was being admitted, but that he was okay. I told him everything would be fine and I loved him. Paul said he loved me, and those were the last words I spoke to this amazing person I'd had for a brother. It is so hard for us to accept that he is gone. I try to find comfort in knowing he is an angel, looking down on us and protecting us. Until we meet again, I am proud to be your sister, and you will forever be in my heart.

Love,
your sister,
Marian

A FATHER AND BEST FRIEND

Our dad was very involved in our lives. He was a supportive, loving dad and a proud, caring nonno. He was the dad you could always count on, and he would drop whatever was going on in his life to help us in ours. Not everyone can call their dad a best friend, but he was mine. He was even the best man in my wedding.

Dad had a huge heart, and "no" was not in his vocabulary when it came to his family. He never complained, wanted nothing in return, and worked hard. He was our number one fan in all our sports, never missing a game. Football isn't the same anymore. Watching games with him or talking about sports was our favorite.

It's not fair that I had to say goodbye to my dad. He didn't have the opportunity to get vaccinated, but I know he would have. The memories will always be there; the little things will remind me of him, but it's just not the same as having him here with us. If only heaven had visiting hours. "Until we meet again, Dad, I love you!"

Love,
your son,
Paul David

MY NONNO, MY UNCLE

My Uncle Paul was the sweetest, most kindhearted, and caring person I ever knew. Growing up, he always treated me like one of his own. He brought so much love and happiness into my life. The memories I treasure the most are of our family trips to the beach. He was happy and content just being with his family, no matter what we did. He was a true one of a kind with one of the purest souls. His memory will live on in my heart forever.

I love and miss you every day, Nonno!

Your niece,
Brittany

A SPECIAL FRIEND

A few years ago, Paul and I talked about when we met. We pinpointed September 1963, the start of sixth grade at Lincoln Elementary. Since we lived on opposite sides of the "big city" and had to stay within shouting distance of our moms, we didn't get to know each other outside of school. Our genuine friendship started in high school when we had some classes together, and we were in the same homeroom in 11th grade. We reminisced about school lunch; no cafeteria, brown bag at your desk; a lot of teenage fun; golfing at Sweet Valley; and summer afternoon card games at Greg's house. Driving gave us independence, which included rides to nowhere special, listening to AM radio, high school "Sandy Beach" dances, and finding our soulmates! Not once did I hear Paul Letizi say anything bad about anyone. I am blessed to have called him a friend! I think of Paul every time I hear the song "Brandy."

– Joe, lifelong friend of 57 years

A SPECIAL FRIEND AND COWORKER

In 1986, I took a job at Nesbitt Memorial Hospital. At the time, I didn't realize I was about to meet someone who would impact my life in such an incredible way.

Going back in time: There was lunch with Paul, and his coworker and sister-in-law, Shelly. He always listened to the two of us rambling on about work and life. I loved the darkroom, which was Paul's workspace. I'd escape there, hide in the corner, or sit on the counter. The people coming in and out never even knew I was in there… bending his ear about anything and everything. He had the patience of a saint.

One lunch time we were sitting at Grotto Pizza, and Shelly, Linda, his wife, and his daughter, Kim, walked in. Linda blurted out, "I was wondering if I'd catch you with your girlfriend." We all got a good laugh out of it! Since then, I was known as Paul's girlfriend. I wouldn't have had it any other way. He was my bud. We were two peas in a pod. His love for Linda was like a fairytale and likewise mine for my husband, John. They were the loves of our lives. We shared stories about our children, bragging about the successes and expressing our concerns and worries.

We brainstormed about how we could be the best parents. We tried to mend their hearts when broken and always steered them on a good path. As time went on, we weren't just friends, we were family.

And then, a day I could never imagine happening, did. I was asked, and very much honored, to join the family FaceTime to say goodbye to Paul before they took him off of life support. Not being able to contain my emotions, all I got out was, "I love you, Paul."

Close in my heart is an image of walking into work and seeing those caring, compassionate, loving eyes of his. A smile from ear to ear. Sometimes a hug. And then being asked, "Lunch?"

"I miss you more than any words could ever express."

– Karen, friend and coworker of 34 years

SCHOOL AND CAREER

From a young age, my dad worked hard to provide a good life for us. His first job was helping his cousin with odd jobs throughout high school. After graduating in 1971, he worked at A. Rifkin Co. and later began a career in the healthcare industry. A dedicated employee, he never missed a day of work. I always said he could retire years early with all of the accumulated time he never used. I remember the days of walking downstairs and being greeted with a friendly "Good morning, honey" and a hug. Many mornings, we sat and chatted before he would head off to work (at least 30 minutes early because he was always punctual!). After nearly 40 years, my dad retired in August 2019.

FAMILY LIFE

My parents were together for 47 years and had just celebrated their 44th wedding anniversary. They shared a wonderful life together and loved each other more than two people possibly could. It warmed my heart how they still held hands while walking and watching television together. They enjoyed each other and the simple things life offered: long car rides, scenic trips, getaways to Atlantic City, walks on the beach, and dinners at their favorite restaurant. It didn't matter what they were doing if they were doing it together. My parents met at a high school dance. Their first dance was to "Stairway to Heaven." I'll never forget the tears of joy in Dad's eyes at their surprise 40th wedding anniversary party, surrounded by all the wonderful people in their life.

Our family enjoyed many summer vacations at the beach. Dad wasn't a fan of the sand, but he loved the ocean and people-watching on the boardwalk. In 2014, we started a family tradition with both Dad's and Mom's families in Mexico. Our last family vacation together was July 2019, in Cape May. Dad sat front row and watched my daughter, Layla, play soccer on the beach. He would spend hours on the boardwalk with the grandkids at the amusement park.

Dad had a special place in his heart for his three grandchildren, Layla, Chase, and Bella. Layla and my dad share the same birthday, February 12th. Her birth on his birthday was the best present ever. With a twinkle in his eye, he took strolls with the grandkids, gave the best piggyback rides, listened to their stories, never said no to special requests, and attended every Grandparent's Day at school. A proud grandpa indeed! He was always the first to call the kids to say, "Have a great first day at school!"

My brother and his wife, Morgan, welcomed a healthy baby boy, Camden Paul Anthony, in late November 2021. I know my dad would have been head over heels in love with this little miracle. He would have beamed with pride. I can imagine him saying "Tell me a story" while holding a fussy baby Camden. It saddens my heart that this boy will never know the special, beautiful soul his grandpa was.

My dad's love for animals impacted me when our family dog was dying. Through the night, he lay on the floor with her, offering comfort and support, so she wasn't alone. Although hesitant to get another dog, he welcomed their new dog, Melody, with open arms. My dad was loyal to anyone and anything that mattered to him. He valued the friendships he made like they were precious gems and regularly helped neighbors by cutting their grass, shoveling snow, and just being a compassionate, loyal friend.

Dad's favorite music was classic rock, and that guy could name every song, artist, and song year. If a song came on that he was into, his pipes opened up, and he sang those lyrics clearly and confidently. He also had a love of classic cars and could identify the make, model, and year in a heartbeat. My parents enjoyed yearly trips to the classic car show on the Wildwood Boardwalk.

Always thinking of others, my dad donated blood regularly and received numerous awards for his many contributions. His small act of kindness helped save countless lives. He was also a registered organ donor, hoping to help others even after he was gone. After he passed, however, the hospital said it wasn't possible to donate his organs, or anything else, because he had been infected with Covid. It broke our hearts that we couldn't carry out one of his last wishes.

COVID

My parents came to visit me and my family to celebrate their 44th wedding anniversary on September 25th, 2020, for a quiet weekend at our house. To spend time in person after months of only phone calls and video chats felt amazing. Throughout the pandemic, we had followed the guidelines, stayed home, wore masks when in public, and remained vigilant. We enjoyed the weekend together, and on Saturday, September 26th, I woke up early to say goodbye to my parents. Before my dad walked out my back door, I gave him a big hug and kiss, and told him that I loved him and would see him soon. I had no idea it was the last time I would ever hug my dad.

A couple of days later, on Monday, our nightmare began. I woke up feeling sick. By the next day, I felt worse; I had a fever and lost my sense of taste and smell. I had a video call with my doctor, and he sent me to get a Covid test that afternoon. I frantically called my parents to let them know they should get tested as well, since we had all been together over the weekend. My dad had an ultrasound done on his bladder for an unrelated issue (or what we thought was an unrelated issue) earlier that morning.

On Wednesday, September 30th, I received the results of my Covid test: positive. I quarantined in our bedroom and scheduled my husband, Jim, and our children, Layla and Chase, to get tested. As a follow-up to my dad's appointment on the previous day, my parents let the doctor know they had been in contact with a positive Covid case. Because of this, the specialist couldn't see him for 14 days. The nurse suggested my dad go to the emergency room immediately, since there was a risk of developing an infection in his bladder, and he could also get tested for Covid. Looking back, the issue with his bladder may have been a symptom of Covid. That evening, my mom took my dad to the ER. Within two hours, his fever spiked, he had increased respirations, and his blood pressure and heart rate decreased. His pulse oximetry was at 84% (normal is 96–100%). They put him on a low dose of oxygen, and his chest X-rays came back negative for pneumonia. Then we received his test result: Dad was Covid positive. My mom stayed with him for as long as she was allowed but then had to say goodbye, assuring him everything would be okay. She left, wanting to turn back around immediately, but she knew she wouldn't be allowed back in. This was his first time, in his 67 years, that he had ever been admitted to the hospital. He was alone and afraid.

On Thursday, October 1st, he continued to experience increased respirations, and he received a high concentration of oxygen. A second chest X-ray came back negative. The next day, there were no improvements, and he continued having rapid breathing. A third chest X-ray came back negative. At home, we were notified that Jim and Layla had tested negative for Covid.

On Saturday, October 3rd, Dad was struggling to breathe. The hospital called my mom for consent to intubate him. He was sedated and placed on a ventilator in a drug-induced coma. We thought it would give his body and lungs a chance to rest. He needed to fight. His fourth chest X-ray came back, confirming Covid-induced pneumonia with emphysema. That evening, the first lobe of my dad's left lung collapsed; it would require a chest tube. At this time, a nurse called to notify me that our son Chase was Covid positive. Shortly after that, my mom called to let me know she was Covid positive. I couldn't even grasp what was happening. It was a domino effect, and I couldn't stop it. The next morning, the second lobe of Dad's left lung collapsed, requiring a second chest tube.

I desperately wanted both of my parents. I needed them. A health nurse gave me the okay to go visit with Mom at her house. I stayed with her for a few days to care for her and offer support. We wore masks, and I continuously monitored her temperature and watched her breathing. At one point, she had increased respirations and a fever. I called her doctor immediately and thought, "This can't be happening. My dad is on a ventilator. I am not prepared to put my mom on one too." I was beyond scared. Thankfully, my mom recovered and didn't need to be hospitalized.

A FIGHTER

Each day, we waited for the phone call of daily updates on Dad. He had good days, and some days he suffered setbacks, but he was fighting. Baby steps were still steps in the right direction. We prayed as a family and remained hopeful. We wanted Dad to still hear our voices, so we scheduled nightly video calls. Otherwise, we helplessly watched, asking nurses to hold his hand, and just kept telling him to fight. We couldn't stand the thought of him being alone in the hospital, but there was no other option. I desperately researched every outcome, probability, prognosis, and top-rated, long-term acute care facility. If Dad kept fighting, he had a chance. His doctor informed us that he was the longest living Covid patient in the ICU. We were so full of hope.

On Thursday, October 15th, nearly two weeks after being on a ventilator, Dad was hitting all his numbers, and they placed him on the lowest ventilator setting. He even gave us a thumbs-up on a video call that afternoon. We screamed with excitement. This was the breakthrough we had been waiting and praying for! They successfully extubated him, but after 20 minutes of fighting to breathe on his own, his team decided to re-intubate. This wasn't the news we'd hoped for. My dad was heavily sedated once again and stopped responding to basic commands. But he continued to fight.

On Friday, October 23rd, his medical team informed us that they could not keep him intubated with the increased risk of infection, and that he needed a tracheostomy and feeding tube. Every day felt heavier and heavier, and any complication that could possibly arise did.

On Tuesday, October 27th, we joined our nightly FaceTime call, and my brother asked to speak to him alone when we were done. Shortly afterward, my brother called our mom in a panic. During his private call, Dad's heart rate had increased, and the team cut the phone call short. The doctor called to let us know Dad's heart was affected, and his organs were shutting down. Within a ten-minute phone call, Mom, my brother, and I had to decide to allow them to resuscitate him should his heart stop. I'll never forget my brother's cries; we just wanted to be with our dad.

The next morning, we met with his team of doctors over a phone call and discussed his options. We made the heart-wrenching decision to remove him from the ventilator and on to comfort medications. I pleaded with the hospital staff to let us all in, but because of visitor restrictions and the hospital's urgent need to conserve PPE, only two people could go in. It was heartbreaking and unfair. As a family, we decided my mom and brother would be with him during his final moments. My last question was, "Will my dad hear me?" His medical team reassured me that hearing is the last to go. We drove to the hospital in silence. I dropped my mom and brother off at the entrance, begging them to hold him tight and let him know how much love surrounded him in that room. I waited as they gowned-up in full PPE to connect me on the video call as we parked outside of the hospital. I couldn't comprehend what was really happening, and that this was how I would say goodbye to my dad. It was not only heartbreaking, but cruel. As much as I wanted him to stay, I knew it was time to let him go. I was blessed to have had my dad for 35 years, but selfishly, I wanted more. Helpless and crying, I watched as the medical staff turned off his machines while my mom and brother held him. This was deep pain, and no one can ever prepare you for this moment. My dad was a fighter and continued to fight even after the machines were off. I played some of his favorite songs, including "Stairway to Heaven," and my mom laid her head on his chest. It was the first song they had danced to, and it would be their last. I just kept telling him how much I loved him. He continued to fight for over nine hours before taking his last breath. I had never known heartache like this. Dad fought a courageous fight, but Covid took him in less than a month. He entered the hospital, not knowing he would never return home.

The hours, days, and weeks following his passing were a blur. We couldn't hold a proper memorial. Covid restrictions limited attendance, and we had to choose who could attend. Many people were afraid to hug and comfort us. This was not a normal grieving process.

The pain remains raw and real. We can't escape the tragedy of this pandemic as it surrounds our daily lives. At the time, I didn't know anyone else who had had Covid, let alone died from it. I began searching for support groups to seek others like myself. My dad was one of a kind, but I found his Covid story was not. As a nation, we continue suffering incomprehensible loss, losing our parents, grandparents, children, siblings, the very members of our families and communities.

TRYING TO MOVE ON

In my grief, I became an advocate and joined various support groups. I started by holding a community vigil at our local county courthouse in honor and remembrance of those lost to Covid. Other grieving families in the community needed to know they were not alone, and our loved ones were NOT just a number. I collaborated on many social media platforms to share my dad's story and raise awareness. In his honor, I publicly spoke to local officials as well as members of the U.S. Senate. I proudly represent Yellow Heart Memorial as a chapter lead in honoring and remembering our loved ones lost to Covid, and I have met some of the most inspiring individuals after our Covid loss, many of whom I now call my friends. In my dad's honor, I promise to continue as a sounding voice to raise awareness, educate the public, and continue the fight to help prevent the spread of this devastating virus.

In honor of Dad, we planted a tree on our first Father's Day without him. The family was together, and we shared stories and fond memories. We will continue our family traditions and celebrations because my dad wouldn't want it any other way. Our lives are forever changed, but we are so thankful he was ours while on this earth. He provided us with a good life and loved us with every fiber of his being. He taught us to love unconditionally and accept others for who they are.

Death is difficult, and it's not something anyone can prepare you for. Some days are harder than others. For me, it's hard to accept his loss, and what he battled during his remaining days. My dad was surrounded by loving family and friends his entire life, but in the end, he succumbed to a sad, lonely death. Covid robbed him of life. I'll never understand why things happened the way they did. I struggle to find closure. One day, I hope to find it. My dad, Paul Letizi, was a beautiful person who shared only love within his heart. Our world shines a little less brightly without him in it. My dad may physically be gone, but he is forever a part of us. It brings me comfort when I hear loved ones sharing stories of him. I smile when I hear his voice on my saved messages that always ended with "Have a great day, I love you". My heart warms when I listen to his favorite songs or wear his favorite T-shirt. As I walk along the beach, I am reminded of him, and it makes me both happy and sad. I will miss my dad every minute of every day for the rest of my life; until we meet again. I love you, Dad.

~

ABOUT KIM

Kim Letizi grew up in Nanticoke, Pennsylvania with her parents, Paul and Linda, and older brother, Paul David. She earned a Bachelor of Science degree with a major in Biotechnology from East Stroudsburg University of Pennsylvania. She currently resides in Tannersville, PA with her husband, Jim, and their children, Layla and Chase.

Kim enjoys traveling, spending time with her family and friends, and loving on her rescue pup, Bia. She stays actively involved with her community.

In addition to working full-time in the vaccine industry, Kim continues to build connections and offer support to others within the Covid community. She is one of the Pennsylvania chapter leads for Yellow Heart Memorial.

Kim would love to connect with you via social media on Instagram @Kim Letizi and @yellowheartmemorialpa

Twitter: @kletizi
Facebook: Kim Letizi
Or email kimletizi@gmail.com

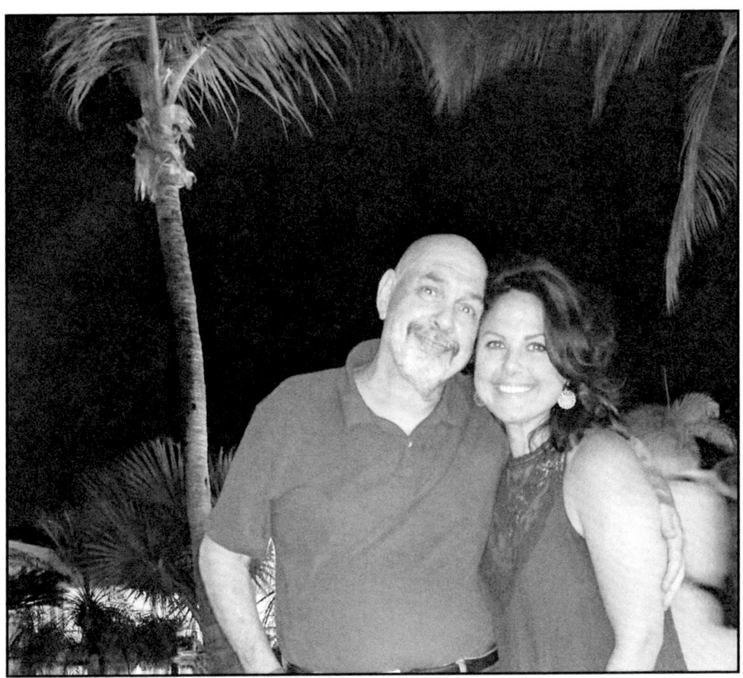

Paul and Kim enjoying a family trip in Punta Cana.

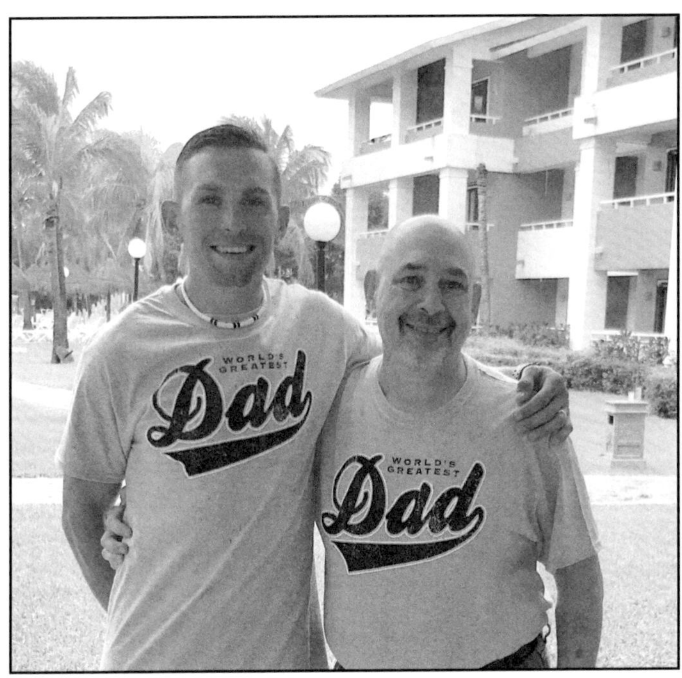

*Paul with his son, Paul David on Father's day,
June 2018 during a family trip to Riviera Maya.*

One of Kim's favorite vacation memories with Paul on their last family vacation together in Cape May, July 2019.

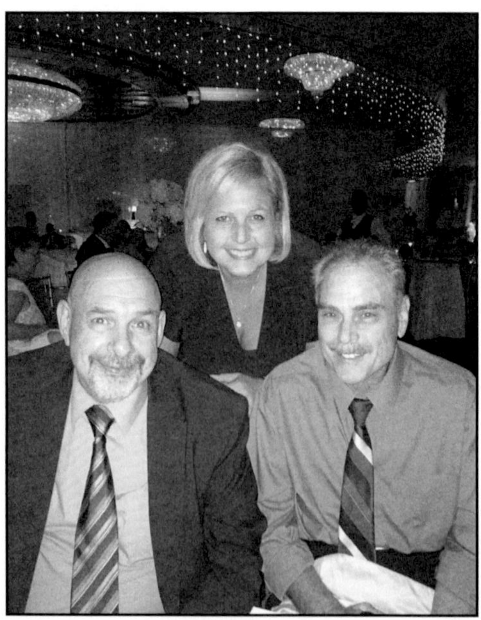

Paul with his sister, Marian and brother, David.

Paul enjoying time with his family on Christmas Day 2019.

Paul and his family having fun at Stroudsburg Winterfest in early February 2020.

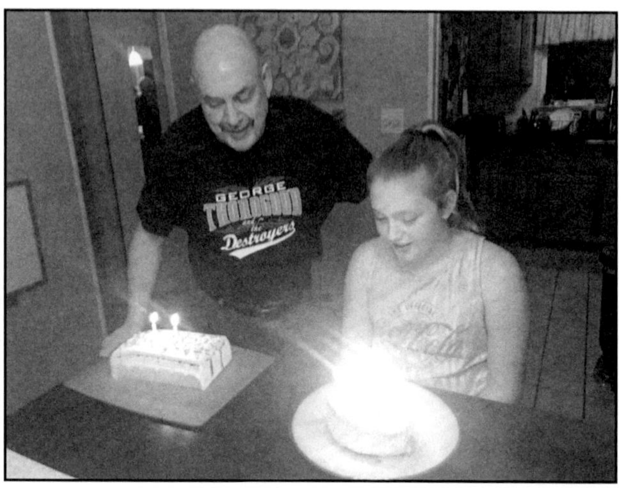

Paul and his granddaughter, Layla, celebrating their birthdays together on February 12th.

Paul and Linda on their wedding day September 25th, 1976.

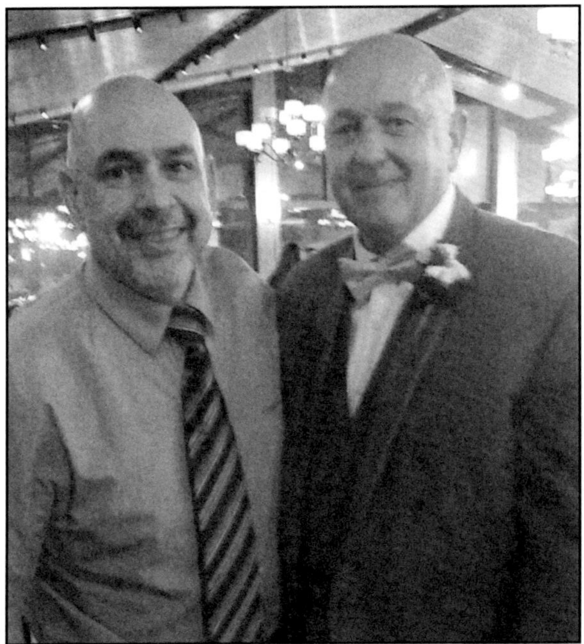

Paul with his lifelong friend, Joe.

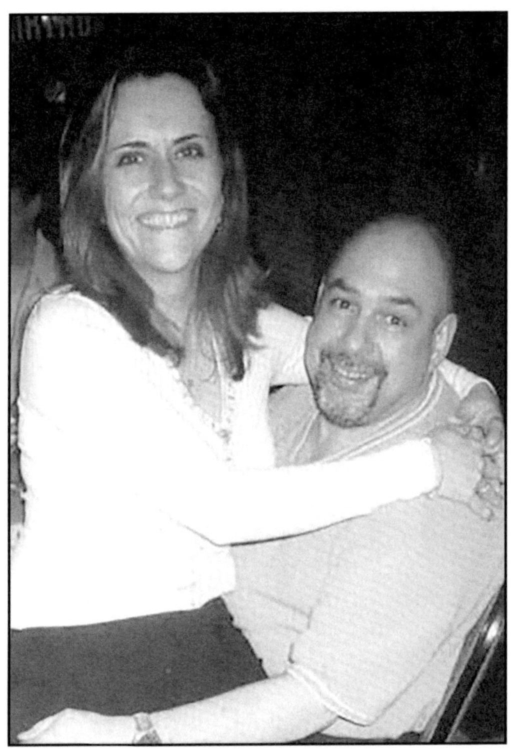

Paul and his dear friend, Karen, celebrating together at her 40th birthday party.

Mary's Story

MARY'S LEGACY LIVES ON

By Rosie Davis

My mother, Mary Castro, was a pillar of strength to all who loved her. She was the strongest person I have ever known. Born on April 9th, 1945, to Dominga Amaro, my mother was adopted six months later by Dominga's older sister Celia Mendoza. Dominga gave birth to my mom at a very young age, and so gave my mom up to her older sister Celia, who was already married. She was the oldest of thirteen siblings, some adopted and some biological. She always made sure to divide her love up equally among all of them.

As far back as I can remember, my mom put all her effort towards being the best mom she could to me and my three siblings. As a single parent, she raised four kids on her own, with a ten-year gap between the second and third child. Hard work did not scare her as she balanced being a mother, father, and friend. My mom worked at the Vans factory and also as a fruit picker. She was never too proud to do what she had to do to support her family. She thrived when surrounded by family and always looked forward to the next gathering.

Her favorite place was the beach, and we spent long days at a beach in Southern California when I was young. Walking on the sand, picking up shells, and watching us play in the ocean brought my mom peace.

My mom loved sewing. It was a gift passed down to her by my grandmother. She also had a green thumb and spent hours outside in her garden, planting flowers and fruit trees. Helping others brought joy to my mom's heart, so it's no surprise she spent time volunteering for the ministry at a women's jail. One thing I remember doing as a child is watching my mom dance; she loved to dance and would always grab my hand and pull me over to dance with her. She also did that with her grandkids.

Outgoing and fearless, my mom brightened any room with her smile or her singing and dancing. She didn't care who was watching! Her laugh created a ripple effect, bringing joy and laughter to those around her.

I will always admire the strength my mom displayed during the tough times. Despite the loss of her two oldest children, her confidence and faith kept her going. She suffered the devastating loss of her oldest son, Ricky, in December 1999 to suicide. Ricky had been diagnosed with HIV, which would later turn into AIDS. He couldn't bear the pain and suffering that had been brought on by the virus. Several years later, she lost her oldest daughter, Renee, to complications of an opioid addiction following back surgery.

With courage, determined to succeed, she started nursing school when I entered junior high. I can still feel her hand on my arm, wrapping a bandage around it because she had a test coming up and needed to practice. Like a proud parent, my heart was full as I watched my mom walk across the stage at her graduation. The biggest of all her smiles (she had an amazing smile!) was planted on her face. With such a loving personality, nursing came naturally to my mom. Her patients adored her. But, because of health reasons, she had to retire early, and it broke her heart. She tried to make the most of her time at home by gardening, crafting, and spending time with family. We were shopping buddies, but my mom didn't know when to stop. I would become exhausted!

As the years went on, my mom's health declined, and she needed me more. Diabetes and early onset dementia gradually took its toll, resulting in the loss of one of her legs. In 2017, the painful journey of further decline began. My mom had to transition into a nursing home, and she did not approve of this decision. My family and I did our best to make it feel like home for her. They allowed her to leave for day trips, which kept her going. She anxiously awaited our visits and shopping trips. Holidays were always her favorite; I would pick her up for the day and both of our hearts would break when it was time for her to go back.

In March 2020, nursing homes went into complete lockdown because of the pandemic. They did not allow visitors, which was a huge adjustment for her and for me, since we had seen each other every day for the three years she'd been living there. For the first time, my mom spent her birthday with strangers. There was no royal treatment from her family to make her day special. We made sure, however, that she still had her tiara and sash to wear on her big day. The last time I saw my mom's face was on Mother's Day. I expected to see her all dressed up, donning her usual bright smile, but she was the complete opposite. No smile at all and still in her nightclothes, she was so weak she couldn't open her gifts or even look up at us. I hated that a window kept us from hugging and kissing each other. I couldn't speak to her except through an iPad a nurse would hold up to the window. I had to make an appointment just to talk to my mom on FaceTime.

Then my worst fear became reality. My mom caught COVID. They transported her to a local hospital on May 12th, and she took her last breath on May 17th at 3:45 PM. I was in complete shock when I got the call, and every memory of her flashed before my eyes as they welled up with tears. How could this be? We had just talked the day before. Looking back, I think my mom knew she was going to die, because her last words to me were, "When you get to heaven, we will look for each other."

This unwelcome journey has been tough, but I knew I had to keep my mom's memory alive. My heart led me to start a memorial called "Yellow Heart Memorial" in honor of my mom, and all the lives lost to COVID-19. My mom will never be forgotten. We have included her in every Yellow Heart Memorial across the nation, and there is a heart in London on a memorial wall with her name as well. There will also be a willow tree planted in honor of my mom in Poland. Yellow Heart Memorial is now throughout the nation, ten chapters strong. We have given communities the opportunity to come together and grieve by holding memorials. Our memorial puts a name and a face to the numbers. We are also working with different cities to grant permanent memorials, and five have been approved so far. Yellow Heart Memorial held the biggest COVID event in the nation, COVID "March to Remember" on August 7th, 2021. More than 400 people came together in solidarity with survivors and long haulers to walk the Brooklyn Bridge, bring awareness, and honor our lost loved ones. Twenty-three other events were held that day in twenty different states. Our goal was to take a step for every life lost to COVID, and for our long haulers who are still fighting. Thirteen landmarks in the New York area, and across the nation, lit up in yellow, including Niagara Falls. It was a beautiful experience. Through the Yellow Heart Memorial, I have started my healing journey and have helped others begin to heal as well.

I love you, Mom! Thank you for instilling knowledge and love in me, with your shining examples of bravery and compassion. I promise, when I get to heaven, I will find you.

Love and miss you so much,
your daughter,
Rosie

~

My mom was a strong, independent woman who gave us all the necessary things in life. Leading by example, she went to school to pursue her dream, and she always believed in her convictions. When I look back, I now realize that my mother had taught me a lot of things, something I wasn't aware of when I was younger. Because of her, I understand that, in this life, you have to work hard towards what you want because no one is going to give it to you. You have to do it yourself!

My mother loved her family and friends with all of her heart. She was a Christian, and knowing she is in a better place brings me comfort. I love you always, Mom. Till we meet again.

Love,
your son,
Abel Herrera

~

The smell of rain and thunderstorms filled the vehicle. I wiped the fog off the back window just as the lightning hit the ground. The white car, as I remember, seemed to be from the 60s and a bit rickety. This is my first memory as we drove to what would be our new life of stability.

Taking care of two kids while in nursing school, and then taking care of her first grandchild, was no simple task, but my grandma made it happen. She was a strong woman of many characteristics.

If any of us made a mistake, she greeted us with her stern reactions and punishments. She made sure to instill respect and kindness in us.

She loved to watch old black-and-white films that would make me think, "What's so interesting about these basic films?" Eventually, they drew me in, and I understood. The smell of home-cooked meals was a constant in our house, along with cheerful smiles across the table. Spoiled, some might say, I enjoyed many gratifying meals on Sundays after church.

Honest (even if you didn't like it), kind, and admirable, she was a lovable human being with an infectious laugh that would linger throughout the room. In all my life, I never once called her "Grandma," which meant a lot to her. She was not only my grandmother; she was my mom.

Love,
your (son) first grandchild,
Alex De La Cruz

~

When I think of my grandma, I think of her green thumb. The fruit trees in the yard, and the many flowers she tended to in the garden, were as beautiful as her smile. Add in her favorite garden décor for the perfect display! Her nurturing instinct and compassion showed in everything she did, from her career as a nurse to her everyday hobby of gardening. My grandma put her all into her work.

As I entered high school, I realized my talent for art. My talent for pottery thrilled her. At my grandma's request, I would bring home clay so we could make something together. I showed her how to make cups, bowls, and more. After they dried, we would spend hours together painting our work. Oh, what I would give to have these moments again.

I miss all the holidays spent with her. Over the years, celebrations became small but very intimate. We painted eggs for Easter and carved pumpkins for Halloween. She enjoyed the interaction we all shared, as did I. Feeling like a kid again, she jumped right in to color or watch cartoons with my niece and nephew. Her entire world lit up when she saw them.

My favorite memory is when I was older. Our family loves wine, and we all enjoyed having a glass with one another. One day, during the summer, I asked if she wanted a glass. "It's rather sweet, so you may enjoy it," I told her. As soon as her lips finished that first sip, her entire mood changed. All bubbly and feeling no pain, she told us all about the crazy times she had danced with girlfriends when she was my age. That wine gave her the gift of gab, and she talked about her life and all the fun things she had done along the way. My family didn't agree with my wine offering at first, but then they saw what a great time she was having. "She can still have fun too!" I exclaimed. Enjoying a glass of wine with my grandmother might seem insignificant to some people, but it truly meant a lot to me.

Birthdays are always a big celebration for our family. Big party, big cakes, and big crowds were a must back in the day. My mother and I would get her ready for her big day. We fussed over her, styling her hair and applying her makeup. She loved every second of it!

As a tribute to my grandmother, I painted a canvas for my mother. Her favorite flowers were tulips, and her favorite color was pink (just like mine). I did my best to create something that symbolizes her and her place in our lives. The center is a yellow heart, just as she was the center of our lives. Her picture sits by my nightstand, and she is the last one I see when I go to sleep and the first when I wake up. I'm at peace with my grandma. She still makes her appearance through butterflies and cardinals. I guess I've trained myself to believe that each time I spot one, it's her. It's the comfort I need, and she knows when to show up. This is for you,

Grandma, the person who helped mold my life. I love you, and you wouldn't believe the impact your life has made here since you left.

With all my love,
your princess,
Alexzandria Pena (granddaughter)

~

When I was younger, my grandma had cherry trees. She had planted them in front of her house in New Mexico. In the summer, when it was time to pick them, my sister and I would rush to the trees to pick cherries with our grandma. With excitement, I would pick them and stuff my mouth full. It was pure delight, despite her yelling at me not to eat them all. My grandma made us fresh fruit roll-ups out of the fresh fruit grown from her trees. Every time I see fruit trees, it reminds me of summers with my grandma.

Love,
Granddaughter Kassandra Merritt

~

Losing my mom has changed me forever. I am forever traumatized by the way she was ripped away from me. Imagining her last moments and thoughts, I am haunted, knowing I was robbed of having this time with her, holding her hand as she took her last breath. All I have left is questions and no answers. She was both my mom and my dad, so I lost both parents when I lost this amazing woman.

It's my life's mission to make sure the world knows she was an amazing mom, grandma, and great grandma. My mom's legacy will live on even after I am gone. The love I have for my mom ignited a movement that is now known throughout the globe. She is everywhere!!! It makes me smile to see people memorializing her (and so many others) all over. She loved to travel, and she is still traveling today. I know in my heart, when we see each other again, she will be waiting with open arms and will tell me how proud she is of me.

~

ABOUT ROSIE

Rosie was born in Garden Grove, California, the youngest of four children. Her family moved to New Mexico, where she graduated high school and went on to college. She started a family in New Mexico and later moved to Texas. There she started a new chapter of her life and a new career as a laser medical skin specialist.

Rosie currently lives in Carrollton, Texas, where she now focuses all her time on Yellow Heart Memorial, a memorial created to humanize the number of lives lost to COVID-19. She also travels the country to advocate for Covid victims and survivors. You can connect with Rosie and Yellow Heart Memorial via social media on Facebook and Instagram under Yellow Heart Memorial and through email at yellowheartmemorial@gmail.com

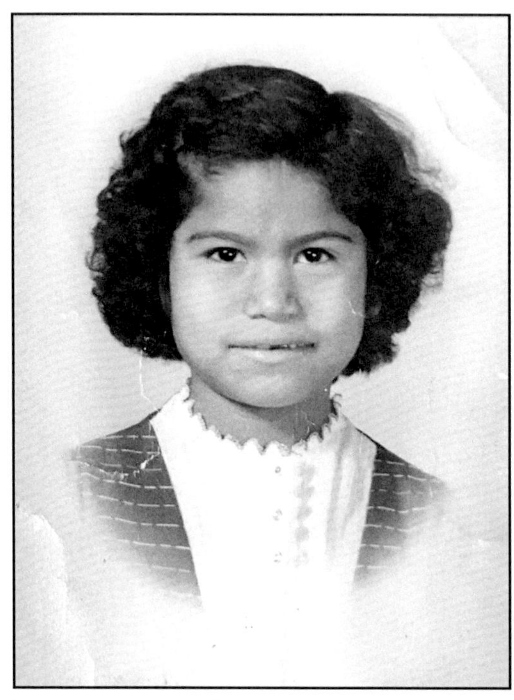

Childhood photo of Mary in elementary school.

Great granddaughter Adalee loves and misses grandma so much she drew a picture of both of them together.

Mary with great granddaughter Adalee.

Mary with first grandchild, Alex, 1979.

Mary with her favorite brother, Jesse.

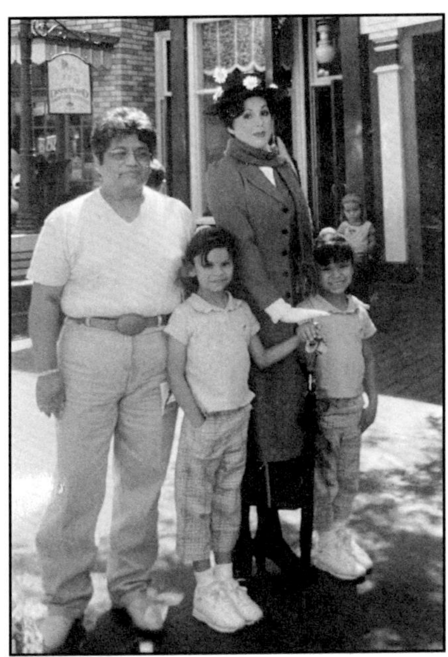

Mary with granddaughters Alex and Kassandra on a family trip to Disneyland.

Mary dancing with her brother Carlos and granddaughter Alex.

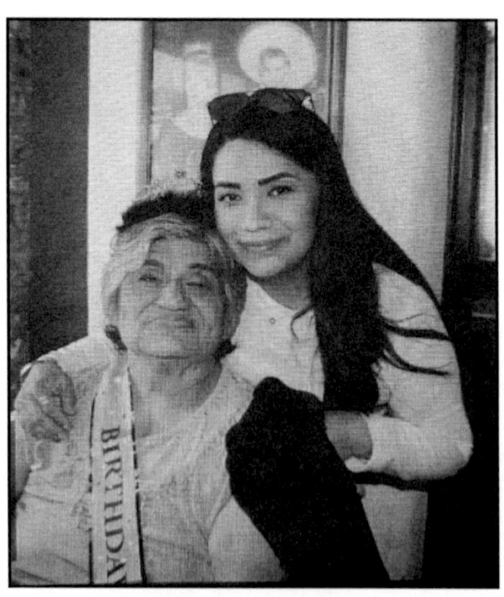

Mary and daughter Rosie.

Mary with her two youngest children Abel and Rosie.

Granddaughter Alex Pena painted a canvas with a yellow heart and Mary's favorite flowers tulips.

Tony's Story

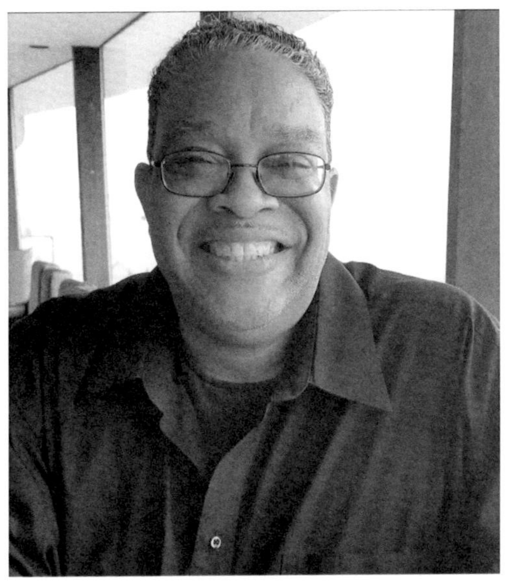

NOT ENOUGH TIME
ANTOINE (TONY) M. NIXON

By Raenell Worrells

"Hey, Raenell. How are you? I just wanted to let you know Tony has Covid." This is the text message I received from my sister-in-law, Heather, on Sunday, May 3rd, 2020, regarding my brother, Tony. I said to myself, "Okay, Raenell, don't panic. Many people are coming through this just fine. He'll be fine. He'll get through this okay."

For the next three days, we texted back and forth, checking in. On Wednesday, May 6th, 2020, I received a text from Heather: "Hey. How's your day? Tony is coughing a bit more. Says his chest feels heavy. His temp this morning was the highest it's been: 102.1. He is as comfortable as can be."

I texted my brother: "Hi, Tony. I'm sorry you are sick. How are you coming along?" He responded: "Hi, Raenell. I'm fighting. Constant fever. Thank you for checking in."

You may be wondering why all the texting back and forth. Why didn't I pick up the phone to call? I wish I had. Tony and I had always been close, but in the past few years, our relationship had become strained and complicated. We were still on speaking terms; we would occasionally check in via text to see how the other was doing. Maybe one of us would send a quick text to inform the other that someone we knew had passed, or that we'd run into someone we had grown up with and hadn't seen in a long time. I wish I had picked up the phone and called him. I would've heard his voice, for what would have been the last time. Hindsight is 20/20.

On the morning of Thursday, May 7th, 2020, I received a text from Tony thanking me for the food I had sent them. I asked how he was feeling, and he responded: "Coughing a lot. Still fighting the fever but working hard at bringing it down." I told him to keep fighting and gave him some suggestions of some holistic things he could do that I thought would help. But what did I know? I was still praying and hoping this would be the worst of it for him. After some back-and-forth texting about tea and ginger, and what he called "Black Death Oil" (that is not what it is really called, but he said that's what it tasted like), I told him to keep drinking hot liquids throughout the day. He responded: "Okay. Thank you. Will do." That was the last time I communicated with my brother while he was conscious.

On the morning of Friday, May 8th, 2020, I got a phone call from Heather. She informed me that she was taking my brother to the emergency room at the instruction of his doctor. He could not breathe. It was not a thought in any of our minds that he would not come out of the hospital alive. She called me back when she got home. My first thought was, *Why is she home? Why didn't she stay at the hospital with him?* I hadn't been thinking about the circumstances, that she wouldn't be allowed to stay there with him. Heather told me they had met her and Tony at the entrance of the emergency room, put him in a wheelchair and took him inside. They said they would call with an update once a doctor had seen him, but she could not come in or stay there with him. That was the last time Heather physically saw and touched my brother, her own husband.

I immediately went into protector mode and told her to stay on top of the hospital. If they didn't call in a reasonable amount of time, I told her to call them for an update. I had seen online, and on TV, that some hospitals were overwhelmed, and that many patients were falling by the wayside. That would not happen to my brother. I was not accustomed to not being there for someone I love. When a loved one is in the hospital, I always make sure they are being properly cared for. My brother was no exception; our complicated circumstances didn't matter. I needed to make sure Tony was taken care of so he could get out of that hospital as soon as possible.

The hospital called Heather with an update; Tony had Covid-related pneumonia, and they were admitting him to the ICU. They were putting him on a bypass machine. His O2 saturation was 86–95%. The bypass machine is 100%. We all hoped it wouldn't drop since that would mean he would have to be intubated and put on a ventilator. At least he was sound asleep and getting some much-needed rest. In my mind, I was thinking all he needed was a little help from the bypass machine and plenty of sleep to help his body fight off this wretched virus that had been causing so much havoc in everyone's life. *He's going to be okay. He'll be home in a few days.* Meanwhile, my brother's 16-year-old son, Jaden, was on my mind. How was he going to handle his father being in the hospital with COVID-19?

Saturday morning, May 9th, 2020, I received a message from Heather telling me she had spoken with the ICU nurse, and they had informed her that there was a strong possibility Tony would have to go on a ventilator today. His respiration was high and his O2 was low, but since he could still talk, they were holding back for now. When they put him on the ventilator, they would also put him in a medically induced coma. At 4:15pm that afternoon I received the text: "I haven't spoken with the nurse yet, but Tony texted me at 3:29pm and said they have to put the tube in now."

I was nervous, anxious, and scared. We had not heard of many people making it through once they got to this point, but I remained positive and hopeful, praying to my Almighty Heavenly Father, Jehovah, to help my brother get through this.

Sunday morning, May 10th, 2020, according to the update, Tony had had a good night and no fever. The ventilator settings were high and had been turned down a bit, and he was doing well. His blood work looked good, and the nurse would call my sister-in-law that afternoon. I thanked Jehovah God and prayed Tony would continue to improve. That evening, Heather sent a group text to our large family with the following update: "Good evening, all. Just spoke with Tony's daytime nurse. Tony had a good day. They reversed the paralytic all the way and woke him up for a bit. The ventilator is currently at 60% and his O2 is good. He couldn't tolerate it going any lower. He wasn't in any pain and could respond to the nurse's questions. They started feeding him through a tube so he could get some nutrients. They put him back under and upped the sedation, especially since night is coming, so he can be comfortable. His blood sugar is high, but they are managing it with insulin. It's high because of the steroids they are giving him. Tony is at a critical point, and this could go either way. He is critically stable and will probably be on the breathing tube for a little while. They will wake him every day to see how he is tolerating all of this. He knows everyone is praying for him, and he knows how much we love him. I'll send another update tomorrow." I was still very concerned after reading this text, yet I remained positive and continued to pray. At this point, I was definitely not thinking about the "D" word.

Monday, May 11th, 2020, at 1:33pm I received a text from Heather: "I just got to FaceTime with Tony! He looks good for being on a ventilator. He winked at me, moved his legs back and forth, and raised his hand. He is very sleepy, but he knew it was me. I told him how much we all love him and that we all are praying for him! I told him to keep fighting, and he is doing great. All he needs to do is focus on healing his body. I told him Jehovah's got him!"

Tuesday, May 12th, 2020, there was no change in Tony's condition. I was thankful he didn't get worse. However, little did I know I needed to buckle up because the roller-coaster ride was getting ready to speed up. Heather was displaying mild symptoms (mild fever, loss of taste and smell, fatigue, and body aches) and had tested positive for Covid. I gave her the same advice I gave Tony, about continually taking in hot liquids and getting as much rest as possible. But who can rest when your husband is in the hospital on a ventilator? She then informed me that Tony had spiked a fever overnight, and they were working to get it down. Hopefully, it was just a minor setback. I remained positive.

A couple of days later, Heather felt better and took the dog for a walk. As she was walking, she felt dizzy and leaned against a tree for support. She reached for her phone to call her son and passed out. On the ground, she was disoriented, not sure what had just happened. Her entire body hurt. Heather stayed in bed for the next week. She continued with a mild fever and could not do much except sleep and talk to the doctors about Tony's condition. Thankfully, she recovered without needing hospitalization.

Thursday, May 14th, 2020, an update text from Heather: "I spoke with Tony's nurse practitioner this afternoon and his vent settings are back up. His lungs are not good, and he's developed MRSA. That could be the reason he has a high fever. They are treating him with antibiotics for the secondary infection. Hopefully, putting him in the prone position (face down) will open his lungs." My brother's fight for his life had intensified, and so did my fear and anxiety, as well as my praying. It was not a good feeling at all, and I wouldn't wish this on anyone. Despite the circumstance that caused my bond with Tony to become complicated, he didn't deserve this. I felt helpless, but there wasn't anything else I could do besides pray.

Saturday, May 16th, 2020, Heather spoke to the hospital about the availability of any treatments they could give Tony to help him. I also told her to ask about any clinical trials. Unfortunately, they didn't offer any at the hospital he was in, and he was too critical at this point to move him to a hospital that did. Still feeling helpless, it seemed they were just going to let him die. Heather said they had told her Tony was getting worse. His lungs barely had any room to move air, and there was a possibility his heart could stop working because his O2 was dropping so low. I wanted to scream: Try something! Anything! If they had said a piece of the moon would save my brother's life, I would've done everything in my power to get him a piece of the moon. It was the worst feeling in the world knowing that my brother was lying there dying and there was nothing I could do about it except pray and hope his immune system would kick in to kick the virus in the butt. It isn't over till it's over. I was hanging on for dear life.

This was not my first time in this situation. In November 2008, Tony and I were in this same situation with our mother, as she lay dying of pancreatic cancer. Despite her being in a coma, her organs failing, and the doctors telling us she would not make it, I held on to hope until she took her last breath and was pronounced dead. I did the same thing for Tony. How could this be happening again? Except this time, it was Tony, and though I had the support of family and friends, I still felt alone. It wasn't fair that I couldn't see him or talk to him or be there with him. I HATED that he was there all alone. Covid has ruined our lives.

Sunday morning, May 17th, 2020, I spoke with Heather on the phone, and she told me Tony's doctor said he was going to die.

My heart dropped into my stomach. I was afraid for my brother's children; Anissa, 28, and Jaden, 16, from his first marriage. Anissa is married and had just had her first child; Tony never had the chance to meet her because of the lockdown. Tony had not seen his son in person since the first weekend in March either, also due to the lockdown. They both lived in Maryland, and Tony lived in Pennsylvania. Because of Covid, a granddaughter will never get to know her grandfather, and a son did not know his last weekend visit with his father would be the last ever.

Heather asked about speaking with my niece and nephew's mother, June, so she could talk with them about what was going to happen. The nurse offered to arrange a Zoom call for any family who wanted to join. We left it up to June whether she felt it was a good idea to have Jaden join in, but she didn't think it was a good idea for him to see his father like that. I wanted to, but I also didn't want to. I was afraid of what he looked like and wasn't sure I wanted that image in my head for the rest of my life. I am still not over watching my mother take her last breath, and I probably never will be. Despite that, I knew I needed to be there with her. I couldn't let her die alone, without me by her side. I felt I needed to talk to Tony, so I told Heather to have the nurse set it up for me.

Heartbroken, confused, and angry, I posted the following message on my Facebook page while I waited for the information to log on to Zoom:

"Not in a good place right now. My heart is aching, head is confused, and I'm in a fog as my brother, Antoine M. Nixon, is fighting for his life. The worst part is neither his wife, me, his kids, nor anyone in our family can be there with him. This virus is not a joke, and it is not here to play games. It is taking lives. If there is anyone who has still not taken this seriously, I'm here to say you need to! I would hate for anyone to go through what my family and I are going through right now. This is real, and while folks are out there complaining about having to stay home, or not adhering to stay-at-home orders, or complaining about having to wear masks, others are losing their lives. Yes, I would love to go get my nails or my hair done, go to the movies, etc., but not at the expense of a human life. STAY HOME, people! Take care of yourselves and each other. I wouldn't wish this on anyone. It's not fun feeling heartbroken, confused, upset, and angry all at the same time."

I mentioned earlier, the strained relationship between Tony and me had become complicated. We had spoken very little during the past few years and hadn't seen each other much. While the circumstances involving our now complicated relationship do matter, there's no point in addressing it here. He's no longer here. I needed to let him know that, despite all of it, I still loved him. I had forgiven him, and I didn't hate him. It was as much for me as it was for him to be at peace. Heather was constantly telling me he knew I loved him. I needed to say it to him. It's a shame this is what it took for me to do so. As my chapter title states, there was "not enough time." I had no clue we would run out of time to fix our relationship so soon in our lives.

Heather sent me the Zoom log-in information and told me he didn't look bad. I was still afraid, so I said a prayer before I logged on. When I got on the Zoom call, the nurse was in the room. She told me to take as much time as I needed, and that he could hear me, but he wouldn't be able to respond. Saying goodbye to someone you love so dearly, someone you shared your life with, someone who knows you as much as you know yourself, and vice versa, is one of the hardest things a person has to do. Tony and I both had to do it with our mom, and it was the absolute hardest thing I have ever had to do. Here I was again, having to do the same with Tony.

I sat there and looked at him on my screen for a few minutes, trying to find the right words to say. I finally began talking to him; I told him how sorry I was that this was happening to him, and no matter what happened between us, I would never wish this on him. "Please fight," I begged him. "Fight as hard as you can, because I'm still hoping for a miracle." I told him that I wasn't mad at him and that I had forgiven him. Then I assured him I would look after his children and make sure they were always okay. For a moment, I sat there with him in silence, not wanting to say goodbye, so I didn't. I simply told my big brother, "I love you." I thanked the nurse for taking good care of him, and I logged off.

Alone, in a fog, I sat there. I couldn't believe what was happening. Was I dreaming? No, this was a nightmare. Later that evening, I received a call from my sister-in-law, Heather, letting me know Tony had passed. I broke down and then went numb. Covid had taken my only sibling, my big brother, Antoine M. Nixon, 1/2/1967–5/17/2020. He was 53 years old. Gone too soon. I love you, Tony!

Who was Antoine M. Nixon? To everyone, he was Tony, who loved people and who loved to help others. He was a loving husband, father, son, brother, nephew, cousin, and friend. To me, he was my big brother who would pick on me, hide my dolls, hide in closets and behind doors to jump out and scare me, yet he was there for me when I needed him. Family mattered most to Tony. Enjoying life and making his family happy was most important to him. He didn't always get it right. I don't know anyone who has, but he did the best he could with what he had and with what he was given. He was human, like everyone else in the world.

Tony was a big kid at heart. One of his favorite places to go was Disney World, even as an adult. Our parents took us a few times as kids, and Tony's love affair with Disney continued to the end. I remember the first time he took his daughter. He was so excited to take her; I think he was more excited than she was. Then, when my nephew came along, he had the same excitement taking him for the first time. In 2010, Tony took all of us to Disney; his wife, kids, and me to celebrate my niece's high school graduation. He spared no expense. Tony booked us the Land and Sea Package, which included both Disney World and a Disney cruise to the Bahamas. From the time he'd booked it to the time we'd left, it was all he could talk about! We had a great time and made amazing memories. Tony and I went on the rides we used to go on when we were kids. Space Mountain was one of our favorites. While we were on the cruise, Tony, June, and I enjoyed a few evenings dancing at the club and singing our hearts out during karaoke after the kids went to bed. Tony and I also enjoyed a few nights sitting together on the balcony of our cabin while everyone else slept. We chatted as we sipped Jack Daniel's and Coke, enjoying the view of the ocean at night. As I reflect on those memories, it felt good to just sit and talk with my older brother as an adult, sharing our feelings with each other.

Spending time with family was one of Tony's favorite things to do. I spent weekends at his house with him, his wife, and kids. We went bowling, enjoyed eating our favorite things, and watched *Star Wars*, *Star Trek*, and Marvel superhero movies all day. When a new Marvel movie was coming out, we all couldn't wait to go see it together. My girlfriends are not into those types of movies, so it was always something I looked forward to doing with my brother. I miss that so much now.

Tony loved playing spades. He and my cousins played spades like it was an Olympic sport, and they were all going for the gold medal! He taught me how to play, and we sat and played with our cousins for hours while drinking whiskey. We had the best times: playing, trash talking, and laughing.

My brother was also a very talented artist. He had taught himself how to draw as a child and later improved his skills by studying commercial art in high school. We had a little business; my classmates would give me a magazine picture of their favorite celebrity, and for a fee, my brother would draw a poster-size replica of the picture. Of course, I got a cut of the profits.

Tony would do anything he could to help people. He and Heather both worked at an assisted living facility. All the residents loved him so much! They still tell Heather how much they miss him. He touched so many lives, which was clear by the countless number of calls, texts, cards, and the hundreds of people who logged on and attended his virtual memorial service. No one attended in person due to the limited number of people allowed because of Covid restrictions. Only ten would have been allowed, but there was no fair way to choose who those ten would be. We decided it was best the entire service be held virtually so that everyone could attend.

Tony's life may not have always been easy, and it certainly was not without trials and tribulations, but it meant a lot to so many. He meant a lot to me, our family, and friends. He's no longer suffering, but I still miss him and wish he and our mom were still here. To honor Tony, I take part in events and memorials remembering our loved ones lost to Covid.

I am thankful for the memories, good and bad. I will just spend a little more time with the good ones. My advice to you is to take one day at a time. Hold on to the memories most dear to you. Grieve for however long you need to. Don't let anyone put a time limit on your grief, or make you feel bad for grieving. For those of us who lost a loved one early on in the pandemic, when we couldn't be with them in the hospital (they died alone), our grief hits differently. It's not the same. But we are not alone. We are all in this together.

I love you, Tony! I will see you, Mommy, and Grandma in the new world.

ABOUT RAENELL

Raenell Worrells was born and raised in Philadelphia, Pennsylvania. She and her brother Tony were educated in the Philadelphia school system, and they both graduated from Northeast High School. Raenell and Tony shared an avid love of music, theater, movies, and travel.

Raenell enjoys spending time with her family and friends, especially her brother Tony's children, Anissa and Jaden, and his granddaughter, Harper. Raenell also devotes time helping others in her community through various volunteer initiatives.

My brother Tony, about 3 or 4, I think. This has always been my favorite picture of Tony. He is such a cutie pie. My mom had him dressed so nice. He looks so sweet and innocent, though I'm told he was a little terror.

Tony with our Mom (black dress, center) and her sisters, our aunts.

Tony, 5th or 6th grade.

A painting Tony did in high school. His teacher asked him if she could keep it to hang in the class. He just got his painting back in 2016. Tony was an amazing artist.

Family portrait, circa 1983 or 1984. Tony, me, and our mother Cheryl.

Tony and his daughter Anissa.

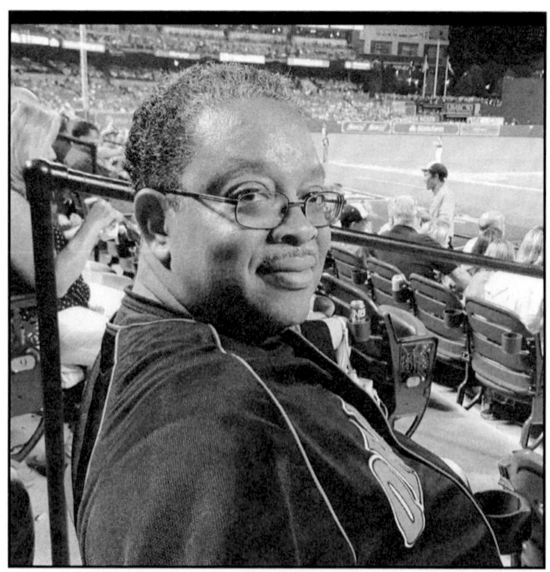

Tony at a Baltimore Orioles game.
He loved baseball, and he loved his Baltimore Orioles.

Me and Tony hanging out.

Family trip to Disney for Tony's daughter Anissa's high school graduation.

Tony and Heather on their wedding day.

Cheryl's Story

MY WIFE, CHERYL…

By David Stedman

Cheryl packed as much as possible into her 59 years on Earth. Her zest for adventure, along with her desire to help and serve others, was clear to all. She created memories for all who knew her. The life she lived had purpose and not a single moment was wasted.

LOVE OF THEATRE

One of Cheryl's true loves was the theatre, both being in the audience and on the stage. Her first acting opportunity was in the Wisconsin Rapids Community Theatre's production of *Night Must Fall*. Playing the part of the maid, she delivered her one-liners with exuberance. Cheryl never cared for delivering her lines exactly as written. She liked doing things "Cheryl's way" and preferred to ad lib or just express the general idea behind her lines. Over the years, Cheryl continued to perform in many plays. When the houselights went down and the stage lights came up, Cheryl shined her brightest, no matter how small or large her role. What she enjoyed most about her theatre experience was the camaraderie she shared with the other actors and the people working behind the scenes. She would often get together with fellow thespians at a local venue after a rehearsal or a performance. They would laugh and share with each other the crazy events that had occurred: the flubbed lines, the props that didn't work, or the ad libs used to cover up the occasional gaffe that happens in any production. By performing and providing entertainment, Cheryl enjoyed giving back to her community, which gave her a feeling of pride.

CHERYL'S PASSION AND "RULES"

No matter what Cheryl was doing, or whom she was helping, she did it with passion and love. Whether it was at work, volunteering at the food pantry, taking part in Lions Club activities, serving on various boards and councils, or helping with church and community events, Cheryl gave it her all. She was the type of person who carried a project through to completion. If someone dropped the ball on a task, Cheryl picked up the load to make sure the project was completed, even when it would mean more work for her. She never wanted to see projects, in which she believed so strongly, fail. When our Lions Club struggled to find new ways to raise funds, it was Cheryl who came up with the idea to sell Terri Lynn nuts, snacks, and sweets, and it was a tremendous success! What I admired about Cheryl is that she never forgot people who worked with her in any capacity. Whether it was a major or minor role, she thanked everyone with a note, a card, or a token of appreciation.

Cheryl, however, preferred things to be done in a particular way. This included everything from the way towels were folded to the rotation of dishes in the cupboard, so they were all used equally!

While entertaining one evening, friends decided it was time to put an end to the latter by rearranging the entire kitchen. Cheryl went along with the joke, and let's just say, the dish rotation was not an issue after that.

Cheryl's "rules" were sometimes hard to keep straight, even for Cheryl! When someone caught her bending or breaking her own rules, the rules were somehow allowed to change in her favor.

She even reminded me of my responsibilities while she was battling COVID-19 at UW Health University Hospital in Madison, Wisconsin: plants needed watering on certain days, bills had to be paid on time, and appointments cancelled or rescheduled in a timely manner. Throughout our marriage, we had the occasional disagreement; however, common ground was always found, even if I had to bend a bit more to Cheryl's way of thinking.

LOVE OF TRAVEL

Traveling brought joy and excitement into our life. Although we didn't go on a honeymoon, because I was a band director in charge of homecoming festivities that happened the week after our wedding, we made up for it with other travels. We made it our mission to see the United States and beyond. From a simple trip around Lake Superior to exploring the Mediterranean on the high seas, we made memories together in many places. Our adventures ranged from airplane trips, hot-air balloon rides, and parasailing to whitewater rafting, helicopter rides, train excursions, amusement park rides, cruises, road trips, and more.

On one particular trip, while staying near the Grand Canyon, we took a nighttime stroll. Cheryl was in awe of the stars. As she gazed at the picture-perfect sky, she remarked, "There are more stars in the sky than anyone could ever count! Their beauty is beyond compare!" We also became ship celebrities on a Mediterranean cruise after participating in the ship's version of *The Newlywed*

Game. The social director needed three couples to take part. They chose the newlywed couple and the couple that had been married the longest, but they also wanted a couple who were somewhere in the middle. A "Kiss Off" determined who the remaining couple would be. Whoever received the most applause would be selected as the final couple. Our kiss definitely caught the audience's attention. We received wild applause and were selected to be the third couple. Our lips were locked for an extended period, which appeared to add to our popularity and applause. It surprised Cheryl how long our kiss lasted, but she didn't resist, and it earned us a coveted spot on the show. Some of our answers might have been embarrassing for some people, although as performers, we were not embarrassed in the least. Our answers entertained and captured the hearts of the audience. Although we didn't win, our participation did net us a nice bottle of bubbly, delivered to our stateroom, as well as a videotape of the show as a keepsake. They even broadcast the game on the ship's TV channel for days, which made us recognizable to the other passengers.

Cheryl collected stamps in a National Park Passport Book, which included stamps to over 182 national parks, monuments, sites, and recreational areas. Before planning any domestic vacation, she always consulted her National Park Passport Book to see which parks we could visit in the geographic area we were going to explore. While on our last major trip in the fall of 2019, we traveled throughout the West Coast. Cheryl collected eight stamps there, the most from any of our trips. This accomplishment thrilled her. However, a bit of contention arose on that trip. Cheryl was adamant about visiting Redwood National Park in northernmost coastal California, which is about 325 miles north of San Francisco. I was concerned about getting to San Francisco in time for our flight home after all we had planned. Cheryl had read a story about the Charles M. Schulz Museum in Santa Rosa, California. Since I am a huge *Peanuts* fan, she negotiated with me. If she could go to Redwood National Park, then we would also visit the Charles M. Schulz Museum. Deal!

LOVE OF SPORTS AND OTHER ADVENTURES

Cheryl enjoyed a variety of sports and was enthusiastic about them all. We cheered on all the local teams by attending Wisconsin Badgers football games, Green Bay Packers games, and Milwaukee Brewers games. If Cheryl couldn't attend a game in person, she would become the team's major cheerleader, glued to the television at home. She loved her Milwaukee Brewers most of all. We attended at least ten Brewers games each season and did our best to attend postseason games as well. No Brewers game was complete without us joining in on the singing of "Take Me Out to the Ballgame" during the seventh-inning stretch. Each rendition immediately made it onto Cheryl's Facebook page for all of our friends to enjoy, so they could feel as though they had been at the game with us.

Although drinking beer is not a sport, reunions at Leinenkugel's brewery were an annual "must" for us. Of course, Cheryl documented our adventures by posting photos to Facebook. Several friends would remark about our adventures; one said, "You two go on the best dates!" Yes, we did…

LOVE OF SERVICE AND VOLUNTEERING

Cheryl thrived when serving others. She embarked on an education career in college and knew the importance of teaching, whether it be in school or for the betterment of her community. She relished the feeling of accomplishment when something she had fervently worked on came to fulfillment and made the community, or the person benefitting, better off than before. She took particular pride in leading the project to provide landscaping for the "Welcome to Fort Atkinson" signs that greeted visitors when they entered town. Cheryl was an active member of Lions Clubs International, the largest service organization in the world. In her five years as a member of the Jefferson Lions Club, she honed her leadership skills by serving in a wide variety of roles. Despite several ongoing health issues, Cheryl served as Membership Chairperson,

Lions Clubs International Foundation Director, and secretary for the club. Impressively, she became the club's first female president in 2018. She was also the club's Service Chairperson at the time of her passing. On the district level, she served as Hunger Chairperson and as Zone Chairperson. To enhance her leadership skills, she received both a bachelor's and master's degree from Lions University. Cheryl loved being a Lion and displayed a strong interest in serving in the areas of environmental, hunger, and diabetes awareness. At district, state, and international conventions, she built a global network of friends through the Lions' world. Friendships came easily for Cheryl, and people felt like they had known her forever after having just met her. Cheryl and I were weekly participants in the Burmester Virtual Cocktail Parties. This event was hosted by fellow Lions Club members, Dale and Jodi Burmester, each Saturday during the pandemic. Cheryl jumped right in during breakout sessions, making friends and leading discussions. Lions participating from around the world enjoyed Cheryl's banter and appreciated her ability to keep others engaged with one another. They described her as a gentle and friendly leader.

As a church volunteer, Cheryl took part as a council member, lay reader, and not surprisingly, given her outgoing personality, a greeter. She was also an active volunteer with the Fort Atkinson Community Theatre and the Council for the Performing Arts of Jefferson County.

LOVE OF DOGS AND ENCOUNTERS WITH OTHER ANIMALS

Cinnamon, Mia, and Lucy were Cheryl's three spoiled canines. Cinnamon, an Australian Blue Heeler, was a rescue from the Humane Society and her first "baby." Cheryl dreamed of winning the lottery and opening a dog rescue. After we lost Cinnamon, we adopted Mia and Lucy. My sister, Bonnie, had adopted a Rat Terrier Schnauzer puppy. When Bonnie told Cheryl that more puppies from the litter were available, we went the next day to see them. It was difficult for her to choose just one to bring home, and the family who owned the pups were smooth salespeople. They explained to Cheryl that if she took two puppies, they could keep each other company. That was all she needed to hear; she was sold! Cheryl "needed" two dogs, so we brought Mia and Lucy into our home.

Cheryl's experience with other animals was interesting. Her encounter with a bison while driving through Custer State Park in South Dakota was priceless. She was recording from the passenger side of the vehicle. This was when video cameras were large and cumbersome. Cheryl was holding the camera awkwardly on her shoulder. The bison came up to the window and was about to stick his head inside, but I rolled up the window just in time! I will never forget the look on her face. On another adventure on Mackinac Island, I was driving a team of draft horses from a surrey and Cheryl was to capture this once-in-a-lifetime experience on video. Unfortunately, her fear of horses impeded her ability to record the event, so our experience went forward without video documentation. However, I give her credit for riding a horse while attending an open house at the Kettle Moraine Equine Lions Club at the Horse Power Healing Center. Despite her fear, this was a Lions Club volunteer opportunity that Cheryl simply would not miss.

LOVE OF FAMILY

Cheryl doted on her family and showered her nieces and nephews with love. A proud aunt, she would snuggle with them, loving them with all her heart. We did not have children of our own, but Cheryl fell in love with the Watoto Children's Choir from Uganda when they performed at our church. The love she felt led her to sponsor one of the children. She lovingly welcomed 9-year-old Rahmah Kabuye Nakayiza into our extended family. She lit up whenever letters and photos from Rahmah arrived, and Cheryl was grateful for the opportunity to support her.

LIFE CHALLENGES

What others might consider fearful challenges, Cheryl always met head-on and never backed down. With her "tell it like it is" attitude, she never feared telling anyone what she thought or how she thought things should be done. If Cheryl came up against a challenging situation, she worked through it. If it meant altering the course of her life or changing a specific task at hand, it became the "new normal" for Cheryl. Health issues were the biggest challenges in her life. Through lupus, Wolff-Parkinson-White Syndrome, kidney diseases, dialysis, then gastric sleeve surgery to prepare her for her kidney transplant, and her actual transplant, Cheryl was a trooper and a fighter. When Cheryl first learned she had lupus, she knew it would mean undergoing some form of chemotherapy. Even though she was fearful of starting treatment, she knew it was necessary for any chance of improvement. When her heart started short-circuiting, causing it to beat out of rhythm, she knew surgery was the only answer. After learning her kidneys were failing (despite feeling good) from the damage lupus had caused years earlier, she knew the recommended kidney transplant was something she had to do. I know others who have confronted many challenges in their lives, but Cheryl always showed incredible tenacity and courage in the many challenges she faced over the years. On the outside, Cheryl projected a brave outlook. I will never fully know how she may have been battling things on the inside, but she always bravely faced adversity and did her best to work through every difficult situation.

THE ULTIMATE CHALLENGE

As with everyone, Covid changed the course of our lives in 2020. A transplant recipient with a suppressed immune system, Cheryl was at a higher risk for Covid, so we were very cautious. The two of us had a quiet Thanksgiving at home instead of spending the day with family, which we normally did. Never did I imagine this would be the last holiday I would ever spend with my dear wife. She started coughing and experiencing shortness of breath the day before. We notified the county health department of her mild symptoms. They suggested she get a Covid test. It was a holiday weekend, and the nearest test location was 32 miles away in Madison. The drive was unsettling and somber as we both had feelings of uncertainty and dread. We knew a very serious situation could be unfolding. Always the optimist, her final Facebook post was on November 28th, 2020: "Brighten my day with the sixth photo in your gallery with no explanation." Forty-three friends responded within a day.

The next day, her test results came back positive. Although devastated, Cheryl and I prayed about this new challenge. Her symptoms quickly worsened. An ambulance was called, which transported her to Fort Memorial Hospital. They assessed her, but since her blood oxygen level was still in the normal range, they sent her home. She spent a restless night alone on the couch. By morning, her blood oxygen level had dropped significantly. We did a videoconference with the doctor, and he asked her to return to the hospital for further tests. A few hours after being at the hospital, they told Cheryl she had pneumonia, and because of her kidney transplant, their staff was not equipped to treat her condition properly. As a result, they transferred her to the UW Heath University Hospital in Madison on December 2nd. It broke my heart, but because of Covid restrictions, I could not be with her… even for a quick visit. Knowing Cheryl was struggling with this dreaded virus, and I couldn't hold her hand, or be by her side, was the hardest thing I have ever endured. I held a constant vigil at home and relied on phone updates from doctors and nurses at the hospital.

Cheryl and I communicated via phone during this time. Five days later, on December 7th, the doctors told Cheryl she needed to be put on a ventilator. She immediately called me. I could tell by her shaky voice that she was frightened. I felt helpless, so I called a friend at midnight just to chat until the hospital called a half hour later to assure me that Cheryl was comfortable and successfully on the ventilator.

During the time that followed, the nurses put me on speakerphone next to her ear when I called. I prayed my voice and words of encouragement would comfort her and give her strength.

On December 22nd, I received a call saying Cheryl would not make it through the night, and I could come to say goodbye. Our pastor drove me to the hospital. We arrived at 11:30 pm. Fortunately, they allowed him to accompany me to the ICU. Wearing protective gowns, masks, gloves, and face shields, we entered Cheryl's room. She was hooked up to monitors and fluid drips, still on the ventilator. My strong-willed, tenacious wife lay there helpless. It was difficult to see her this way, but I still wanted to let her know I was there. With my gloved hands, I stroked her hair and held her hand. It was hard to hug her while wearing a face mask and gown. I put my body as close as I could to hers, just to touch her one last time. Covid was the one challenge Cheryl could not overcome. She fought hard, but the virus and pneumonia that developed in her lungs were too much. We stayed with her until the end.

Cheryl died at 3:10 am on December 23rd, 2020. I took a few more minutes to be with her, then I said one last goodbye.

Cheryl was one of the most fun-loving, adventurous, big-hearted people I will ever know, and I loved her with all my heart. We were together, through every adventure and challenge, for 38 years. Covid did not define her life. All the wonderful things she did for others, and the way she made people feel, defined her life. In sharing her story, I hope others feel inspired to be like Cheryl… to get involved and make a difference as she did.

Cheryl's passing has forced me to be more self-sufficient. It's been years (since college) that I've had to do my own housekeeping and bill-paying and maintain a household. Cheryl had handled these things so wonderfully. Losing my beloved spouse made me realize how many things she took care of that I took for granted. I advise other couples to talk often about each other's end-of-life wishes. It is important for both to have a firm grasp on financial and insurance information, as well as passwords and other important documents a spouse may have filed away.

Not a day goes by that I don't talk to her. I have received several signs that my guardian angel, Cheryl, is making sure I stay on the right path, even though I now face that path without her. It can be a reminder to pay a bill, or a phone call from someone checking in on me. Sometimes, a cardinal shows up at our bird feeder. It is said that cardinals are a sign that loved ones who have passed are visiting, and they usually arrive when they are most needed. Cardinals can also make an appearance during times of celebration, or despair, to let us know our loved one will always be with us.

I am proud Cheryl's memory is being honored in many ways. Our Jefferson Lions Club planted a sycamore tree and dedicated it to her memory. The Jefferson County Humane Society placed a memorial brick at their facility in honor of her love of animals. The Lions Eye Bank of Wisconsin flew their "Donate Life" flag at half-staff in honor of Cheryl being a cornea transporter and an advocate for organ/tissue/eye donation. She was the posthumous recipient of their Legacy of Sight award for 2021. They also awarded Cheryl a Melvin Jones Fellowship, the highest honor awarded by Lions Clubs International, courtesy of Lion Daniel Marney Elkins from Delaware.

These honors will be constant reminders of Cheryl's generous spirit and strong desire to make a difference in the world. I hope her legacy inspires others to live a life full of gratitude and service to others.

ABOUT DAVID

David Stedman is a retired music instructor and lives in Fort Atkinson, Wisconsin. David is an active member of Lions Clubs International, and he has been active with the University of Wisconsin's Health OTD (Organ and Tissue Donation) Department as the "Dottie Donor Dot" Mascot. He also enjoys public speaking to promote organ and tissue donation.

You can connect with David on Facebook: David Leon Stedman, or email: tubabuzz@charter.net

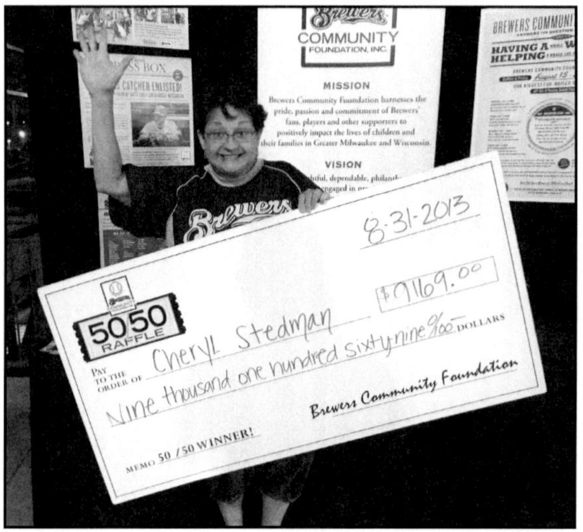

Cheryl wins the 50/50 raffle at Miller Park on August 31, 2013

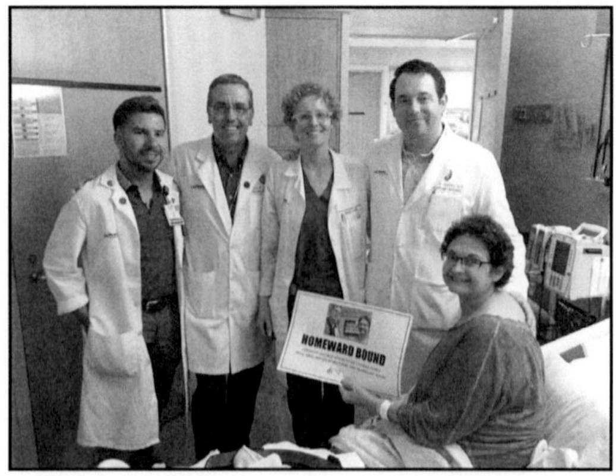

Cheryl with her kidney transplant team, May 2016.

Cheryl And David with their Watoto Children's Mission sponsor child, Rahmah Kabuye Nakayiza from Uganda, Africa, in 2019

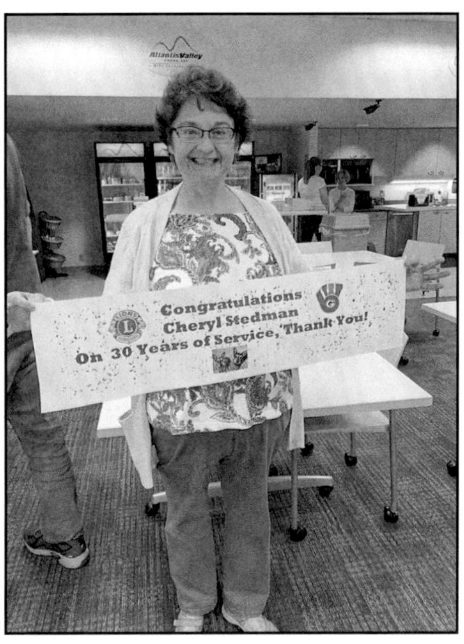

Cheryl celebrating 30 years of service as a bid sales representative at Demco in 2019.

Cheryl As Jefferson Wisconsin Lions Club's first female president.

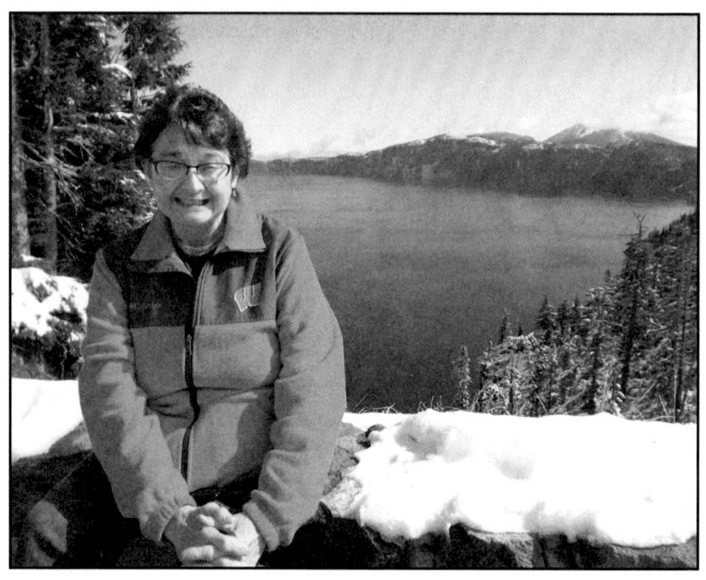

Cheryl at Crater Lake National Park in Oregon, 2019.

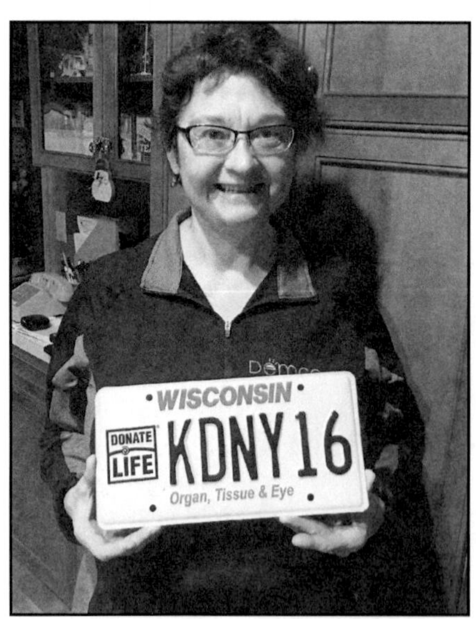

Cheryl with her Donate Life license plate December 2019.

Cheryl participating in the National Kidney Foundation of Wisconsin Capital City 5K event in Madison, Wisconsin, 2018.

Cheryl in one of her many theatrical roles with Fort Atkinson, Wisconsin, Community Theatre.

Cheryl Panning for Gold in Alaska, 2002.

Angelo's Story

THE STRONGEST MAN I KNOW

By Patty Mazzola

At five feet, five inches, Angelo was not tall by most standards, yet his presence loomed large in my life. In my family, we all looked up to him. He was the person I went to for advice, to share a funny story with, and to get a reaction from. He was the first person I received a text from each morning and the last person I talked to at night.

Angelo spoke in a calm, thoughtful voice, and he had a signature way of answering the phone; "Yello!" With a relaxed demeanor about him, he never seemed rattled by much. He ran on "Angelo time," which meant he ran late; usually 15–20 minutes. Like a turtle crossing the road, he'd get there when he got there. "Why rush?" he asked. "What's the hurry?"

People gravitated toward him. Beloved son, favorite brother, friendly neighbor, loyal husband, dear uncle, proud business owner, valued coworker, dedicated stepfather, and adored papa; an array of titles earned throughout a lifetime. His most cherished role was "Dad," and like an all-star player, he was the best of the best. As dad to his three daughters, he anchored our family with his strength and loving support. Like the sun setting in the ocean, he was a source of endless joy. Not only was he my dad, he was my best friend. This is his story.

Angelo was born on January 20, 1950, in Pietraperzia, Sicily to Maria (née DiDio) and Salvatore Mazzola. He had four brothers; Ciro, Joseph, Philip, and Salvatore. At the age of ten, he moved with his family to the United States and settled in East Boston, Massachusetts. After several years, his parents and three younger brothers moved back to Sicily, but he and his brother Ciro stayed in the U.S. where they married and had their own families. Angelo often spoke of the "old country" and the farm where he grew up. Pietraperzia held a special place in his heart, and he visited whenever possible. Growing up, life was tough, and his family had little, yet his memories were always fond. One of his favorite pictures from childhood was one of him with his family when he was chosen to be "the Angel" in one of the local Sicilian feasts.A proud Italian American, he loved the Italian flag, Italian food, Italian music, the feasts in Boston, movies that featured Italian culture; he even liked to eat tripe… now *that* is a true Italian. If you were Italian, he felt an instant connection to you and wanted to sit down and talk about the "old country."

As a young adult, Angelo settled in Medford, Massachusetts, to raise his family. To me and my two sisters, he was a good mix of disciplinarian and "fun dad." He led with strong morals and would often state, "It's the principle." He doled out punishments, and celebrated our achievements. Like children waiting for the ice cream truck to come down their street, we would wait for him to get home at 6:00 pm (often with candy bars from the train station). When he was home, we reveled in his attention as we took turns vying to be the center of it. Happy to put a smile on our face, he never said "no" to our requests for an ice cream or slush. We could easily sway him, and we knew it. He had nicknames for each of us: "Peanut" for Angela, the youngest, I was "Patty Lyn," and my older sister, Laurie, was "Sonny." Despite his easy-going demeanor, the suppressed Sicilian temper reared its head occasionally, and when that happened, we knew we had better run.

The "family man" title included our extended family, so it's no wonder we spent many weekend nights and holidays with our uncles, aunts, and cousins. The adults played cards, smoked cigarettes, and drank coffee while the kids played games. Summers flew by with weekly outings at amusement parks, beaches, mini-golf courses, and drive-in theaters. Every summer, we spent a week at Weirs Beach in New Hampshire, always hitting the fun tourist spots like Santa's Village and Story Land, as well as the arcades, water slides, and go karts. My Dad was a "young Dad," and was known for his affable personality. My friends would ask, "That's your Dad? He looks so young!" as he made us laugh with his funny comments and witty remarks. Always looking handsome and put together, he made me proud. It made sense since he was a clothes guy and loved shopping, but it also had to do with his business.

Aside from family, Angelo's other true love was his clothing business. He began working for H&B Pants Co. on Essex Street in Boston, on the edge of Chinatown as a teenager and shared a special bond with the owner, George. When George passed away in 1975, Angelo became co-owner of the business with another employee, Willy. Over time, he bought out Willy and became the sole proprietor of H&B Pants Co. Each morning when he unlocked and lifted the big metal security gate, he lit up with pride. It was a large, dusty old space, yet he walked around like it was the Taj Mahal. When it was my turn to go to work with him, he would either close early, or take an extra-long lunch break, so we could walk around Boston, check out the Common, or the Frog Pond in the Public Garden. When his building was sold for new construction, he moved to a new space in Medford Square, but it never felt the same. The excitement of the commute, the nostalgia of the old building, and the hustle and bustle of downtown Boston were gone. Angelo closed his business altogether in 1990, but he truly missed it like an old friend who had moved away.

Angelo was no stranger to health challenges. He endured major back surgery in the early 1970s, when it was more complicated and painful, and the recovery more intense. Mental health issues challenged him in his twenties, but he came out on top after seeking professional help. We received dismal news in 1992, when we learned he had kidney failure and would eventually need a transplant. He was married to his second wife, Rose, and she was wonderful at guiding him through this difficult, scary time. Before his transplant, he suffered a heart attack and needed double bypass surgery. Once healed from that surgery, he could proceed with his kidney transplant at Massachusetts General Hospital on May 23, 1995, at the age of 45. Knowing I needed this great man and reassuring presence as a guiding light for my future, I offered him one of my kidneys. In the beginning, Angelo was not in favor of accepting his daughter's offer to donate a kidney. Ferociously protective of his children, he was also too proud to accept help. After careful consideration, he ultimately said yes, and I became his living kidney donor. We were already the best of buddies before the transplant, and that bond became even stronger afterward. It was the best decision for both of us, and "our" kidney worked beautifully for the rest of his years, allowing us extra time (26 years) to make more memories. Throughout this time, Angelo had the support of his family, and also Rose's family. He was a stepfather to three boys; Joey, Denny, and Kevin, and he loved Rose's family as his own.

Angelo continued to be a pillar of strength for his family. He was our driving instructor when we were teenagers, our taxi when we needed a ride to the airport, and our skilled negotiator when we were buying a car. Without hesitation, he happily performed these same duties for his grandchildren. He first became a grandfather, or "Papa," at age 42, and he reveled in this new role. It brought him such joy to amuse his grandkids with practical jokes and to engage in games of chance with them. Angelo loved traveling with his daughters and grandchildren. Trips to Disney World, the Jersey Shore, Ocean City, Old Orchard Beach in Maine, Niagara Falls, a cruise to the Bahamas, and New York City made us appreciate life and family time. Angelo craved the oceanside. He appreciated a good boardwalk where he could eat seafood, play carnival games, and soak up the ocean air. Casinos and staying up late filled him with delight. If a deal was to be had, Angelo found it! A bargain hunter through and through, he stopped at every yard sale, slowly scoured through flea markets, and would drive past stuff left in front of someone's house at a snail's pace, just in case there was something he could use. He sure had an eagle eye for a deal!

When the grandkids were younger and in Little League, you would find the proud grandpa with a snack and a bottle of Diet Coke, cheering on his grandkids. Angelo was an enthusiastic Boston sports fan and enjoyed watching games with his son-in-law, Bob, and his grandkids; Justin, Tyler, Kenna, and Bobby. The excitement of attending a Red Sox or Celtics game with one of us planted a smile on his face for days.

In his last decade, Angelo thrived in the routine he had created. Every morning, he would meet his brother Ciro, his friend Tom, and other acquaintances at Dunkin' Donuts. It was then on to the YMCA gym to work out (and socialize), and home to spend time with his beloved cat, Khloe. He always ended up back at Dunkin' Donuts in the late afternoon. At night you could often find him at one of his favorite restaurants with his family. Every Sunday, he attended Mass at St. Raphael's in Medford, and every other Thursday, he met a group of guys for his "breakfast club." Saturday nights were spent with his brother Joe at Café Sicilia. On Sunday mornings, he talked to his brothers, Philip and Salvatore, in Sicily, and between these routines, he would text or call his daughters and grandkids. He liked to text about his favorite shows; the *Chicago* series or *Parenthood* with Angela, *Walking Dead* or *Blacklist* with Laurie, *Shameless* or *Seinfeld* references with me. We could laugh for days about George from *Seinfeld* or Larry David's quirks, but the character he loved most was Frank from *Shameless*. Gracefully opposite, he often joked he wanted to be more like Frank. Whenever I felt embarrassed by some of his actions, he would just grin and say, "What would Frank do?"

Once, during a car ride, he said to me, "I wish I had a guy best friend, like they do in the sitcoms, someone who just pops by. We hang out together and tell stories and laugh." I replied, "Well, you have me. I'm your best friend." He responded with, "That's not right. My daughter shouldn't be my best friend." He pondered silently for a few moments and came back with, "No, I take that back… it's been great for me, but not so much for you because I won't be around forever." I came back with, "Come on, Papa, you're stuck with me. We're best friends forever!" Under his breath he mumbled, "Oh boy," but I think he was secretly happy. Reflecting on this now, I'm sure he knew in his soul it was going to crush me one day to be without my best friend.

Strong and resilient, Angelo fought through the many health challenges that had befallen him, but starting in 2015, these challenges proved especially difficult. Luckily, "our" kidney was still doing well after 20 years. However, the immunosuppressant drugs he was on to keep his kidney from rejection made him more susceptible to cancer cell growth. These diagnoses all seemed to come at once; skin cancer, colon cancer, and lung cancer. He underwent four major surgeries and suffered some complications, but he battled through and endured each setback like a warrior. Everybody was always hoping for that "break" for him… a break from health worries and surgeries. Angelo referred to his long list of doctors at Mass General as "my team," and he believed he was getting the best care possible there. Through all of his health struggles, Angelo always kept a brave face and positive attitude. When asked "How are you?", his unwavering reply was always "Doing great! Life is good!" Living life to the fullest, he never took a single day for granted. A true champ with the ability to bounce back from major health issues, he was finally cancer free, and we were all looking forward to that well-deserved break. Then came 2020.

Happy and in good health, Angelo turned 70 on January 20, 2020, and we had a blast celebrating with him at Encore Casino. In February 2020, he became aware of the health crisis sweeping across continents. He often spoke to his brother Philip in Sicily, and Philip had been sharing with Angelo the dire story of the situation in Italy. They were in lockdown, scrambling to buy necessities because of a new virus, COVID-19. Stories of people dying, especially the elderly, made Angelo uneasy. He began shopping and stocking up on supplies. When the news started coming in of cases popping up in the U.S., we knew we needed to keep this virus as far away from him as possible. I spoke to his doctors and heard all I needed to hear in just two words: "Isolate him." And so it began.

Angelo lived alone and embraced his independence but wasn't thrilled about having to quarantine in his apartment. Thriving in the company of others, he was a social butterfly. The loss of independence that came with isolation proved difficult for him. I became his "person," dropping off what he needed at his door, and my sisters would also help if necessary. Obeying COVID precautions, we would only sneak a peek at him through the door. Keeping him safe became my number one priority, so I too isolated myself. We were in a tight bubble. Angelo struggled without his family nearby, and he fiercely missed his routine and weekend outings. He would complain that I was going overboard with these rules. I understood it was difficult for him, but I also knew if the villain came near him, the outcome would not be good.

Early on in the pandemic, he developed a cough. They tested him for COVID twice and the results were negative. However, he had a lung infection that required hospitalization. It was the first time he had been in the hospital without family by his side. Being alone, knowing there were patients fighting the virus and seeing the nurses and doctors looking more like astronauts in their full protective gear, planted the biggest fear in him. Luckily, he fought off the infection, and once back at home, he did not challenge me anymore. Safe inside his cocoon, Angelo kept busy doing word search puzzles, listening to music, cooking, surfing the internet, chatting with people on Facebook, and enjoying the company of his cat Khloe.

Though I never wavered in my belief that being isolated was the safest scenario for him, I worried about his mental health, as being isolated all the time was wearing him down mentally. For a change of scenery, we took daily drives. Donned with our masks, gloves, and sanitizer, we drove to Revere Beach, Horn Pond, or Lake Quannapowitt, but our first stop was always the Dunkin' Donuts drive-through. I would wipe down his cup, keep the windows open as we drove, and wear my mask at all times. He would roll his eyes at me, yet I know he appreciated it all. "Okay, Nurse," he would smirk. We also enjoyed some serenity on our walks in the woods or around Horn Pond. With excitement, Angelo searched for special rocks, especially painted ones.

May 23, 2020 was the 25-year anniversary of his kidney transplant, but none of that mattered when, unexpectedly, his ex-wife Rose passed away. They had remained close friends, so this really shook him. He needed family, so we did our best to be near him and support him, while trying to be socially distant. We got creative with outside visits with the grandkids, picnics on a park bench, and more strolls through our favorite nature spots.

In August, the family headed to Cape Cod and Angelo was delighted to have his daughters, son-in-law, and three of his grandkids all together in the same place. Soaking in the ocean air, eating seafood, swimming in the pool, and playing board games was just the vacation we needed. We were happy to be together, even if it meant wearing our masks at all times, taking our temperatures each morning, keeping six feet apart, and driving in separate cars.

In September 2020 and then again in December, Angelo needed to have a heart procedure to unblock a stubborn blocked artery. The procedure was more involved and daunting than expected. He had to stay awake and lie still for a combined total of 12 hours. The surgeon let me know it was successful and raved about my dad being one of the strongest patients he had ever come across. I was grateful one visitor could be with him, but shortly after this, COVID cases began to rise, and hospitals would once again be on lockdown with a no-visitor policy.

Once home, Angelo had a new routine and continued to stay COVID safe, only venturing out to the grocery store or run errands and always wearing his mask and gloves. He enjoyed watching Hallmark holiday movies and began a new hobby of rock painting. His brother Joey brought many of his meals, and I would go by most nights to visit and go on our car ride.

The holiday season was a favorite of Angelo's, especially the sparkling Christmas lights. Driving around and admiring the spectacular light displays put a smile on his face. He longed to be with family for the holidays, so we did a "modified" Christmas Eve at Laurie's house, with the kids and grandkids, to exchange gifts. As the New Year approached, we went for one of our night drives. I thought having mostly just me for company must bore him. As we drove, we now wore two masks each and continued to keep the windows rolled down because of the recent surge in COVID cases. One of Angelo's favorite songs, "Hey there, Delilah," came on the radio. He turned up the volume, saying, "Come on, Patty, we need to have some fun!" He sang along, doing a little dance, and as I looked over at him, I knew he was smiling under his masks. Without hesitation, I joined in and sang too. When the song ended,

I exclaimed, "Next year is going to be an exceptional year! 2021! Your birthday is coming up, we'll be getting a new president, and the vaccine is on its way!" We were both excited, like children anticipating their birthday or summer break.

For his birthday on January 20th, I brought him dinner, dessert, and a balloon, and we watched the presidential inauguration on TV. In noble spirits and looking forward to the new year, he scheduled his first COVID vaccine shot. He had a cough again, and it seemed persistent. He had taken a COVID test the previous day, and it was negative. With no fever and no other symptoms besides a cough, the doctor didn't seem concerned. Then on Friday, he admitted to me he was tired; in fact, exhausted. I begged him to go to the urgent care, but he wasn't having it. Normally, Angelo was quick to seek help, wanting to get ahead of any health concerns, but he only had one thing on his mind: his first COVID shot was scheduled for Monday, Feb. 1st, the first day that he was eligible to receive it. He didn't want to miss it.

A snowstorm attempted to sabotage his plans, but a determined Angelo made it to his vaccine appointment and went straight home to rest. When I went by that evening, he was resting and sleepy, so I dropped off the food and spoke to him briefly from the doorway. On Tuesday morning, he sounded better, joking as usual. Angela went by to check on him, and the next morning, she mentioned to me that he had sounded out of breath when he came to the door to speak to her. That was all I needed to hear. My sister Laurie brought him to the emergency room immediately. He didn't fight it this time; he was calm and in no hurry. Only patients were allowed in the hospital, so it was a long day of waiting for news. I called the hospital many times but was always told they were waiting for an available room for him. That evening, I finally received a text from him; "COVID test positive." My heart sank. I replied, "Don't worry, they'll take good care of you. You're in the right place," but in that moment of anguish, I broke down, crying a river of tears. Despite my efforts and Angelo's faith, my worst fear had come true. He had survived 2020 and was so close to being fully vaccinated.

How could this be happening?

Late that night, they admitted him into a room, and he called me. A glimmer of hope shone through as I heard his calm, somewhat cheerful voice. He was chatty, proclaiming he didn't feel that bad. They had him on supplemental oxygen and had begun the Remdesivir treatment. I was in constant contact with his nurses, and Laurie kept a close eye on his online test results and oxygen levels. I would call the team if we noticed any major changes. His breathing was more labored, and they kept increasing his oxygen intake level. Texts from him became less frequent and shorter. On Friday, when I spoke with him, he was upset, and I could feel his fear in my soul. I wanted with every cell in my body to be there with him, by his side. My heart broke, knowing he was alone, fighting for his life. All I could do was call his doctors to voice my concerns and beg them to let me visit him. The strict no-visitor policy was still in place, and they couldn't break it. Early that Saturday morning, anguish filled me when the doctor called to tell me they were transferring him to the ICU and would begin high-flow oxygen treatment. On Monday, February 8, 2021, they put Angelo on a ventilator. The nurses and doctors kept me updated, but it wasn't good. My dad was struggling and fighting the machine. He was tired and suffering. The next days were a nightmare. My sisters and I would talk to him via speaker phone each day with pained hearts, trying to be there for him, like he had always been there for us. But COVID had robbed us of that. How could a virus be so cruel? He deserved better. So many people were praying for Angelo and expecting him to pull through like he had so many times before. Angelo's fight for life, and the quest to keep our dad alive and well, ended on February 19, 2021, an ending that left us shattered and broken.

One of the last things he said to me was, "Everyone has their time. We can't live forever, but I just want one more year." I think he would have always said, "One more year." Despite his slowing down a bit, he was a young 71 with a passion for life.

Because of COVID, our dad is gone, and we miss him tremendously. We will never forget his exuberance for life, his quiet enthusiasm for experiencing new things, his never-ending patience, his fun spirit, and his generous heart. We will miss hearing his laughter, his steady guidance, loving advice, and constant check-ins. The sun was always brighter with Angelo by our sides. We will forever embrace his memory within our hearts.

RIP Angelo
1/20/50–2/19/21

~

ABOUT PATTY

Patty Mazzola lives in a suburb of Boston. She has been an early childhood educator for 32 years and also a nanny for the last 24 years. In the past, Patty has volunteered as a Big Sister, Aids Action Buddy, Soldiers' Angel, Playspace Activity Leader for Horizons Initiative, and for the Homeless Coalition of Massachusetts. She has also volunteered for many other local organizations that she holds dear to her heart.

What brought Patty the greatest joy in her life was donating her kidney, in 1995, to her best friend and favorite role model, her father. She is grateful to be able to honor his memory and keep his legacy alive by sharing his story.

Patty would like to remind people that, during a pandemic, utilizing simple precautions, like wearing a mask, getting a vaccine, and social distancing, can save lives—especially lives of those who are immunocompromised like her father was.

You can connect with Patty via email: plyn449@gmail.com

Maria and Salvatore Mazzola with 3 of their sons: Ciro, Angelo (The Angel), and Joseph at the Celebration of the Feast of St. Joseph in Pietraperzia, Sicily.

1973. Angelo and Patty. Father and daughter, and best buddies from the start.

♥

1976. #1 Girl Dad. Angelo and his three daughters, Laurie, Angela, and Patty.

1990. Ciro, Joey, and Angelo at Ciro's house in East Boston on Christmas Eve.

1991. Angelo visiting his father and youngest brother, Salvy, in Sicily. He adored spending time with Salvy, and wished that he could have seen him more often.

1992. Angelo with his daughters, Angela, Laurie, and Patty, on his wedding day to Rose in Las Vegas.

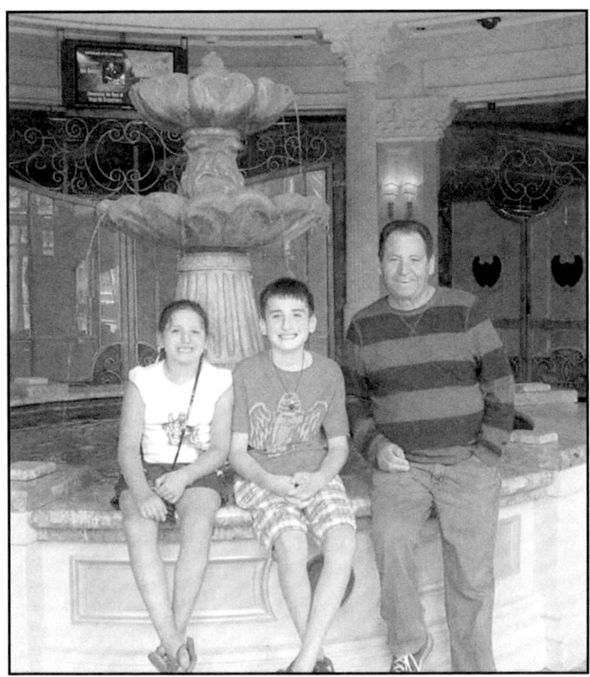

2014. Jennifer, Timothy, and their Papa, on vacation in Niagara Falls.

2015. Angelo on vacation with Rose, his daughters Laurie and Angela, son-in-law Bob, and his grandkids at one of his favorite places — Disney World.

2018. Angelo with his grandkids, Tyler, Justin, and Kennady, at Kennady's high school graduation. He never missed a family event.

2019. Hanging out with his brothers, Ciro and Philip, at Dunkin Donuts.

Isabelle's Story

ALWAYS OUR HERO

By Fiana Garza Tulip

As we walked around my Brooklyn neighborhood on a sunny spring day before my mom's flight home, I felt heartbroken. I was going to miss her. Her visit had gone by too fast, especially since I had spent most of the time sick in bed. But, as I lay in bed, it was comforting to hear her in the next room, laughing with my six-month-old daughter, Lua, my mom's first grandchild.

It was time to say goodbye, and I remembered we hadn't taken any photos. She said it was fine and we could do it next time. "No, no," I said. I wanted her to at least take a picture with Lua, so I handed my daughter to her. They pressed their cheeks together and smiled. Lua giggled and my mom looked the happiest I'd ever seen her. I quickly took two photos, and we said our goodbyes. It was March 2020, the same time the pandemic began to erupt across the country. This was the last time I would see her alive.

THE YOUNGER YEARS

When I was about three or four, I spent most of the day wondering when my mom would come home. She was my best friend, and I idolized her. I remember her walking through the door with pink Mary Kay boxes, so full of energy. We were always so delighted to see each other. My mom and I loved to sing. I'll never forget how we marched around the house, clapping and singing to various songs she had taught me. A Mary Kay song stands out in my memory the most. Then we'd transition into a chant my mom had made up. This chant has been, and will be, my north star until the end of time.

Fight! Fight!

Fight for what you know is right!

Fight! Fight!

Fight for what you know is right!

Isabelle Odette Hilton Papadimitriou was born on April 1st, 1956, in Brownsville, Texas. She was given the name Isabel Odette Garza (her name would go through many changes throughout the years). Born to a single mother, she grew up independent and strong-willed, and she proved to be a bit of a handful for my grandmother. When a friend offered to take care of my mom while my grandmother worked, her days with this other family turned into weeks, then months, and then years. It didn't go unnoticed by my mom that she was the only one of her four siblings being taken care of by another family.

At 14, my mom, a baton twirler and flute player for her high school band, became pregnant with my half-brother, Isaac. She married Isaac's father, Richard, and they moved from Texas to Chicago when Isaac was a newborn. My mom found herself a thousand miles from home, with no family or friends to lean on for help. She rarely saw her husband, who was in medical school, and she practically raised my brother on her own while living on Doritos and Coca-Cola. Six years later, she caught Richard having an affair and divorced him.

My mom was beautiful inside and out. She beamed with joy despite having had a tough childhood. I'm sure I don't know even half of her story, but what I do know is she was a fighter and, sadly, a magnet for misfortune.

FAMILY LIFE

My mom attracted many suitors, including my father, Paul Garza. I likely romanticize their courtship, mostly because I know little about it. From the photos, it seems my dad was the cool guy. He sang in a band, had long hair, and wore bell-bottoms. After serving in the Navy for a brief time, he dove into real estate and found his passion. My dad was the guy who was going to save my mom from hardship and give her the life she desired and deserved.

When I think of my younger years, I remember little. But I have technicolor memories of my mom, my dad, and my brother and me playing silly games in the backyard and twirling to whatever music danced from the record player. Those were happy times. I can hear my mom's laugh now. Sometimes her laugh was big enough to wake me up from my deep toddler slumber when my parents had friends over. I loved how fun-loving they were.

EVERYTHING WAS OKAY UNTIL IT WASN'T

My dad's job had us moving from city to city in Texas. His relationship with my brother (who was settling nicely into teenage rebellion) was nothing short of a challenge. My mom switched careers and left her bank-teller job to become a respiratory therapist. She wanted to do something more lucrative and meaningful. This endeavor also meant going back to school and spending less time with us. The arguments between my mom and dad grew worse. After one fight, I screamed, "Get a divorce! Please!" I was seven years old.

My mom cried every day after my dad told Isaac (he was 16) to move out. I could hear her through the bedroom door. I missed our life. All I wanted was for us to sing those Mary Kay songs again. One Saturday afternoon, I played her favorite song, "Downtown" by Petula Clark, outside of her bedroom door. I hoped it would lift her spirits. Instead, she sobbed even more.

Every summer, we spent the week of July 4th with some of our closest friends and family on South Padre Island. It was just a 30-minute drive from home. Still, it felt like a real tropical vacation, and my mom was most cheerful when she was with people she loved. We spent our days hopping back and forth from the beach to the pool and playing card games until very late in the evening. On the 4th of July, we all put on our matching red, white, and blue T-shirts, and we drove to the McDonald's around the corner to watch the fireworks. "Proud to be an American" blasted through our car stereos, and we kept our eyes peeled to the sky. I can see my mom's beautiful smile now as she looked up with those dark brown eyes.

When I was 15, my parents got a divorce. My mom gave me far more details than a teenager would ever want to hear about their parents' breakup, and I think, at that moment, we both wanted to die.

MARRIED AGAIN

Shortly after my parents split, my mom began dating a man with the same name as my dad. I found him awkward (sorry, Paul!) though he seemed nice enough, and he treated my mom well. To my surprise, they got engaged right away. I just wanted her to be loved the way she deserved. He seemed to be the guy for the job.

I graduated from high school and began my freshman year at the University of Texas at Arlington to stay close to my mom. Things were going well until she came home with some news. "I'm engaged," she said. "I know," I replied. "No, I'm engaged to Dimitrios. I met him at work." She was giddy. It baffled me. Who was Dimitrios? Paul, my mom, and I were living under the same roof, and now she was engaged to Paul *and* another man. My mom and I had had a complicated relationship up until this point, but this took us to another level. That same day I decided to move out.

My mom and Dimitrios (from Greece) eloped. He had zero respect for her (and me). I know this because of the bruises he gave her on her body, on her face, and in her heart. After a few years, with the help of the authorities, my mom moved out and filed for divorce. For reasons I can't explain, she kept Dimitrios' last name. She said it was because she loved the Greek Orthodox religion and thought Greek culture was captivating. Isabelle (sometimes Isabella at her church) Odette Hilton Papadimitriou is the name she took to her grave.

MORE DIFFICULT TIMES

As the years went on, I distanced myself from my mom. I wanted to live my own life and not worry about her anymore. But the distance didn't matter. At all hours, I'd receive calls from her; she would be crying on the other end, telling me that she was lonely and still not over how my dad had hurt her. Often, I wished she would disappear so I could breathe. I hated thinking this way, and I will carry the guilt of those feelings with me forever.

My mom saw many doctors for her mental health, and she took various antidepressants that helped and didn't help. It wasn't until she moved in with my brother that things changed for the better. I thought them living together would be a colossal mistake, but it ended up being a blessing because she spent her last week alive with him by her side.

THE LAST YEARS

Things were looking up for my mom in her last several years. She was smiling again and spent a lot of time with a close group of friends from work. They went bowling and enjoyed holiday dinners and birthdays together. My mother and grandmother reconnected, and she also began speaking with her father, who had left before she was born. She even made a rare visit to Brooklyn to cheer me on as I ran the New York City Marathon in 2017. Her grand gestures and cheerleading antics made me feel like a star.

In September 2018, I told my mom I had met someone. His name was Charlie. Two months after I met him, he called my mom to ask for her blessing to marry me. Charlie revealed to her that we planned to elope within the next month. I had *somewhat* prepped her for this, but still she wasn't pleased. After a very awkward and choppy conversation between her and Charlie, she finally said, "Okay." Her reaction hurt my feelings, but I understood since I was marrying a man I had just met.

Charlie and I married on December 14th, 2018. Six days later, we discovered I wasn't experiencing a prolonged hangover from our wedding celebrations; I was pregnant. We revealed the news to my mom on Christmas Day and her reaction was… well… inconclusive. It was overwhelming for her.

My quick pregnancy understandably caught her off guard, but she wanted to be there for the birth of our daughter, Lua. Unfortunately, her demanding job as a respiratory therapist made that challenging. Time off required at least a month's notice, and she could only take two weeks at a time. Sadly, she never saw me pregnant and didn't get to be there for my daughter's birth. Looking back, the quickness of everything felt like it had all been for my mom since she died a year after Lua was born. I had never planned on having a baby or getting remarried, so these things were a blessing for my mom while she was here on this earth.

PROUD GRANDMA

When Lua was born, August 25th, 2019, it seemed as if every fear or doubt she had held about her life disappeared. It was clear that a grandbaby was the "happily ever after" she had always wanted. The following month my mom landed in Brooklyn for her two-week stay. I was experiencing a fever, chills, and complete exhaustion. I couldn't wait for her to arrive, so she could help me navigate motherhood. Instead of jumping up when she walked through the door, I remained on the couch with Lua in my arms and said, "Mommy… help me." She couldn't have arrived at a better time.

For the next couple of weeks, I labored my way through the hard days of newborn life. My mom took the day and night shifts. I knew she was tired, even though she tried her best to hide it. One night, we had the worst argument ever. I'll never forget that night and how I had screamed at her while holding my daughter. We both cried ourselves to sleep and never spoke of that night again. Just writing about it makes me feel so uncomfortable. I'd do anything to have the chance to tell her I am sorry.

My mom visited again in March 2020, days before we knew Coronavirus was a "thing," and a few months before she died. I couldn't wait to see her! I wanted to make up for the last trip. I had notions of us walking through Prospect Park, dining out while drinking mimosas, and even getting our hair and nails done together. We finally had the chance to have the relationship I had always wanted. When my mom arrived, I was giddy. She picked Lua up and started dancing. We all laughed! This was going to be a great visit.

The following day, my mom planned to watch Lua for a couple of hours while I went to work. I realized I didn't feel well, so I stayed home. For her entire visit, I lay in bed while my mom made me chicken soup and looked after Lua. Hearing them giggle together warmed my soul.

Before she left, we learned someone in New York had been diagnosed with COVID-19. We didn't know enough about the virus yet, other than it was mainly in China and primarily affecting older people with underlying conditions. Looking back, I will always wonder if I had COVID-19 during her stay.

On her way to the airport, my brother texted my mom and me, telling her to be careful as she headed home.

Isaac: *Hey, by the way, none of you guys have the Coronavirus, right? Mom, be very careful at the airport and on the plane. Try not to breathe. And when you get here, I'll have a mask for you to wear.*

Mom (trying to be funny): *I promise I will not breathe at all.*

Isaac (not getting my mom's joke): *Cool*

Mom (clarifying her joke): *Well, I will be dead since I will not be breathing. So don't spend your money on a mask. However, Coronavirus is now everywhere!*

Isaac: *What!!?? Omg!! Mom, seriously, it's everywhere. Wash your hands.*

Mom: *It's fine. No worries. I'm stronger than an ox.*

As Covid ravaged the country, the hospital where my mom worked in Dallas remained quiet. In April, the governor of Texas started reopening (too soon, in my opinion) after a month of temporarily closing schools, bars, gyms, nursing homes, and long-term care facilities. The hospital my mom worked at started laying off staff. Just a year away from retirement, she had (thankfully) kept her job.

Meanwhile, in Brooklyn, my daughter, husband, and I were spending a lot of time together and enjoying it. Day in and day out, we watched the news, and with the surge in our area, we couldn't help but wonder if we should go to Texas to lock down with my mom and brother so they could spend more time with Lua. However, the moment our idea was blossoming was the exact moment Texas saw the number of COVID-19 cases skyrocket.

As her hospital filled up, my mom did her best to keep her spirits high. She posted photos of herself wearing her new face shield on Instagram, and she sent messages to friends about getting ready to go fight Covid. She even joked about how respiratory therapists were the new rock stars.

At the same time, I was receiving updates from her about how she didn't have enough PPE, how she was having to reuse her masks, and how the ER didn't have any available beds. She shared a story of a woman who was visiting her father (my mom's patient) in the rehab clinic. My mom asked her to wear a mask, but she refused. There was no longer a mask mandate at the hospital, but it was recommended. The daughter's response was, "If my president doesn't wear one, why should I?" This was annoying for my mom, but she never openly expressed fear. As far as I knew, she trusted her place of work and believed they would protect her.

We all agreed my mom should cancel her return visit to Brooklyn in June, since traveling wasn't safe. I felt guilty about this, but I didn't want to put anyone at risk. I later learned she had told my father, with whom she was now friends, that she'd be visiting me in August for Lua's first birthday. She had never told me this; it made me smile when I found out.

Now that my mom was no longer using her time off to visit us, she had volunteered to pick up extra shifts to help with the surge. In a text to her colleague, she said she wanted to work more hours to help my husband and me since we weren't working. Unfortunately, it was during these added shifts that she caught Covid.

THE FINAL DAYS

On Saturday, June 27th, 2020, my mom came home from her shift like always: through the back gate, her dogs, Shadow and Gauner, wagging their tails, ready to greet her. The next day she told my brother she wasn't feeling well. In her journal, she kept track of her symptoms: dizziness, lightheadedness, chills, body aches, huge headache, shaking and drowsy, and fever at 100.8 degrees. "All at once at 10:30 pm," she had written.

My mom was the person who always put others first, so when she was sick, she kept it to herself. Her texts to me remained lighthearted and focused on Lua. I had no idea what she was going through. She tested positive for COVID-19 on June 29th, the third day she had been experiencing symptoms. She wrote in her journal about being in constant prayer for my brother because she feared he, too, would catch the virus. After initially testing negative for Covid, my brother later tested positive the day she died.

My family and I were staying at an Airbnb in upstate New York for a change of scenery from our one-bedroom apartment. While sitting at dinner, I received a text from my brother. Despite my mom's protests, he wanted me to know she had Covid. He mentioned she was having trouble talking and breathing, so a text to her would be better. My mom reassured me she would be okay and fight it. She sent this text on July 2nd.

Mom: *I wish I could feel better, but I am not. I didn't want you to think of me during your trip, that's why I hadn't told you. I love you, and that sweet Princess is my reason to fight this.*

In the days after she was tested, my mom dismissed pleas to go to the hospital. When her sister Vicky told her to go, she responded, "You don't understand. The hospital is worse."

In her journal, she had written:

July 1. This was not a good day. I had a fever of 102 in the evening. I spend most of my day in bed. I rotate to drain the lungs from side to side and stomach to back. Isaac brings Wendy's chicken sandwich. I can barely eat it.

July 2, 2020. Still not feeling well today. I have lots of coughing this morning. Feel weak.

That was my mom's final entry.

Despite my mom telling him it would be too expensive, my brother called for an ambulance. They raced her to Medical City Las Colinas in Irving, and by the time they reached the hospital, my mom had lost her pulse at least three times.

It was the morning of July 4th, and I'll never forget how I felt when I saw that my brother was calling me early that morning. I seldom answer my phone, however, this time, I knew it was necessary. "Fiana… Fiana…" he cried. "I'm so sorry. I'm so sorry." I fell to the ground. I didn't get to say goodbye to my mom the day she died. I hadn't even spoken with her during the last week she was alive. Most painfully, I didn't get to tell her I loved her.

A death in the time of Covid is a tricky one to navigate. When my mom died, funeral homes were full, burials were being scheduled weeks in advance, and everyone seemed too flustered to help. One woman I spoke with seemed annoyed with me for asking so many questions. I had to remind her that I had never planned a burial before.

As my husband and I packed up the rental car on July 19th, strapped Lua into her car seat, and began the drive from Brooklyn, New York to Dallas, Texas, I couldn't help but wonder how in the world we had gotten here. I was going to Texas… by car… on my 40th birthday, with plenty of masks and hand sanitizer in tow, to say a final goodbye to my mother.

My brother and I held her memorial at her favorite Greek Orthodox church in Dallas. We had waited a couple of weeks until he was Covid-free. I had to ask the mortuary questions like, "Will my mom's body hold up for that long?" Immediately after her memorial at the church, the funeral home drove her nine hours south to Brownsville to be buried. We followed.

The funeral home in Brownsville had flooded the night before her ceremony, and there was no air conditioning for visitation hours. It was a hot summer day in Texas. The fans were blowing loudly to dry the floors, and everyone was sweating through their clothes. My mom, in her open casket, no longer looked like my mom because of the heat and humidity and the fact that she was being buried a month after she had passed away. She deserved so much better than this.

After she died, I dedicated every waking hour to sharing my mom's story. Her selflessness and compassion deserved global acclaim, and I owed it to her to make sure she got it. I also wanted people to know, during a time when we couldn't physically gather, that they weren't alone.

I joined a grassroots movement called "Marked By COVID" to help others amplify their story. With their help, I wrote an obituary that held our leadership accountable for my mom's death. Even though my husband and I were unemployed, I paid $2,000 to run it in the *Dallas Morning News,* and Marked By COVID funded the second one that I ran in the *Austin American Statesman*. In a blink, major news outlets from around the world asked me to talk about my mom and give my thoughts on Covid. My mom's name was in the *New York Times*, the *Dallas Morning News*, and the *Washington Post*. I appeared on CNN, BBC, Al Jazeera, and several local news stations. I repeated to myself "Fight! Fight! Fight for what you know is right!" to help keep me going, as I was also being harassed by those who felt I was spreading lies and insulting politicians.

Even President Biden featured her story on his social media pages during his presidential campaign. She would have been thrilled since she had planned to vote for him in the upcoming election. I also started a Facebook group called "I Lost my Loved One(s) to COVID-19," to bring all of us who were suffering together.

As the death count grew higher, I hosted a handful of outdoor memorials in my mom's honor. I teamed up with the Floral Heart Project, a COVID-19 memorial effort where floral hearts were laid in cities and towns across the United States. I spoke in front of groups of people at New York City landmarks, like Herald Square and Times Square, about how my mom would often sit and stay with patients, giving them someone to talk to amid their recovery.

Her love for her work was the reason my brother said she wouldn't quit when he pleaded with her in March to retire early. She wouldn't even consider it. Her work was her life, and she insisted she would stay safe as the pandemic unfolded. Now, my brother and I wonder if we should have pushed harder.

I spent the first year after her passing running at full speed on an empty tank. My world had been flipped upside down, and I was going to do everything in my power to keep her spirit alive and bring her back to me. It was as if my naïve child brain thought she had gone away for a little while, and she was just taking a really, really long time to come home.

There's a nightmare children have, awake or sleeping, in which they worry their parents have died if they're late to come home. It's in our nature to experience separation anxiety over our parents, particularly our mothers. We expect our mothers to be there always.

Grief is a strange thing. The more time that passes between her being here and not being here, the more I long for her physical presence. In a daze, I even considered taking my own life to be with her. I thought grief was supposed to get easier with time, but it only seems to get harder.

To others, her career was her job as a respiratory therapist. To me, her full-time job was being a mom. After becoming a mother myself, a shift happened in my relationship with her. I saw my mom as an independent human being, separate from her role as a parent (which I now have even more respect for). It's like I finally realized she had a life before the day I was born, and I appreciated her for it. I awoke to the reality that being a mom is a choice, and it's a choice that comes with many sacrifices.

My mom deserved more time to travel the world and enjoy her granddaughter and newly born grandson. When they are older, I will tell my children about their Abuelita Obie (what she wanted to be called). I will tell them what a brave woman she was, a woman who gave her life to save others. They will know she was also a loving mother and grandmother, whose life was cut short at age 64 by a virus called COVID-19. She was a hero… she was my hero.

Since I wasn't able to tell her so, I designed a memorial bench for her graveside that includes a plaque of that last photo I took of her and Lua during her last trip to Brooklyn. It reads: "Live so that when your children think of fairness, caring and integrity, they think of you."

Every year on July 4th, the anniversary of her death and her favorite holiday, when America is celebrating its independence, I'll be celebrating my mom's life on the Texas beach my family had visited countless times when I was a child. Just like we did for the one-year anniversary of her passing, my brother and I will drop a wreath of yellow roses into the waves so that she can once again light up the world with her beautiful spirit, just like she used to do.

ABOUT FIANA

Fiana Paulette Garza Tulip is a communications professional by day and an aspiring author by night. She received her bachelor of science in communications from The University of Texas at Austin and her master of arts in fashion marketing from Parsons School of Design. A Texas native now residing in New Jersey, she is a lover of naps, beaches, cookie dough, the color pink, the borough of Brooklyn and cleaning everything like her mother taught her.

Fiana became an activist with Marked By COVID within days of her mother's passing on July 4th. Since then, she has committed her energy toward ensuring the country takes Covid seriously, urging everyone to wear a mask in unity (#MaskOnForMyMom).

She credits her resilience to her mother, who taught her at a young age a chant that has been a lifelong mantra for both women: "Fight, fight, fight for what you know is right."

Outside of this important work, Fiana spends time juggling life with her husband Charlie, their two-year old daughter Lua, and newborn son Albie (named after Abuelita Obie). You can find her on Instagram or Twitter with the handle @itsmefi

Isabelle Odette Hilton as a toddler, Circa 1959.

The last time Lua saw her "Abuelita Obie," and the last photo I took of my mom.

Me and my mom happy together.

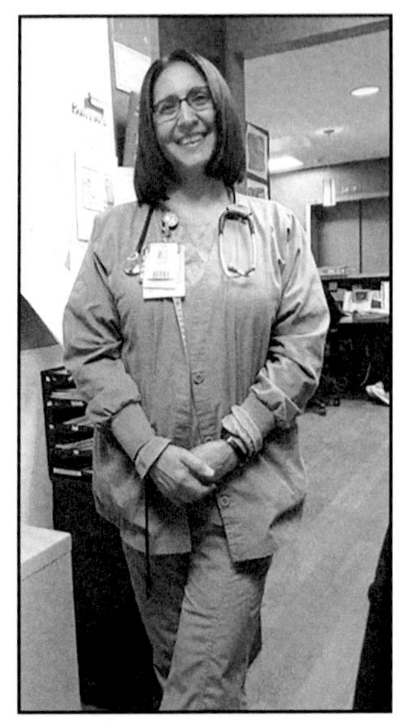

Mama always smiling at work.

My mom at her job as a bank teller.

That time she made me and my brother wear matching outfits for a photoshoot in Dallas, Texas, Circa 1996.

My husband Charlie and daughter Lua laying a rose on my mom's grave the day after she was buried in Brownsville, Texas.

My mom and dad on their wedding day in Brownsville, Texas.

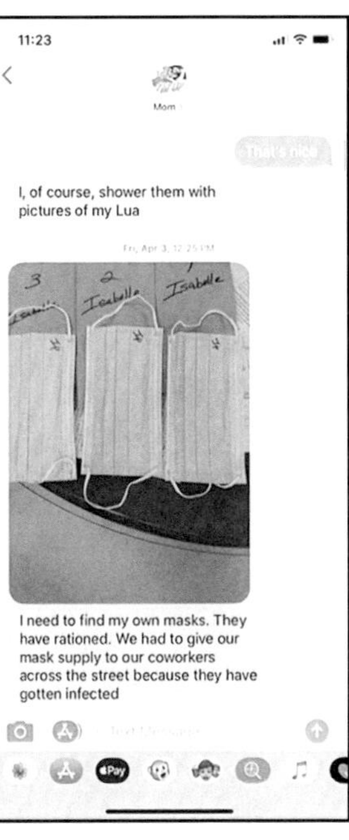

A text from my mom at the onset of the pandemic, updating me on the mask shortage at the hospital where she worked.

When my mom came to visit me in New York to watch me run the New York City Marathon for the first time.

Vince's Story

SIMPLE, RAW, AND SWEET

By Bert Foreman

October 25, 2020, is a day that will forever be ingrained in my soul. It is the day my life changed forever. Outside the window of the hospital room of the COVID ward is where I painfully witnessed my brother, Vince, take his last breath. Due to the severe restrictions on visitation for COVID-19 patients, his loved ones all gathered outside his window to be with him. Vince's wife, our mom, his daughters, our brother Terrell, and I, along with grandkids and other family members all waited with anticipation of what we knew was about to happen. Since only one person was allowed to visit him at a time, my sister-in-law allowed my mom to go in and say her final goodbyes. As she held his hand and watched the tears roll down his face, she knew he was ready. With a prayer, and in a soft voice that only a mom would have, she gave him permission to find peace and join our grandparents in the next chapter of his journey. Just before Mom left the room, they removed Vince from the ventilator. As she watched him painfully labor and fight to breathe, she continued to pray. Finally…my brother, her son, found peace and left us with the memories of his life, his journey, and his love. There is nothing that will ever be able to fill that space. Vince was my rock, my protector, and just simply, my big bro.

I find peace in the memories we made growing up. The times at home in the summer, riding our bikes to our grandparents' home, exploring the surrounding forest, or simply hanging out in the front yard dreaming about the future. All of these moments are what I have left to fill the void left by his absence. From the very beginning of my life to the end of his, I will never forget where it all started and how it came to a painful end.

In a very humble home in Southern Arkansas, across the street from the church where my mom played the piano and my brother and I sang in the choir, is where my brother first taught me about dreaming and goals. As we stood along the highway watching the cars and trucks go by, we would play a game we called, "Mine," where the first one to say the word *mine* was the one who would own the car. We both would always compete for the sports cars and luxury cars (which was a bonus because there were very few in rural southern Arkansas). However, there was one vehicle I always conceded to my brother.

"You can have that one," I would say. You could hear it from almost a mile away. The deep growl that became more intense as it got closer. With every level of intensity, my brother's smile grew just as large and intense. It was the very distinct sound of a semi-truck barreling down the highway.

My mom had a rule that we were to never set foot on the highway. But when the semis came, my brother would drag me as close to the road as he could just so we could get a close look. If we were lucky, the driver would give us a blast of the air horn after we dramatically gestured with a pulling motion as if we had our own air horn. That…THAT was the ultimate for Vince.

I would often ask why he liked trucks so much, and he would always reply with the same answer, "Maaaannn…they are so cool! You get to drive them and travel. Plus, you can make ten dollars an hour so you can take care of your family."

I would sit there in wide-eyed amazement as I listened to my brother share his dreams. But more than that, I can still see the excitement in his eyes as he shared his passion with me and reminded me of what's truly important in life.

Vince lived his life simply. He focused on the things that mattered and at the top of his list was family. There was no greater gift on earth than family. Just like his passion and dreams of becoming a truck driver, which he did for over 30 years, he had a greater passion for having a family. If you recall, one of the key reasons he wanted to become a truck driver was because it gave him a means to take good care of his family. At the time he was sharing his dreams about driving trucks, he was also sharing dreams of having a family. Those are the only things he ever truly wanted in life. Thankfully, he got them both.

Vince and I were the typical boys growing up—always getting into things and testing the limits. We would often go to our grandparents' house and play with our cousins in the woods that surrounded their home. Full of wildlife, bugs, and plants, there was no shortage of things to occupy two young boys and their cousins in the woods. Often coming home with ticks and chiggers attached somewhere on our bodies was no deterrent. It was more a badge of courage and toughness as it showed we knew the risk of being out there but were brave enough to do it again. I later decided that there is a fine line between bravery and foolishness. As we ran through the woods chasing squirrels and rabbits, or when we just pretended we were like Tarzan living in the jungles of Africa, we felt a sense of freedom and closeness. Vince would always look out for me and made sure I didn't get too extreme in my adventures. I was the more reckless, overzealous one, while Vince was the cautious one, always watching over everyone. He was always the "watchful dad" of the group. Looking back, I'm so thankful that my big brother was always watching over me. Much like he's doing now.

Once, when he, my cousin Bobby, and I were on one of our adventures, his watchful eye saved my life. There was an abandoned train near our house that we were forbidden to go to. Of course, that simply meant we definitely had to explore it. As we ventured off to the forbidden land, we hopped on our bikes and grabbed our BB and pellet guns, of course. I mean, we are true southern boys. It's practically illegal to grow up without some type of gun in Arkansas. So off we went to explore the train and see what type of adventure we would discover. As I almost always did, I took off in the lead; I was fearless and unaware. I was in heaven! Another grand adventure with my big brother! What could be better? As we walked along the train, from car to car, I became so wrapped up in the time with Vince and with the thought of being on such a ginormous train that I was completely unaware of the danger I was suddenly in. As I walked ahead of Vince and Bobby, taking it all in, I heard Vince scream, "Bert!!! SNAKE!!" Within a split second, I looked down to see a water moccasin in striking position aimed directly at my leg. And just as fast as I saw it, I saw the deadly snake fall. As soon as Vince yelled and alerted me to the snake, Bobby raised his pellet gun and killed the snake in an instant.

I was so thankful my brother's keen eye and awareness were looking out for me. That moment sums up how I always felt: Vince looked out for me and protected me. He was always there when the snakes would try to attack. And if he couldn't get to them first, he had someone or something available to pull me through.

There were so many times my mouth wrote checks that my body couldn't cash. It was not uncommon for me to get into verbal altercations with boys much older than me. Yep, I was that kid. However, I knew all I had to do was tell one of my friends to go get Vince. Once he got there, it didn't take long for the situation to de-escalate. A few times, Vince put a good beating on a couple of guys. I couldn't believe what was happening, mostly because it was my mouth that got us in the predicament, but my big brother was there to back it up. I later grew to appreciate what my big brother was willing to endure and sacrifice for me. We should all be so blessed as to have that one guy who is always there. Even if it is YOUR mouth that gets you in trouble. Yeah, he was my first true ride or die.

Vince was quite the athlete, and teachers loved him. It was hard to find anyone who didn't love him. He was just that kind of guy. Even when you wanted to be mad at him, that innocent smile and boyish charm softened you up. Now, because he was so loved, I spent most of my childhood days hearing, "That's Vince's little brother." Trust me, I used that to my advantage as often as I could. I would get away with things they would immediately punish others for. But not Vince's brother. Yes, the benefits of riding your big brother's coattails! However, the greater burden came in the way of expectations, mainly in sports. Vince excelled in multiple sports. Basketball, football, and track was where he excelled. He was a great running back, he could jump through the roof, and he was as fast as a rabbit. Some called him "black rabbit." It was a name given to him by one of his track coaches. (His teammate, Robbie, was "white rabbit," and I'm sure we can all figure out why they got their nicknames.) Following in those footsteps was a tough road to travel, but I did my best. After all, I couldn't let my big brother down.

Now, as I face this journey without him, I still try to walk that road, doing my best to live up to the expectations of being Vince's little brother and continuing his legacy. I mentioned Vince was a stellar track athlete. He was a sprinter and did various other field events, but he was primarily a sprinter. There was one race in particular that I will never forget. Vince was a member of the mile relay team, and he ran in the anchor position. He was the last line of defense for winning the race. The team that the coach had assembled for the relay was outstanding. It included guys like my good friend Sonelius, Robbie ("white rabbit"), and Vince ("black rabbit"). They had become the team to beat, and on this particular day, their opponents came ready to knock off the champions. But it wouldn't happen without a hard-fought battle.

The race started similar to how they normally would: "White Rabbit" leading off, another sprinter in the second spot, Sonelius in the third spot, and Vince as the anchor. The team started out near the front of the pack; however, this time, they lagged behind. It wasn't a huge concern, since they had a history of making up time. But this time would be different. Instead of making up time, they lagged further behind. No matter how hard they tried, they kept getting further and further behind. Each leg of the race put them more at a disadvantage. Going into the last leg of the race, they inched into second place, with the lead team being at least 50 or more meters ahead. As I stood there in the stands with my mom, cheering them on, I knew it was coming up on Vince's leg of the race. All we wanted (including the home team fans), and expected, was for him to not blow second place.

Well, obviously we were not Vince. He had a different expectation. Vince approached sports like he did everything else in life. You don't run the race to lose or just to come in second place. You run the race to win, or why run? As Sonelius rounded the final turn of his lap preparing to pass the baton to Vince, I saw Vince do something I'd never seen him do before. Instead of his normal routine of stepping on the track and loosening up, he slowly walked on the track to his position, never taking his eyes off Sonelius. By this time, the lead team had done their exchange and was even further ahead than before. Vince never looked at them. He stayed focused on Sonelius to make sure they had a successful handoff of the baton. The details of the race were his only concern. You see, if the exchange didn't happen properly, it would disqualify them, thus ending the race for them and negating the hard work it took to even get them to this position. As he prepared himself to take the handoff, I could see an intense look on his face. A look of pure determination. When Sonelius approached and gave Vince the baton, Vince took off in an all-out sprint! The crowd cheered more, encouraging him not to lose second place. We all knew he could not possibly catch the lead team…except someone forgot to tell Vince that. Just as he had focused on Sonelius handing him the baton, he now set his focus on the sprinter in front of him, who, by this time, was nearly 100 meters ahead of him. Within seconds, Vince narrowed the gap by at least 25 meters. Suddenly, a crowd that thought they had to settle for second place believed we could win the race. The cheering became louder and louder as we watched my brother close the gap. Down to 50 meters. 40 meters. 20 meters!! By the time they got to the last turn, Vince had gotten his team as close as 10 meters or less! We couldn't believe it! He could win!! I saw the determination in his eyes. He gave it all he had. In the final straight away, we all believed we were about to see something beyond special.

However, that was not the case. "The bear" jumped on his back and ended one of the most amazing individual efforts I, and many of us in the stands that day, had ever witnessed. What he accomplished that day went well beyond the track field. That relay team represented his family, and he treated them like he would any other family member. He did everything in his power to put them in a position to succeed. No matter the sacrifice. And he did it to the bitter end. For Vince, it was more important that the entire team had success than it was for him individually. If that happened, he considered it a success for him.

The other key thing Vince did, as he ran his race that day, was he inspired others to always run the race to win. Don't settle for second place just because that's the expectation others have of you, or because you feel like the gap is too much to overcome. You may not always win, but never fail to put yourself in the best position to get a win. Although they didn't win the race that day, it felt like a victory because everything Vince showed that day is everything it takes to win and succeed.

Off the track, Vince lived every day like he ran that race. So many times, I leaned on my big bro for support and encouragement. He was never one to just offer random words of opinions and suggestions, but when asked, he would definitely share how he saw it, always in a very polite but very direct way. You knew how he felt about it or what opinion he had. He would always follow it up with something like, "But, hey, that's just me. You do whatever you want. Do you, Boo." That was his way of saying, "If you mess up, don't blame me. I tried to tell you."

He had his share of missteps, too, and he would reach out to me for support and advice. Each time he did, it always made me feel a bit of pride and accomplishment that my big bro would lean on his little bro for support. Yeah, I had earned his respect—the ultimate dream of a little brother. I mean, the guy you looked up to from day one is now asking your opinion about something important in his life. That's one of those "Ahhhh… I'm just going to sit back and enjoy this moment" points in your life. This time, I was the anchor in the race, and he needed me to win. Now, I did nothing like he did that day in that race. But man, it sure felt that way sometimes. Vince had a way of making you feel you were special and had a purpose, and when he asked my opinion, I felt as if that very action was my purpose. Vince lived each day with purpose and intention—always having a plan, but always willing to pivot. I remember when he started his trucking company. It was a goal of his, ever since he started driving for major truck lines. He often thought, *Why report to someone else when I know the business and know how to drive?* He soon learned there was more to it.

One thing he did not take into consideration was the behavior of other people. You can know everything about an industry or a specific thing, but you can never fully predict the behavior of others, even those you may call friends, as my brother soon learned. He had purchased a few trucks and hired some drivers, but he soon found out that not everyone had the same work ethic that he did. He quickly realized some people are just out there to come in second, third, fourth, fifth, etc. Not everyone wants to win or cares to win, and definitely not everyone wants to do what it takes to win and succeed. Whereas Vince was *all-in*, others were just *in*, and sometimes not even *in*…just *there*. They were content to be, but Vince would challenge them.

This complete existence mindset came mostly from our grandfather, whom Vince and I followed around everywhere when we were growing up, Vince on one side and me on the other, just like two six-shooters strapped to his sides. He started calling Vince and me his two guns. We would always hear, "Here comes Dallas and his guns." Vince and I would always glow with pride and joy each time we heard that, and it never got old.

Our grandpa taught us what it meant to have character and integrity. He was not a tall man, but we pictured him larger than life. His presence filled a room, and when he spoke, he commanded respect. Everyone knew Dallas Ford and his family. On some levels, they became the epitome of what a family should be. Grandpa would teach Vince and me things like the value of hard work, how to be "the man of the house," to never waiver in your beliefs, and to always put your family first. We soaked it up. Vince, more than me, since he was older. Grandpa never stopped teaching. I recall one time when Vince and I were helping him in his cornfield, and we were mimicking all his actions. If our grandpa did it, we did it. He watched and smiled and went on about his business. At one point, he stopped us as we were walking in the footprints he made while detasseling the corn.

He looked at us and said, "Boys, never walk in anyone's footprints. You'll get a headache."

I did not know what that meant, so I just kept walking. Right after that, he called us over to a stalk of corn. He broke off an ear of corn and shucked it. He then had us take a bite.

I remember saying, "But it's not cooked, Grandpa."

He just smiled and said, "Take a bite."

To this day, I can still taste that corn in my mouth. It was the sweetest corn I had ever and would ever taste. Vince and I were so amazed. How could it taste so good without being cooked and with nothing on it? It wasn't until later in life that I figured out what Grandpa was teaching us. It was only after watching my brother live his life that I realized he never tried to walk in anyone else's footsteps. He made his own. When you walk in someone else's footsteps, the headache comes when you try to travel their road and experience their journey. Trying to walk in someone else's footsteps can cause frustration because their feet may be smaller or larger, so the shoe may not fit and may cause you discomfort and possibly cause you to trip. You may not be going in the same direction. Even if you are, their stride may be different than yours and cause you to rush or delay your travels and not allow things to happen as they are supposed to in your life. As for the corn, it was simple. Like the corn, sometimes things are best just as they are. Simple, raw, and sweet.

There are so many things I could share about my big bro, but no matter what they are, they do not truly show what an amazing man Vince was. And more so, they don't bring him back. So, it's up to me to continue to share his story and carry on his legacy. He had so much life left in him and so many accomplishments he had not yet completed. But the greater plan saw it a bit differently. It's no longer about his physical presence. It is now about his legacy and the lessons he left us with. It's about living your life to the fullest and running the race to win. It's about finding peace in who you are and helping others do the same. That's how Vince lives now…through all the people he's touched and all they touch. He is resting now and at peace, but he is missed. Yeah, Vince may not have been perfect, but he was a perfect example of how to live your life. Simple, raw, and sweet. Miss you Big Bro….

ABOUT BERT

Bert was born and raised in a small town in Southern Arkansas. He grew up idolizing his big brother, Vince, and his grandfather, Dallas Ford. They both had a huge impact on him and heavily influenced his life's path. He moved to Phoenix, Arizona, his senior year in high school. Bert graduated in the top 4% of his graduating class and attended Arizona State University after graduating. After college, he served in the US Air Force for seven years as a radiology and ultrasound technologist. After serving in the Air Force, he continued in that profession in the civilian sector. Bert later left the clinical setting for the corporate world. He has had rolls ranging from clinical specialist to global marketing director. He currently serves as a vice president of sales for a major imaging corporation.

Bert's passion for sharing his thoughts in print started at an early age. He wrote a comic book at the age of ten. Although it never went to print, it was quite an accomplishment for a young boy, writing and creating the characters, developing the storyline, and providing the artwork. Bert's most recent work has evolved into inspirational videos focused on inspiring and encouraging others. After the loss of his brother, Vince, Bert turned the focus of his videos to include creating awareness of COVID-19 victims, and keeping his brother's name and legacy alive. It was one of those videos that inspired the creator of this book to reach out to him and to share Vince's story.

Connect with Bert:

LinkedIn: www.linkedin.com/in/bertforeman

YouTube:youtube.com/channel/UCC-Kf2ogrsmGcGreFHQKUw

Twitter: @foreman_bert

Vince and his brothers.

Vince and Grandma Marie….Unbreakable bond.

Family.

Vince loved his mom! They had a long time dream of taking a cruise. Thankfully, they were both able to fulfill that dream a year before he passed. They went to the Bahamas to celebrate their October birthdays.

Vince was proud to continue the family history of serving our country.

Vince loved family more than life...especially his grandkids.

Vince and his childhood sweetheart Wilma. They would later go their separate ways only to reunite and marry later in life. They were married until his untimely passing.

Vince with his brother and dad.

Joni's Story

MY LOST LOVE

By John Lancos

A bundle of joy entered the world on March 23, 1956, and her parents named her Joni Ilene Arkin. Born and raised in Brooklyn, New York, she fell for a guy from Astoria (Long Island City), Queens. Joni would eventually become my wife and touch the lives of so many. This is her story.

Joni came into my life on October 15, 1977, while I was working as a Park Ranger with the National Park Service at Federal Hall National Memorial on Wall Street in lower Manhattan. She worked as a temporary clerk-typist in the Manhattan Sites administrative offices. From the moment my eyes saw her I was instantly stricken. One day, I finally introduced myself to her. For someone who types with four fingers, I was very impressed with her typing speed of 63 words per minute. Within a few days, I worked up the courage to ask her out, and to my surprise, she said *yes*! I invited her to see the one-man Broadway comedy show of Danish pianist and comic, Victor Borge, and I got tickets for November 3rd.

I knew we were destined for a unique relationship when we lost out on our first kiss in the back of our taxi because of a fungal infection in my mouth. Joni would often remind me of this, but it often gave us a good laugh over the years. She said these memories never get old, and she was right. We both had a wonderful time at the show, but Joni was concerned about workplace gossip, so our budding romance almost ended there. We remained friends, but I didn't give up hope. After work one January day, we finally kissed at her bus stop. With my head in the clouds, I headed home to Astoria, a very happy man.

Shortly after our relationship blossomed, in early 1978, I secured a position at Richmond National Battlefield Park in Virginia. This turned our new romance into a long-distance "Amtrak" love affair, complete with huge long-distance phone bills for me and for Joni's parents ($300 in one month!). We were now a seven-hour Amtrak ride apart—from Brooklyn, New York, to Richmond, Virginia. Every time I picked Joni up at the train station, my heart raced as I anticipated her arrival. During my five months in Richmond, I was able to return to see her for a couple of short, but sweet, visits. Fortunately, my rusty 1972 Ford station wagon survived those road trips. Joni's parents were gracious enough to allow me to stay with them instead of my having to stay in a hotel!

By the Fall of 1978, I had resigned my position in Richmond and was back in Astoria as our "trek to the alter" continued. It was a leap of faith, but it felt right to both of us. By the end of that year, Joni and I made wedding plans for the following April. I proposed to Joni in my car on my block in Astoria. It was not a surprise and not the most romantic proposal of all time! All that mattered was we were happy.

On April 8, 1979, we were wed at the Regency House in Jamaica, Queens, before 130 of our family, friends, and coworkers. Joni radiated beauty that day, and honestly did every day from then on. With sincere appreciation, Joni and I thanked each person for their presence on our special day. As she walked down the aisle, she looked so beautiful and happy. I could hardly wait the few more minutes until she would be "Mrs. Joni Lancos." My entire existence took a breath as I held Joni tight as we danced to our wedding song, "Love Is a Many Splendored Thing." I even sang "Portrait of My Love" to her, with the help of the fine band we'd hired. Tears of joy ran down my face as I sang my heart out to my beautiful bride who was also weeping. I made it through the entire song despite the tears. Fortunately, my singing didn't clear the room!

I was blessed to have both of my parents at our wedding. We didn't know at the time, but my dad was suffering from the effects of many years of smoking. In November 1979, he passed away from extremely advanced lung cancer. With Joni by my side, and my mom's side, to help ease the pain, we made it through this tragedy together as we did with everything life threw at us. She and my mom became closer after dad's death. My dad left this earth knowing I was happy and in good hands.

In 1981, my career took a major turn when I switched federal agencies to the Bureau of Land Management. After working at a less than fulfilling desk job for them in Manhattan, I saw a vacancy announcement for a Park Ranger position at Red Rock Canyon National Conservation Area in Las Vegas, Nevada. I knew this pivot would be a positive career move for me, and Joni supported this decision. Joni had been working office temp positions, so leaving wasn't a great burden for her, and we were both excited about starting a new life in an exciting place like Las Vegas. While living in Vegas for nearly two years, Joni kept herself busy with volunteer work with the Clark County Library system. We both found wonderful doctors there, and Joni continued to see her rheumatologist and ophthalmologist back in New York.

Living in a destination city like Las Vegas brought many visitors our way, from both her family and mine. We enjoyed our time in Vegas, but it was time to return to New York. Joni missed her family and Brooklyn, and I missed my mom. Plus, we had both experienced enough of the awful desert heat!

In 1983, I was named Unit Manager of Theodore Roosevelt Birthplace NHS on 20th Street in Manhattan. Joni supported my role and was a great help. She volunteered at the Information Desk and also helped during concerts and other special events. Joni also continued her education, completing her Associate in Arts degree from Kingsborough Community College in Brooklyn in August, 1987. She and I were both very proud of her accomplishment. In 1986, tragedy hit our family once again when my mom suddenly died of a malfunctioning mechanical aortic heart valve. The valve had been implanted just eighteen months earlier. Once again, Joni was my strength during this sad and difficult time.

Throughout the 1980s and 1990s, Joni's Rheumatoid Arthritis took a toll on her health. Her joints became stiff, leading to a total knee replacement a few years later. This included at home therapy for weeks on a Continuous Passive Motion Machine to improve and maintain the range of motion in her new knee. I wanted to take her pain away. I wished it was me wincing in pain while on the machine, but she worked through it like a champ and came out on top. Her Uveitis and Glaucoma issues also became difficult for her, which eventually led to the loss of any usable vision in her left eye. Joni continued to have correctible vision in her right eye, which allowed her to drive until a few months before her death. Joni's positive attitude throughout all of her joint and eye surgeries, hospitalizations, tests, and treatments gave her the strength to get through it all. Despite daily applications of several eye drops, hospitalizations, and frequent doctor visits and exams, she was a real trooper. She believed in the power of prayer, but I'm sure most of those prayers were for me, her family and others, since Joni always put others first.

In 1993, we made another move, this time to Everett, Massachusetts, just north of Boston. I transferred to Boston National Historical Park, where I supervised and gave tours of both USS Constitution and the World War II Destroyer USS Cassin Young. Thankfully, Joni was fortunate to find excellent local doctors to supplement her continuing care back in New York.

In 1996, we moved back to New York, where I became an Education Specialist at Gateway National Recreation Area. Then in 1997, we lost Joni's mother, Frances, to Emphysema. Her final months were hard for her mother, as well as for Joni and me. To see an active and vibrant person having difficulty breathing and needing to use a nebulizer frequently was tough for Joni. Joni ended up using a couple of those same medications later in life to aid her breathing.

As the years went on, Joni continued with health issues. There was a melanoma scare when they found the most dangerous form of cancer on Joni's left leg. I was terrified, but Joni was optimistic. The tumor was removed successfully and did not return. She eventually developed lung issues and difficulty breathing, and they diagnosed her with Pulmonary Fibrosis. She was prescribed oxygen, which she used both at home and outside.

After I retired in April 2009, Joni and I made a point of travelling upstate or to New England at least a few times a year. We also enjoyed trips to Lambertville, New Jersey, and Lancaster, Pennsylvania. These became premier vacation destinations for us. Our three-to-five day trips to Lancaster usually included a dinner theater performance, and in Lambertville we enjoyed walking the Delaware and Raritan Canal, the view of the Delaware River, and lunches at the Lambertville Inn's fine restaurant. We also went fishing.

In late 2012, Joni's dad Rudy passed away at 95 from Gastroesophageal Cancer. She was heartbroken to have both of her parents gone. She and her sister Cheryl became even closer, and

Joni was an immense help to her since she was now living alone and dealing with clinical depression.

In early December 2018, tragedy struck Joni's family again. A car (distracted driver) hit her sister Cheryl while crossing the street with a friend, just a block from her apartment, and two short blocks from where we live. Her friend suffered a serious eye injury, which she fortunately recovered from, but Cheryl suffered massive cranial trauma. Part of her skull was removed, and they placed her in a medically induced coma. She never regained consciousness. Cheryl passed away seven days after being struck. This devastated Joni. She was now the only surviving member of her nuclear family. We attended two court proceedings for the distracted driver, but all he was charged with was failure to yield to a pedestrian and fined only $300. There was no jail time, and his license was never even suspended. This man killed someone and received no real consequences. It was very depressing and stressful for Joni. Cheryl is laid to rest in Beth Moses Cemetery on Long Island, near her parents. It was hard after that, driving past the driver's house and seeing his white panel van that hit Cheryl parked outside of his brother's house in our neighborhood.

For the year prior to Covid, Joni's health had been declining. She began losing weight, which she simply could not put back on. By the time of her death, she weighed an alarming 72 pounds. Her long battle with Pulmonary Fibrosis and other ailments had taken its toll, and she was having trouble walking more than fifty feet outside without having to rest.

Early in the Covid pandemic, on April 12, 2020, I was feeling ill with some trouble breathing, pain around my heart, and a slight fever. The next day, I called our primary care physician, who is also our cardiologist. He tested me for Covid that Wednesday, and I received the news I was Covid positive on Friday, April 17th. Joni, however, was unfortunately not tested with me. My chest pains and other symptoms lasted a few weeks, but to this day, I still have some memory impairment.

We both did all that we could to protect each other, especially Joni, from Covid. Joni did not venture out at all after lockdown began in late March 2020, but this horror still found its way into our home and into her. On Wednesday, April 22, 2020, at around 3:00pm in the afternoon, Joni was folding laundry in our bedroom. She came into the dinette to sit down, because she was tired and needed to rest for a few minutes. This did not concern me because she seemed fine otherwise. But ten minutes later, I turned to check on her, and she was unconscious at the dinette table, drooling onto the floor. I tried unsuccessfully to wake her, as did several first responders from the New York fire department, and private paramedics who responded to my frantic 911 call. My Joni was whisked away to the hospital. Who knows how many Emergency Room doctors and nurses also tried to save her. I rode to the hospital in one ambulance, and Joni in a separate one. I knew in my heart when she was wheeled up the ramp at Mt. Sinai Hospital's Brooklyn Unit on Kings Highway, I would likely never see her again. With Covid lockdown restrictions in place, I was not allowed into the hospital to be with her. My head was spinning and everything was a blur. This all took place a mere eighteen hours from her first signs of being sick. At the hospital, she tested positive for Covid-19. Joni died, while still in the ER, at 7:25am the next morning. Our doctor called to inform me around 9:00am.

Because of the very strict Covid protocols in place then, there was no wake, and I could not attend her burial. Our cemeteries were closed to the public for many months. It was just the Rabbi, the funeral chapel, and the cemetery staff in attendance. The funeral chapel emailed me several still photos of the Rabbi praying over her casket at the grave. God Bless them for that, but it breaks my heart. I could not be there for her! No one could.

My beautiful wife, Joni Ilene Lancos, was gone from the world at the young age of 64. The love of my life was taken from me way too soon. We had more memories to make, more dreams to fulfill.

There will never be another like her, and having her by my side for over 42 years made me the luckiest man in the world!

Since Joni's passing, I have added her name to several Covid victim memorials, both online and "brick and mortar." There are so many of us who will not let our loved ones be forgotten. These people are now my extended family!

~

ABOUT JOHN

John Lancos is a New York City native, born, in Astoria, Queens, in 1951. He is a retired National Park Ranger, and a graduate of William Cullen Bryant High School, NYC Community College, and Hunter College. He holds a BA in Geology. John still pursues fossil collecting as a hobby.

John's main hobbies are freshwater fishing, traveling, and amateur photography. Today John is trying his best to cope with losing Joni, his beloved wife of 41 years, to Covid-19 and lung disease in April of 2020. He spends most of his summers in the northern Catskills at the Sunny Hill Golf Course and Resort in Greenville, New York.

My western girl.

Our special day. April 8, 1979.

Joni light on her feet.

The happy couple. ♥

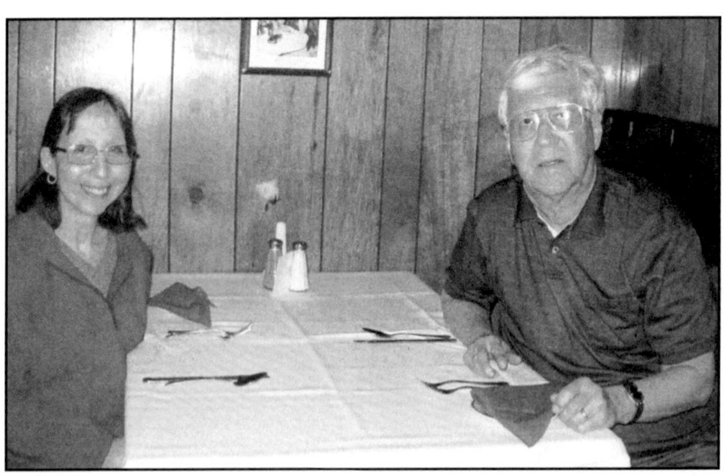

We both loved to eat!

Ray's Story

MY DAD, RAY MASKELL

By Annette Allen

My dad died of Covid-19 on 27th April 2020. He was locked away in his care home where we were told he was 'safe'. Never to be held in our arms again …

Dad was born in 1931 in South London. He was the youngest of four children. His family was very close-knit and loving, and aunts, uncles and cousins all lived on the same street. There was so much support and genuine love for one another. When the Second World War came along, Dad, like so many children in London, was eventually evacuated, but he hated every minute of being away from home. Frightened and lonely, he managed to get word back to his mum from where he was. She hopped on the next train and brought him home. Back in London, danger loomed everywhere, but the family managed to stay safe. Sirens blared often, warning of impending bombs, and they immediately shuffled under the dining room table or under the stairs. Dad's eldest brother was at war in Europe, but he managed to survive and made it home sometime later. My warm-hearted grandmother, Lily, opened her home to soldiers with nowhere to go. To boost morale, she also laid on street parties with singing and dancing to distract from the reality of the war. Lily was your go-to if you had a problem! My dad adored his mum, and his love of family clearly came from his role models.

Dad's eldest sister, Sylvia, fell in love with a U.S. soldier, Jimmy, who was a distant relative of Dad's mum. He promised his own family he would seek out his UK family once stationed in London. It was then when they met, and Sylvia became one of the GI's brides, eventually travelling over to Florida where she stayed for the rest of her life. Dad missed his sister terribly. It would be years until they met again. I never saw my dad cry, but when they finally reunited, tears gently fell down his cheeks as they embraced. He cried again when they had to say goodbye. That day is forever etched in my memory. Sylvia lived into her 90s and passed away in Florida where she had a very happy life.

Life continued. Dad did his National Service and was posted to Egypt to work in the logistics division of the British Army. He hated it, just as he had hated the evacuation when he was a boy. I can only surmise that he really didn't like being away from home. He kept to himself and took a liking to watching the boxing matches that were part of their downtime. He carried on his love of boxing for the rest of his life, including going to see the Ali versus Cooper fight in London, which he spoke of often. When I was younger, he took me to a few fights. Even now, I love watching boxing. Dad liked sports generally, and once back home from Egypt he took up athletics and cricket, amongst other sports. It was at his local athletics track that he met and fell in love with our mum, Peggy. She was a very good athlete, participating in County competitions and winning many medals and trophies. She and Dad dated for a couple of years, then became engaged. They married in 1954 and moved into the family home with Dad's parents.

Dad worked hard to save for a deposit to buy his and Mum's first home. He worked in the construction industry, and was a plasterer by trade. He worked in London on many projects over the years, including many of the royal residences, of which he was very proud. I remember, as a child, watching him leave on his bicycle with his tools in a bag on his back. Sometimes he worked six days a week, but he always had a family day on the weekend. Everything Dad did was for his family. When I was twelve, he took us all to Florida to stay with his sister, Sylvia. It was quite exceptional to do back then, and we became the talk of the neighbourhood!

I have two brothers, Alan and Ian. Both Mum and Dad's love of sport carried on through to us kids. And even more so to Ian. I swam a lot, as did my older brother Alan, but Ian followed in Dad's footsteps and took up football and athletics. Mum and Dad helped set up Norwood Little League Football when Ian was younger. They ran the League for more than twenty years, watching boys from all backgrounds—many from underprivileged families— enjoy a football game every Saturday morning. It became a big part of our lives, and we were very proud of our parents for providing this opportunity to many children over the years.

When my parents retired, Dad wanted to leave London and move towards the Southeast coast. Mum found the move really hard, but, as always, supported Dad's wishes. I will never forget the day they moved. My brothers and I helped, and then watched them leave. We had never lived more than a couple of miles apart, and now we would be a couple of hours away. I cried all the way home. After Mum and Dad settled into their new home, Mum's twin sister, Pat, bought the bungalow that backed on to Mum's garden. They were together again, and it made a big difference to Mum's life. To this day, they remain as close as ever and have been a constant support to each other. Dad and Uncle Bob had each other, too. They were like brothers. It made me so happy!

Eight years ago, our world changed forever. Dad was diagnosed with vascular dementia. It really is the cruellest disease, and I personally wouldn't wish it on my worst enemy. Over the years, the man who had been the head of our family, slowly disappeared, turning into a shadow of his former self. Mum was his sole carer and deserves a medal. Dad eventually forgot who we were. His personality changed over time, and he became very difficult. It became clear it was almost impossible to continue tending to his needs at home. Still, Mum carried on her own, until one day the family unanimously agreed enough was enough, and decisions needed to be made. At 84, Mum was mentally and physically exhausted and had to look for help. My mum is my absolute hero, and I am in awe of her strength and devotion to the man she was married to for more than sixty years, now like a toddler in every possible sense. He was 'her boy', and she would honour her marriage vows if it was the last thing she ever did. But, after Dad became impossible to deal with, Mum spoke to us, and we all agreed she needed some respite. It was the hardest decision of her life, and one she has not fully come to terms with yet. She found a care home she liked, and Dad went there for a week, whilst Mum had some much-needed rest. However, she fretted the whole time he was there, so she didn't rest much. When Dad came back home, he got worse. Between us all, we decided he needed full-time professional care, and so he permanently went into a care home. Mum visited him every other day, but she was heartbroken. She felt guilt beyond comprehension, but there really was no other choice as Dad had become impossible to deal with. In fact, we were all broken-hearted at this point but could see no other way.

That was in October 2019. In March 2020, everything was changed forever again.

Dad's care home, along with hundreds of others, shut their doors to outsiders when Covid struck. They said our loved ones would be safe inside, away from the virus. How wrong they were.

Untested patients from hospitals were moved into our care homes, as hospitals ran out of beds. One of those untested patients arrived at Dad's care home and soon became ill. Mum received a call saying residents were being kept in their rooms, due to a suspected case of Covid. One of our worst fears had become a reality. At the time, none of the residents were being tested, as the home didn't have any tests available. Then, Mum was told that Dad was being sat in the communal area, alone, because there was a worry he might fall in his room. How very confused he must have been—it breaks my heart. He was completely on his own. Although he didn't necessarily recognise us anymore, Mum was his constant. He must have felt so lonely without her.

On 22nd April Mum got a call from the care home staff—Dad was unwell. A doctor called to discuss his symptoms with the Care home staff, not with us. It was thought he may have a UTI. Antibiotics were prescribed over the phone. By the next day, he was worse. He was neither eating nor drinking. A doctor was called again, and via a FaceTime consultation, the doctor decided, there and then, that Dad should be placed on end-of-life care and all medications should be withdrawn. Wait, we thought. What? How can this be? No doctor called Mum to explain, just a member of the nursing staff at the care home. We were in disbelief.

The end of Dad's life came quickly. I had, by this point, broken all the Covid lockdown rules and had driven 120 miles to be with Mum. Nothing could stop me from being with her. We rang the care home, and I asked to facetime with Dad. But the carer said we wouldn't "want to see our dad like this."

"I don't advise it. I would not want to see my father like this."

What, was all I could think? That statement stayed with me. I can only imagine the fear and desperation Dad experienced. No intervention was made, except to ease his passing. No oxygen, no medications, except eventually morphine. We called again, and this time a carer held the phone to Dad's ear. He was unconscious by this point, but we were able to speak to him. His wife of 66 years said goodbye. The carer cried with us. I have often thought of her and the risks she took daily. The carers were absolute angels.

On 27th April, Dad was close to the end, and we were allowed to facetime with him. He was peaceful and had his best shirt on. We spoke to him and showed him his garden full of flowers. He moved his head very slightly towards our voices. We have to believe he heard us as we said a final goodbye. Earlier the day before, I had driven to his care home and stood in the car park, shouting out his name and telling him I loved him in the hope he might hear my voice on the wind. I could not bring myself to enter, as I would likely bring Covid out to the rest of my family. All I wanted was to hold Dad's hand, so he wasn't alone. I'm crying as I write this. My biggest regret is not having been able to hold his hand as he left this world. He deserved so much more.

Dad took his last breath at 7:30 pm on 27th April 2020. A young lad (a carer), aged just 19, sat with him and held his hand. He spoke to Mum straight afterwards and told her what a lovely man Dad was. He said Dad's bed tray was filled with family photographs. He held up a picture of Mum and Dad at their 50th wedding anniversary to show to Dad as he passed away. How can we ever thank this young man? But it should have been us with him.

Dad was taken to a funeral home storage facility and kept there for some time due to Covid rules, so we still couldn't see him. Eventually, we booked a date for his funeral, and they moved him to the funeral parlour. We were luckier than some, since we were allowed to supply his own clothing. We were even allowed to see him in the Chapel of Rest. Many families were denied even this. I clearly remember taking tiny steps towards him, so scared of what I might see. My overwhelming memory is that he looked like a wax model, having been embalmed. But his hair was fluffy and soft, and though his skin was so cold to the touch, I finally got to hold his hand. Mum and I spent a while with him and placed a number of personal items in the coffin, including a letter from his beloved sister Sylvia, and photographs of us all together. How hard it was to watch Mum say her final farewell. It should never have been this way. It's cruel, it's beyond sad, and it is life-changing.

The funeral was restricted to only ten people in the chapel. It would have been full to bursting any other time. My brothers and I all spoke about Dad, and I was deeply proud of us all. The service was live-streamed so others could watch around the UK and in Florida. I was initially against it, but then realised people who could not attend also needed closure. We went back to Mum's, and the weather was kind, so we sat in the garden and shared memories. We were finally able to have a celebration of Dad's life in November 2021. It was attended by more than 50 friends and family, and it was an afternoon full of happy memories. We all sang some of Dad's favourite songs. Mum printed out song sheets, and we had the original music playing. Old photographs were displayed around the room, which kicked off some great conversations. We shared food and had a few drinks. It gave Mum, especially, a lot of comfort.

Initially, I was very angry about how Dad died, and I found it hard to comprehend. We all dealt with it differently, in our own way. I came across a group on Facebook called *Yellow Hearts to Remember*, whose members were all grieving due to Covid losses. It was started by David Gompertz, whose wife had passed of Covid. He suggested to his family that they tie yellow ribbons to trees to acknowledge their loss. His granddaughters said that due to lockdown, it would be impossible for people to go out and buy yellow ribbon, and suggested people put yellow hearts in their window. Thereafter, the yellow heart became a recognised sign of Covid bereavement.

I loved this, so I wanted to promote it. I live in a quiet side street, so who was going to see my yellow heart in my window? I decided I wanted to wear a yellow heart for people to see wherever I went instead. I wanted people to know my dad died of Covid, and tell them about him. To honour my dad, I came up with the idea of a yellow heart pin badge—everyone would see it and ask me about it. Then I could tell them about Dad! Our loved ones were not just numbers on a screen, we needed to say their names.

I began my journey with the yellow heart pin badges, and was soon contacted by a guy promoting the *Remember Me Memorial* at St. Paul's Cathedral. It's a permanent, physical memorial being built to recognise all lost to Covid in the UK. I decided that all proceeds from the sale of the yellow hearts would be donated to this memorial. It was perfect! Dad loved London, and visited all the key monuments, royal houses, and cathedrals as a child. Dad was very proud to be British. This was just the perfect place for him to be remembered, and to be part of British history forever. For my dad to be a part of this iconic and world-famous cathedral for eternity brings me and my family so much pride and joy. Our loved ones will be remembered and honoured for their battle against this disease. They were warriors who fought until the end, and we will remember them forever alongside historical figures such as Lord Nelson. So far, I have sent out over 10,000 yellow heart badges and raised almost £30,000 towards the memorial. I shall continue until they are needed no more, but sadly that seems a long way off right now.

I am honoured to have been asked to take part in this book and share my dad's story. He was a good and honest family man who did not deserve to die this way; alone and confused. I will forever be grateful for the role models that Dad and Mum were (and she still is) in our lives. My brothers and I will continue their legacy of love forevermore. Mum inspires me every day of my life, and I am in awe of her devotion to Dad, through the last few years especially. Her unwavering love and dedication to him were immense and I am so proud to call her my Mum. We all feel that we lost Dad twice: first, dementia took the person, the dad we knew and loved; and then, Covid took him physically.

Not getting the chance to say goodbye is just not right in any sense, and it's my biggest regret. So, until we meet again Dad, sleep well and know you are loved… always. ♥

ABOUT ANNETTE

Annette Allen lives in Bournemouth, England. She is married to Terry, and has a daughter, Sophie, and a stepdaughter, Lisa, who sadly passed away aged 45 in November 2021. She is a full-time teaching assistant in a primary school situated right by the beach in Bournemouth. Annette has two dogs and enjoys long beach walks, dining out, and entertaining her family. Following the loss of her father, Annette spends a lot of time raising funds for the *Remember Me* permanent memorial being built in St. Paul's Cathedral, London, to acknowledge all lost to Covid in the UK. To-date she has raised in excess of £30,000.

You can follow Annette's journey on Instagram:
@remember_me_yellow_hearts

Dad on one of many visits to his sister, Sylvia, in Florida.

Happy days when we were children.

Me and my dad.

Mum and Dad.

Mum and Dad.

Family meant everything. Mum, Dad, Alan, Ian, and myself.

Carmelina's Story

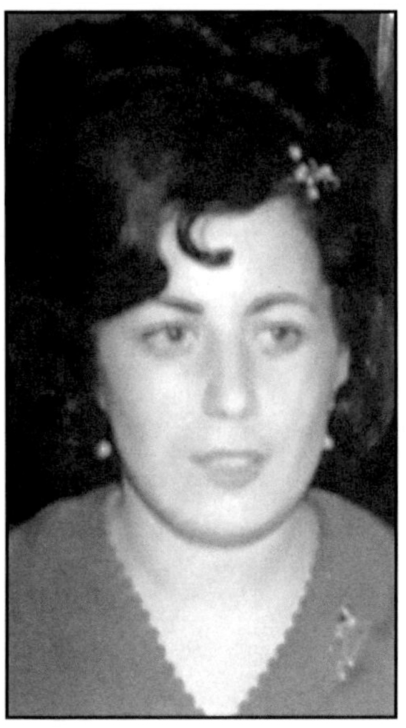

NON TI SCORDAR DI ME

Do Not Forget About Me

By Mary Cabanillas

INTRODUCTION

When asked to write a chapter in this book, I immediately accepted since it would be a way to honor my amazing, beautiful mother, and it was the least I could do. I only hope these words can paint a picture of the wonderful woman she was. I also hope that sharing my mother with you will bring some peace and comfort to me and my family.

ITALY

Carmelina Sierchio was born on January 17th, 1942, to Carmine and Teodolinda Sierchio in Calabritto Frazione di Quaglietta, Italy. As the oldest of five children, she practically became a second mother to her younger siblings. At an early age, my mother had mastered the art of embroidery, which was taught to her by the nuns at her school. Talent could have been her middle name, as this was just the first of the many talents my mother demonstrated. Since I did not inherit any of her talents, I've always said it must skip a generation. Anytime she spoke of growing up in Italy, her face lit up like a Christmas tree! She reveled in reminiscing about her adventures and about how beautiful Italy was. I regret not visiting Italy with my mom. Someday I hope to cross it off my bucket list. I only wish I had done it with her.

EMIGRATING

In 1958, my mother emigrated from Italy to the United States with her family, and they settled in Newark, New Jersey. She had three younger sisters, and their brother, the baby of the family, came along after their move to the United States. All the sisters doted on him, but my mother more so, and he knew it. He would wait for her to come home from work to buy him ice cream from the Mister Softee Truck. One day, thinking she had outwitted him, she purposely came home late, but he said, "You think you are smart. Dairy Queen is down the street, so you can take me there."

Being the oldest, she went to work as a seamstress to help support her family. My mother took great pride in her work; perfection was her highest priority. She also possessed an eye for fashion, knowing immediately, just by looking at someone, what would look good on them. It's no wonder, according to my aunts, her hair was always styled nicely, and everything she wore matched perfectly, like a model. Purple was her favorite color, but she was in awe of all vibrant colors. In fact, my mother always reminded me of Elizabeth Taylor; so beautiful, with jet black hair and incredible green eyes. As beautiful as she was on the outside, she was equally beautiful on the inside.

LOVE AND MARRIAGE

My dad, Carlos Cabanillas, worked at a butcher shop when they met. The owner, wanting to play matchmaker, pulled her aside one day while she was picking up an order and said, "I have a nice guy for you!" His matchmaking skills were perfect indeed. My parents married in September 1970 and settled in Belleville, New Jersey. Carmelina became the mother of three girls; me, Lisa, and Carla. Growing up, my mother made many dresses for me and my sisters. I have fond memories of going to grade school and everyone asking me where my mom had bought my clothes. With pride in my step, I exclaimed that my mother had made them for me! She was the typical classroom mom, always baking cookies and cupcakes for our birthdays and for school bake sales. In third grade, I eagerly tried out for the class Christmas play and happily landed the part of a stuffed animal elephant. My mother spent weeks fussing and working on my costume. She created the most beautiful costume with a pink tutu. My teacher was amazed. That costume was worthy of an award, hands down!

Growing up, we never stayed sitting around in the house. There was too much fun to be had outside, playing with the other kids. In motherly fashion, my mom took care of all the kids in the neighborhood; her door was open to everyone. Whatever we had for snacks was freely provided to other kids as well. She took joy in feeding everyone. You could smell her cooking down the block, and the neighbors would know Carmelina was cooking. Her generosity went even further; she would always pack up the leftovers for our neighbors.

PERU AND BACK

The year I turned eight, my dad moved us to Peru, where he was from. He wanted us to get to know his family, his country, and his roots. Talk about culture shock. We arrived in April 1976. Shortly afterward, my dad had to come back to the states to settle some affairs, so he left my mother to take care of three small children in a foreign country. My grandfather, who I remember as a kind and gentle man, lived upstairs from us, and thankfully, he loved my mother. She adapted quickly to life in Peru, which made things easier. Our neighbors were very curious about the Americans. They embraced their new neighbors and fell in love with the Italian woman from New Jersey. Mom quickly made friends with a few women in the neighborhood. Every weekend, our home became a gathering place where she would teach them how to cook Italian food, and they would teach my mom how to cook Peruvian food. A true master in the kitchen, not only could she cook, but she was also a phenomenal baker. She made all of our birthday cakes from scratch, but they looked like they had come from a bakery.

We spent four years in Peru and returned to the United States in 1980. I was 12, and we once again settled in Belleville, NJ. It was January, and the start of seventh grade for me. Until this point, Mom had been a stay-at-home mother. She always had dinner ready for us and clean clothes. That year, my mother went back to work. I don't know how she worked, cleaned, cooked, and took care of three girls and a husband, but like a magician, she did it all. Everyone else's needs always came before her own. This was also the beginning of marriage issues for my parents. They separated and divorced in 1992. My mother had sacrificed so much to make sure we were taken care of. I was old enough at that point to help her out. She didn't drive, so my grandfather took her to work in the morning, and I picked her up as needed.

FAMILY TRADITIONS

Growing up, our extended family all lived close to each other. We were a close-knit group with my mother's side of the family, and we spent every Sunday and holidays at Nonna's house for dinner. My mother's favorite holiday was Christmas. Sticking with tradition, each year she would transform our dining room into a winter wonderland, tirelessly creating a Christmas Village. It was a spectacular work of art, worthy of belonging in the window of a department store, like Macy's in New York City. At the same time, our kitchen would turn into a bakery. A few weeks before Christmas, my mother would bake three or four different types of cookies. She would put them together in dishes and wrap them up so beautifully to give out to family and friends. Giving to others truly filled her heart. I, however, wasn't allowed to help her wrap or put the cookie dishes together. Unlike her perfectly wrapped gifts, with ribbons, bows, and cards, I was (and still am) the worst gift wrapper! She never forgot a birthday, and even though she had very little, whatever she had, she shared with everyone.

There was always a soft spot in my mother's heart for the boys in our family. Don't get me wrong, she loved her nieces, Pina and Linda, and great-nieces, Larissa and Kayla, very much, but it was different with her nephews. She adored my cousin Frank, her oldest nephew, who was the only boy for the longest time. Somehow, he always made her laugh. Then came my cousins Daniel and Michael, and she fussed over them as well, especially Michael. He was like the son she never had. With a bit of jealousy, I often teased her, saying she should have had boys. She babysat a lot for my cousin Michael, so he was always at our house. He adored his "Zizi Carmela," as he called her. His poor mom, every time they passed the Dairy Queen, he had to stop to get his "Zizi Carmela" her ice cream.

My mother had so much love for her family, and it hurt her when she was unable to attend special events, such as Daniel's and Larissa's weddings. Mother had a unique relationship with her sisters and brother, and she was very close with my Aunt Vanda. Like best friends, they talked almost daily. My Aunt Mary is the fashionista, and my mother was always eager to see what trending outfit she would be wearing. Aunt Patty always looked to my mother for her words of wisdom and advice. Uncle Pasquale was the baby, and my mother always had him under her motherly wing.

A GROWING FAMILY

I married on September 25th, 1999. We relocated to Tennessee because my husband was stationed at Fort Campbell. My being gone was very hard for my mother. As the oldest child, I had done a lot for her. We both depended on each other, so the move wasn't easy for me either. I became pregnant in April 2000 and longed to be with my family. It thrilled me when my mom, Aunt Vanda, and cousin Larissa came to visit me in Tennessee. The minute she arrived, the first thing she said to me in her Italian accent was, "What do you want me to cook for you?" That week, I indulged in the best food I had ever eaten while living in Tennessee. We moved back to New Jersey, and I gave birth to my son, Justin, on January 11th, 2001. Crazy enough, within a year and a half, my mother had three grandsons, and they were six months apart. Joseph was born July 2000, Justin in January 2001, and then Christian came along in August that same year. Finally, a girl entered the picture when Ava was born in April 2006. Her grandchildren brought so much happiness into her life.

My husband and I divorced when Justin was three years old. Justin wasn't really talking yet, and the doctors thought he was speech delayed. We began speech therapy at one of the public schools in town, but one day, a teacher pulled me aside to share that she thought something else may be going on with my son. The school district sent Justin to be evaluated by a neurologist, and they diagnosed him with autism. This completely stunned me, and I felt as if a truck had hit me. How could I deal with this and the divorce at the same time? Feeling overwhelmed, I cried for months, wallowing in my sorrow. One day, I was crying while talking to my mother, and she assertively said to me, "Mary, that's enough. No more crying. You need to be strong for your son and fight for him. You are the only one that can do this for him. God wouldn't give you anything you couldn't handle. He chose you to be this baby's mother!" That day, my pity-party ended, I stopped crying, and I started doing everything in my power for my son. Without my mother's strength and compassion, I would have been lost. I am so proud to be her daughter, and truly blessed to call her my mom!

HEALTH ISSUES

In January 2016, I was walking into work when I received a phone call from my sister Lisa that my mother had collapsed on the kitchen floor. In a panic, I darted out of there so fast, and by the time I got to my mother's house, the first responders were already there. The fear I felt that day was overwhelming and something I will never forget. As we followed the ambulance to the hospital, they pulled over. I rushed to the ambulance to see why, and they told me my mother was having a stroke and the paramedics from the hospital were on their way. After the doctor assessed her, he pulled me aside. My mother had suffered a hemorrhagic stroke, and she had bleeding in the brain, but they could not operate. The next 48 hours were going to be critical. They brought her to the ICU. Tubes and wires were everywhere. We called everyone in the family, and within minutes, half of them were at the hospital. The doctors shared the grim news that less than 20% of people who suffer this kind of stroke survive. He also informed us that, if she survived, the woman we had known before would not be the same. We prepared for the worst and prayed for the best. My poor mother spent almost three months in the hospital. She lost all movement on her right side and had to have a feeding tube because she couldn't eat. The side of the brain that the stroke had affected is known for handling emotion.

When my mother was strong enough, they transferred her to a rehab facility. She experienced a setback there and wound up back in the hospital with sepsis. Once again, my mother was in the ICU, fighting for her life. Thankfully, she made a miraculous recovery and was soon out of danger. The doctor decided the rehab center next door to the hospital would be a good place for her since they were affiliated with the hospital. They moved her to the facility for rehab, and she remained there on a full-time basis. Not being able to care for my mother broke my heart, but the staff was wonderful, and my mother seemed happy there. We made sure someone was always with her. It was hard watching her when she was in pain. She cried, and we cried right along with her, wishing we could make it all better for her. She constantly told us how much she loved us, which was something she had rarely done before the stroke.

Once she had mastered dialing the phone, she called all the time to ask when I was coming and what I was bringing her to eat. The food offered at the facility was less than desirable, so we brought in food for her. Christian, her grandson, brought her happy meals from McDonald's, which she loved. He had to be sure his precious Nonna had her favorite happy meal! She adored her grandchildren and often asked when the girl was coming. The girl was Ava, her granddaughter, who would cut her nails for her. My mother always asked me if I was bringing the baby, which is how she referred to my son. She spent the next four years at the rehab center, and then Covid hit like a tidal wave.

PANDEMIC

In February 2020, when we started hearing about COVID-19, the rehab center required us to wear masks while visiting my mother. Shortly afterward, lockdown was declared, and we couldn't see her at all. It didn't go well when we explained to her that there was a terrible virus, and the lockdown was for everyone's safety. The only comfort we felt was knowing she wasn't alone in her room. A lovely woman named Pat, who was a spry 99, shared her room, and my mom had grown quite fond of her. We called daily to be sure Mom was ok. One day, they informed us that there were several cases of Covid, but we should not be alarmed.

Easter of 2020, we called the rehab to let them know we were going to go by my mother's window to see her. We asked if they could please make sure her shade was up. My sister Carla, my nephews and niece, and I all went to see my mother. We put together a beautiful Easter basket, which we left in front of the entrance, and the aide came out to get it. As we peered through the window, my mother looked good. She was waving to us from her bed, and we yelled to her that we loved her, hoping she could hear or understand what we were saying. We let her know we had brought her the Easter basket, and she blew us kisses, as did we. Little did we know that that would be the last time we would see her alive.

The following day, I received a phone call from a nurse letting us know they were going to test my mother for Covid. I asked why, and to my shock, she told me they had over 50 cases, and it was just a precaution. I asked how my mother's roommate Pat was doing, but she avoided answering my question. Something wasn't right, and I could feel it in my soul. Within 24 hours, I received another phone call informing me my mother had tested positive. They were moving her to a secluded area of the rehab center with other patients who were also positive for the virus. Frustrated, I asked how this could happen when she never leaves her room, but again, they assured me she was fine and had no symptoms. We found out later that my mother's roommate, Pat, had passed away from Covid the day after Easter. Desperation set in, and I knew I needed to speak with my mother. I insisted she have a phone wherever they were moving her to. For the first few days, I was able to speak with my mom, but she sounded horrible. By the end of the week, I could no longer get a hold of her. Finally, the following Monday, an aide answered her phone. I demanded to speak with my mother, but she could barely speak. We hung up, and I tried getting a hold of the nurses but couldn't. Out of panic, I called every number I could and left messages. Finally, that evening, the nurse called me back and tried to convince me again that nothing was wrong. I went back and forth with this person several times that evening until I finally shouted, "My mother needs to be in the hospital! Call the doctor and insist she be seen, or I will come down there with the police and take her myself!" That evening, at 10:00 p.m., the emergency room doctor called me. My mother's blood pressure was dangerously low, and her kidney function was failing. She was so dehydrated that they couldn't get an IV in her. He needed my permission to do a PICC line in her neck to get fluids in her as soon as possible. If I had not insisted that she go to the hospital, he told me that she would have died at the rehab. She was in dire condition, and if he couldn't get her blood pressure up, she would not make it through the night. They couldn't do anything about her failing kidneys because she had Covid. In disbelief, I contacted my sisters to let them know about this unthinkable situation. I didn't sleep a wink that night, thinking I would miss a call from the hospital.

GOODBYE

The next week was a roller-coaster ride. April 29th, 2020, I received a call from a nurse who told me that fluid was building around my mom's lungs, and they needed to drain it. I gave my permission and went back to work. At 1:00 p.m. that day, I received a phone call from the doctor telling me my mom had passed away. "She went into cardiac arrest, and we lost her," he said. I went into hysterics, and from that point on, everything was a big blur. The hospital allowed my sisters and me to go there to see our mother, one at a time, from the window of her ICU room. We weren't allowed to go in. We could not hug her or tell her goodbye. All we could do was stare through the glass as she lay there, lifeless.

It was the height of the pandemic, so we couldn't even give her a proper funeral. Her funeral was on May 5th, 2020, and they were only allowing ten people in the funeral home at a time. No one could go near the casket. The wake and burial had to be on the same day. Because they were so inundated with funerals, they gave us a brief window of only an hour and a half. When it came time to go to the cemetery, they said only two of us could go in. My Aunt Mary tried to reason with the funeral home director. Our mom had three daughters. How could we choose who doesn't get to say goodbye to their mother? How cruel, I thought, as I cursed this monster virus 100 times over. No matter how hard we pleaded, my younger sister Carla was not allowed to go into the cemetery with us. My mother deserved so much better. She deserved a proper funeral with a church mass. Tears are staining my paper as I write this. I can't help but cry. My family and I have never experienced so much pain and heartbreak. We lost an incredible human being!

Today, I carry on through the tough times, trying to find peace in knowing my mother is in heaven with my grandparents and her grandfather, whom she adored. Pots and pans are probably banging as she cooks for everyone and sings to them in her heavenly voice. Oh, how I miss that beautiful voice. The only comfort I have is knowing she is not suffering anymore. To this day, I struggle almost daily with the fact that I wasn't able to be with her on her final day to say goodbye. I didn't get to tell her how much I loved her. This virus cheated me, my mom, and my family of so much. I didn't get to thank her for being the best mother a daughter could ever have! Until we meet again, Mommy!! Ti voglio bene!! I love you all the way!!

ABOUT MARY

Mary Cabanillas lives in Nutley, New Jersey, with her son Justin. She grew up in Belleville, New Jersey, and is a 1986 graduate of Belleville High School. She is employed by the Township of Belleville and is starting her 19th year with the township. Mary is the eldest daughter of Carmelina Cabanillas, and she has two younger sisters, Lisa Appice and Carla Ramos. She enjoys spending time with her family, especially her son Justin, her nephews Joseph and Christian, and her niece Ava.

In her spare time, Mary enjoys Broadway shows, traveling, reading, shopping at the outlets, occasional trips to Atlantic City, dancing, and being around family and friends. Having grown up in a big Italian family, Mary enjoys Italian cuisine, and being part Peruvian and living in Peru for four years, she also appreciates the Peruvian culture and cuisine.

To my beautiful mother: *Not a day goes by that I don't think about you. It's not, "Goodbye"...it's, "Until we meet again!"*

My sister Lisa's wedding, 1998. From left to right Mary, Lisa, my mother, and Carla.

My mother with her siblings. Vanda, Patty, Pasquale, and Mary at her surprise 65th birthday party.

My mother at my sister Carla's christening, with her godparents, Zizi Vanda and Zio Carlo.

Just my beautiful mother.

My wedding in September of 1999 with my mother.

My mother with her grandchild, Ava.

My mother with her grandchildren, Joseph and Christian.

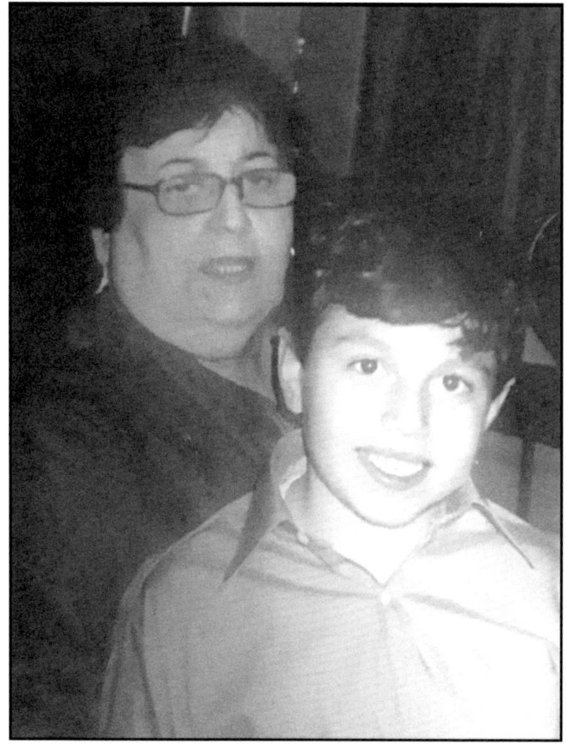

My mother with her grandchild Justin.

My mother with her daughters and her grandchildren, in the long term facility after suffering her stroke.

Louis's Story

By Marla Sarrel

Louis, I know you will always continue to move the puzzle pieces of my life. When I was first approached about writing "Louis's Story," I got goosebumps because one of the last things my husband, Louis, and I had spoken about was his desire to write a book about his life and experiences. I assured him we would sit on the beach over the summer and write his story. Unfortunately, his desire to write his book never came to fruition, but clearly, he still wants me to write his story for him. I hope I can do it justice.

Louis passed of COVID-19 on April 21st, 2020, just three days after he "celebrated" his 58th birthday. It was the furthest thing from a celebration since Louis was on a ventilator, fighting for his life. While standing outside with some immediate family members, I was able to sing "Happy Birthday" through a phone that a nurse had held up to his ear. I know what we all wished for as we let the wind blow out his candle on the chocolate cake that we had gotten for him. I last saw him on March 30th when I dropped him off at the barrier to the emergency room. Because of Covid restrictions, I sat helpless in the car, unable to go in with him. A feeling of despair lurked in my gut. Louis was one of the first in our circle of family and friends to suffer from COVID-19, and the first to pass from this horrid virus. I am not sure how I even drove home, because I know I was in major hysterics, terrified that I would never see him again.

Louis was always the life of the party, and he thrived in the presence of others, helping whenever he could. The irony is that he passed away alone, after spending eighteen days on a ventilator. Not one visitor was ever allowed in. He had wonderful nurses and doctors, but they weren't his family. It's a very different experience than a loved one saying how much they love you, while they hold your hand and stroke your forehead as you pass from this life. We all felt so helpless and waited anxiously for our one call of the day, praying endlessly for great news.

Immediately after his passing, Louis's friends from childhood needed an outlet for their grief. They wanted to honor him and do something special because we could not hold any of the rituals that usually surround the passing of a loved one. His friends quickly got to work on a car parade (similar to all the birthday parades that were going on during lockdown) for the following evening. Tears streamed down our faces as the 50 cars passed by in honor of Louis. We were standing on the front lawn of our house. There wasn't a dry eye as friends and family paid their respects to our family. It was beautiful and sad at the same time. We held the funeral four days later. Only me, our two sons, our rabbi, and Louis's brother were allowed to attend. We set a phone up on a tripod to Zoom the funeral. Zoom was still fairly new to many, but over 300 devices signed in to attend what was probably their first virtual funeral. So that there was never more than five people at a time, the rest of our immediate family parked in their cars at the gravesite, waiting for their turn to pay their respects. How is that fair?

When we arrived home, the family and friends who would have attended the funeral had planned another drive-by. Three-hundred-and-fifty cars, filled with lots of air kisses and "I wish I could just hug you" sentiments, overwhelmed us with love. This was not the goodbye Louis deserved, but everyone did their best to show how much they loved him. This makeshift send-off left a hole in my heart, but I also felt so much pride for the person Louis was to me and to so many others.

Louis Sarrel was born in Brooklyn, New York; he was very proud to tell everyone he was born in Brooklyn. He never let the story get to the part about how, after he had left the hospital, his parents brought him home to suburban New Jersey. He grew up in a modest house in Northwest New Jersey with his mom, dad, older brother, and younger brother. The boys were all close in age, only five years separating them from top to bottom. His aunt and uncle also lived with them for a time after his grandparents had passed away. From what I was told, the house was always open to whoever needed a place to stay, or to anyone needing advice. Many friends lived in the house from time to time. Clearly, it was a haven for anyone needing a place to go. That is probably where Louis got his overly large and caring heart from. Imagine three rambunctious boys growing up in the 1970s and 1980s, a time when you left your house in the morning and had to be home when the streetlights came on. Now take that up a notch or 20 notches; that is what Louis's childhood was like.

Growing up, all three boys shared one tiny room. Louis kept the room freezing cold and said it was easier for others to use an extra blanket. He was always the peacemaker between his brothers (which really was a full-time job), as well as between friends. He was the first one to protect someone against a school bully, or be the voice of reason when friends had crazy ideas. Louis's father worked very hard to give his children a wonderful childhood, including a summer home in Lake Wallenpaupack, Pennsylvania. For many summers, they left for Pennsylvania with their mom when school ended and came home to New Jersey the day before school started. His dad came up on the weekends. Louis had summer friends from the lake and school friends from New Jersey. He never lost touch with many of those friends, even though the house sold over 40 years ago.

Louis loved to organize spring break trips to Mexico and Florida for a large group of him and his friends. His famous line "You do what you want to do?" came from one of those trips. We could never convince him to do something he didn't want to do, nor would he stop someone from doing what they wanted to do. Louis continued on with his sleek organizational skills and helped plan reunions and functions. With a smile on his face, he gladly helped with any task that was asked of him.

Once, while playing football in high school, the team was watching film from their game the previous Saturday, and one coach said, "Look at Sarrel pushing everyone around. He is like a tank!" Since then, they gave him the nickname "Tank," and it stuck with him for the rest of his life. He continued playing flag football with many of his high school friends until he was 32.

Louis loved to cook, especially during the games on Sundays. Smoking brisket on the smoker and whipping up a cheesecake was his favorite. He also enjoyed a glass of good scotch or tequila. Louis grew up a diehard Steelers fan, and because of proximity, he also became a Giants and a Yankees fan. Skiing and snowmobile riding were some of his other hobbies. He loved boating and made sure he received his auxiliary coast guard certification before he ever drove the boat. Working out made Louis happy, and he was very proud of his amazingly defined calves despite never having done squats a day in his life. Poker nights with the "boys" were another favorite of his, and I know there were lots of laughs among friends because, more than anything, Louis loved to laugh. I can still hear his laughter, and my heart fills with joy. Louis certainly had the gift of gab, and he was born to be in charge. We would laugh at his ability to tell anyone how to do something, such as carpentry or fixing things around the house, despite being physically unable to do any of the tasks himself. Another special trait, or should I say "talent," was his ability to fall asleep anywhere.

I met Louis at one of his large family reunions. My dad and Louis's mom went to elementary through high school together and were working on their 25th reunion. I imagine at some point there was talk about his mom having three sons and my dad having two daughters, but we never confirmed that. Somehow, we met on our own at a ski lodge. Louis was so kind and sweet. We continued an on-and-off relationship for two years before I graduated college and moved back home to New Jersey. I always knew he was the right one for me, but I wasn't ready to commit just yet. He was four years older, and I wasn't ready to settle down. We spent many months as friends, talking about everything and really getting to know each other. Despite me knowing exactly how Louis felt about me (he told me it was love at first sight), he never pushed the issue. A few months after I graduated, we both went to Florida to celebrate New Year's. I went with a friend and Louis went with his younger brother. We each stayed at our grandparents' house. We celebrated New Year's Eve in Ft. Lauderdale, together, on the water. It was magical! Our New Year's kiss felt so different, so passionate. All of my built-up love for him came out that night. He asked my dad for my hand in marriage ten months later, to which my dad replied, "What do you think she will say?" Louis always talked about how scared he was to ask me after that. He always joked that he would propose when he found a ring in one of the eggs in a toy machine. Proposals back then were not quite what they are now. We went out to dinner at one of our favorite restaurants on a Thursday evening, and when we got back in the car, he handed me a very big bag. He had filled it with those silly plastic eggs. He made me go through every egg, looking and playing with the items: rubber balls, stickers, temporary tattoos, and even toy rings. He had carefully mixed the engagement ring in with the other eggs, and when I found it, he asked me to marry him. I replied with, "Is this real?" Once I said yes, we went back to my parents' house, where both families were waiting for us. We married in August 1990. My love for Louis ran deep in my veins as we stood at the altar and confessed our never-ending love for each other. Our ceremony and reception were perfect, and our hearts full, as family and friends surrounded us to celebrate our love. Louis promised to always love and take care of me… at least for the next 50 years! He always joked he would have to re-evaluate after that.

Louis and I are so lucky to be parents of two amazing boys: Eric, born in 1995, and Jacob, 1999. He adored his sons more than anything. Pride beaming, he never missed a school function or a sporting event. Louis also spread that love to his nieces and nephews; he attended their sporting events, school plays, recitals, and other functions whenever possible. He had developed an individual relationship with each of them that he cherished dearly.

Louis graduated from college with a degree in communications and went into sales. He was swift, a born salesperson who could talk to anybody about anything. He was especially fond of food, restaurants, and sports of any sort. In 1992, Louis found his passion in real estate and property management, and his career thrived until his passing. Meeting new people and networking was his ideal, and the flexibility to set his own schedule allowed him to coach sports for our children. Football was Louis's favorite sport to coach; he had started coaching when he was in college. He continued coaching even after our sons were done with youth football. Everyone who loved Louis knew his love for the game. Our brother-in-law Steven, a medical doctor who was working in Manhattan in the trenches during the height of the pandemic, became our point-of-contact while Louis was in the hospital. He sent out updates using football analogies each evening. This is the final text message he sent out to family and friends:

3:52am. April 21st, 2020: Update Sweet Louuuu!

Oh, sweet Louis. A battle reminiscent of your days in the gridiron. Battling in the trenches. Fighting hard. Always giving 110% no matter what the score. Never stopping. Never giving up until the final whistle blows. Your effort was always inspiring to those who fought beside you and to those who admired you from the stands.

I believe the game is coming to an end soon. We are inside the two-minute warning now. We are out of timeouts and down by 14, yet you are still coming out of the huddle and lining up, looking for a way to create a turnover and narrow the score. While some fans have left the stands already, and some teammates may have just decided to phone it in, bruised and battered, tired and determined, you line up again and wait for the snap. You wait for your chance to get after the quarterback and create a turnover. Getting the ball back gives your team hope… gives your team a chance. But when the ball is finally snapped, the quarterback simply takes a knee. Out of timeouts, there's nothing you or anybody else on your team can do but watch the clock tick down.

The way you played the game will never be forgotten. You will be unanimously selected first-team all-conference, all-state, all-life, and a first ballot hall-of-famer for sure. The legend of Sweet Louis Sarrel will live on with us forever. You will be named the MVP of this championship game, and even though you did not win, you will always be a champion!

We've been texting for a few weeks now. We've had a lot of ups and downs. The clock is winding down. Louis's body is tired. He needs to rest. The docs have hit him with the kitchen sink.

I believe we need to understand that the deficit on the scoreboard appears insurmountable, and with the clock ticking down and no timeouts remaining, the game is coming to an end.

I believe Louis can hold on a little longer, but we are talking hours and minutes… not days and weeks.

He is resting comfortably. He is sleeping. He is at peace.

He is an MVP, an MVD (most valuable dad), MVH (most valuable husband), MVB (most valuable brother), MVF (most valuable friend)... and the list goes on and on.

I know none of this makes sense. We will ask ourselves over and over, "How did this happen?"... "Why did it happen?"..."What if?"... None of it makes sense. None of it is right. Quite frankly, it's pretty messed up.

I know Louis is standing in that huddle right now, all fired up, yelling at his teammates and trying to draw up a play that will help his team get the ball back... but if the opposing quarterback keeps taking the snap and taking a knee, it's simply going to make that a lot more difficult to do.

In the words of our nephew Scott, "We are all left with a Louis-sized hole in our hearts."

Philanthropist, volunteer, supporter, planner, Louis donated both his time and money to others in need. When I first met him, he was helping with a leukemia organization started by his extended family. Volunteering at our synagogue and helping the homeless put the brightest smile on his face, and he considered everyone he helped a friend.

"Unofficial mayor" was a title bestowed upon him wherever he went, fulfilling his duty to help whoever called upon him. This is why his passing has left such a gaping hole in the lives of so many people who relied on him. No matter who I spoke with, his friends from all walks of life have told me he was the most loyal friend a person could have. Truthful in his words, he shared his honest opinion when asked, even if it wasn't what you wanted to hear. Louis's bursting personality and love of life made people feel comfortable. But that overzealousness for life and sports sometimes meant I had to wind him in a bit to keep him out of trouble. His deep voice carried great distances and embarrassed our boys often.

This is a post from our 21-year-old son on Father's Day 2020:

Happy Father's Day, Dad. Not a second goes by that I don't think about you. There truly is a Louis-shaped hole in my heart. I know you are watching down over us and guiding us through all endeavors. Your large personality is still shining, even though you are not physically here with us. When I think of what it means to be an amazing father, you are the perfect match. You were tough, but so loving. A knuckle touch may have been how you said you loved us, but that was so special to me. You would push me past my limits, all while saying how proud you were of me. I will never forget the long phone calls about lacrosse, where I would get about five words in and you would finish the conversation by saying, "I know you'll make the right decision and I will stand by any decision you make." You raised me to find the good in any situation, no matter the circumstances. That said, I want to say "Happy Father's Day" to all my father figures out there. You all know who you are, and I am extremely thankful for you. Dad, wish everyone up there a "Happy Father's Day" and keep showing us signs you are okay. I love and miss you like crazy. I know you would be proud of how Mom, Eric, and I are holding down the fort. I would do anything just to hear your voice or even see you from a distance. It is crazy to believe you left us two months ago. Some days it feels like so much has changed and it's felt like a lifetime. Then, other days, I can close my eyes and picture seeing your last breaths through that little window in the ICU. It was very nice going to the cemetery today. We want you to know that we are all okay, and we want you to enjoy the day with all the wonderful fathers in heaven. Just know I love you and will always be thinking about you. Enjoy some double chocolate cake and watch some TV with Pop. I love you, Dad. ♥TCB♥ (taking care of business).

Our sensitive 24-year-old is much more about feelings than words. He has Louis's big heart and love of laughter and life. Friends and family are everything to him as well. He always refers to his dad as "big guy." They would sit and watch sports for hours on end together. His father was everything to him, and I know Louis will continue to guide him in whatever he does in life.

Wanting to keep me safe from harm's way, Louis did everything in his power to make me feel protected. He was my protector and voice of reason. I also know that he felt safe and comfortable with me. We always said that we could make it through good and bad together. We were each other's rock and support. Louis was always the first one I called to share my thoughts or good news with. I called him every day when I left school to chat about our day. I didn't want to wait until I was home to hear his voice. In all of our years together, we never went to sleep or left the house without saying we loved each other. After almost 30 years of marriage, my heart would still skip a beat when I saw his name appear on my phone. Louis made me feel special. He was my best friend, and we talked about everything together. It is so strange when someone so close to you passes. They were your person, and now they are just gone. I still talk to Louis daily. I let him know how much I miss him and that I hope he is okay. About six months after he passed, I sat thinking about him (as I do all the time) and said, "Wow, you must be so proud of me." I am doing this crazy thing called life and making decisions on my own. These things have never been my strong suit; they were my husband's. He may not recognize the person I have become. I feel Louis's love and guidance from the other side, and I know he is crazy-proud of me. Louis's name is spoken often in our house. My boys and I say, "Daddy would have loved this," or "Daddy would be so angry."

When Louis passed away, I sought ways to keep his memory alive, ways to make sure he will never be just a number or a statistic. Less than a month after his passing, I found a story about a family in the UK that started a yellow heart project. Reading that story inspired me, and it was my first step toward helping myself and others. I immediately put up a yellow heart in my window, and it is still there. Every morning I look at it as I come down the stairs, and it warms my heart. I have also become involved with a Covid-loss group called "COVID-19 Loss Support for Family & Friends." This became a comfortable place for me to be right away. Through the group, I have met wonderful friends and continue to talk to them often. It is amazing to be able to talk to other people that just get it.

Our amazing family also started a social media campaign to honor those who were lost to Covid, and also those affected by Covid. As my brother-in-law was getting his vaccination, he was feeling emotional and thought, "This jab's for you, Louis." That saying stuck, and we created a webpage, Facebook page, and Instagram profile called "This Jab's for You." People can print out our logo, and post who or what they got jabbed for. There were many jabs for Louis, as well as for many others who lost their lives to this virus. People posted about getting jabs for going back into classrooms, attending concerts, going to bars, traveling, seeing grandparents again, and for countless other reasons. We felt as a family that Louis would have been the first in line to help himself and keep others around him safe. This campaign has been a wonderful way to honor Louis and to keep fighting for him. One of Louis's amazing friends felt the need to continue to honor him and held a golf outing in August 2020 in Louis's memory. The love and feelings at that golf outing were a true indication of Louis's legacy, so much so that they held a second annual golf outing the following summer. This was the perfect way to honor an amazing man, and our boys and I loved hearing the wonderful (and sometimes very interesting) stories told to us. A scholarship in Louis's name has been started at our local high school.

Loving, helpful, boisterous, determined, teddy bear, friend for life, and devoted family man are just a few of the words to describe Louis. He will be in the hearts and minds of everyone who knew him. It's impossible to think about Louis and not smile! We all are blessed to have had him in our lives. He left one heck of a legacy behind. His boys will never doubt that their father loved them unconditionally and that he will be proud of them forever. Although Louis was a best friend to so many people, I was the lucky one to call him mine.

ABOUT MARLA

Marla Sarrel is an elementary school teacher in Morris County, New Jersey. She earned her undergraduate degree from The University of Maryland and her Masters degree from Seton Hall University. She married her best friend at a beautiful ceremony on August 19, 1990 and loved the life that they built together. She lives with their two sons.

Marla could not have made it through this traumatic experience without the unconditional love of her family and friends. She is so grateful to share Louis's story so he never becomes a statistic. He was so much more. She has met the most amazing people through her covid loss journey that are now friends for life.

Louis, Marla, Eric and Jacob at Eric's Bar Mitzvah, 2008.

Louis at his nephew's bar mitzvah with the family.

Louis (with white hat) in Cancun with his brother and friends.

Louis and Marla August 19, 1990.

Louis's funeral with just us and over 300 devices.

Louis in his glory days!

Louis with Eric and Jacob.

Louis with his brothers and parents.

Louis, far right with his two brothers.

Sarrel Family at Jacob's Bar Mitzvah.

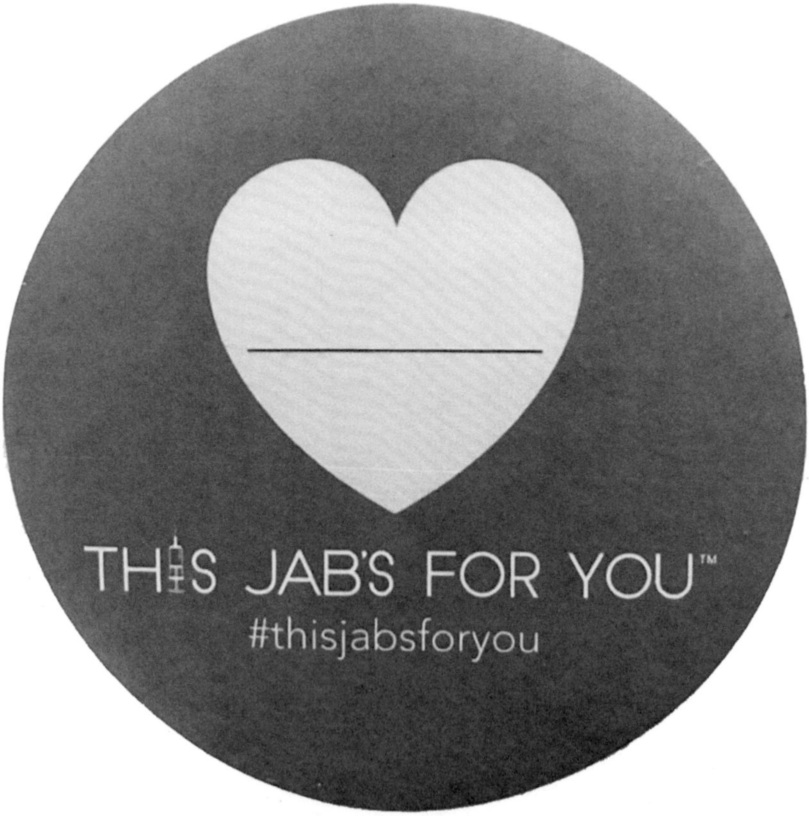

THIS JAB'S FOR YOU™

#thisjabsforyou

The campaign that was started by our family to combat vaccine hesitancy. We can be found on Instagram, Facebook, and at www.thisjabsforyou.com

Frank's Story

FATHER, FAMILY, FRIEND, FISHERMAN—FOREVER LOVED, FOREVER MISSED

By Gina Sirico

MONDAY, JULY 13, 2020 - 11:28AM PST: "IT'S COVID."

My dad's text confirmed our worst fears. In the middle of my workday, in my living room in Los Angeles, I dropped to my knees and sobbed.

My dad hadn't been feeling well for a few days. He'd gone to his local urgent care in Florida to get a Covid test but hadn't received the results yet, so his doctor suggested he go to the ER, where he got the full work-up; blood test, Covid test, chest X-ray. All came back normal, except for the Covid test.

For 98 days—74 of them on a ventilator—he fought an unthinkable battle, before finally succumbing on October 18th at 3:26pm.

Dad was my hero. My rock. He was the best father, husband, friend, and colleague. He was many things to so many people.

"When certain people die, it leaves a void in your life that can never be filled. Frank's loss is that void for me. He was a great friend, a GREAT friend," Joe DellaPietra told me.

Frank Sirico was born in Brooklyn, NY in 1938 to Mary and Salvatore Sirico. He was the third of four children; two boys, two girls. He was a fighter from the start, a street kid from Bensonhurst who worked hard and played harder. He originally went to drafting school but felt the need for speed early, and ultimately, he became a renowned engine builder.

Growing up, Frank was a gifted athlete and captain of his high school gymnastics team. "We were in the band together. He played the bugle, and I was a baton twirler," said his sister, Josephine DeGiaimo. "He was so cute, but always mischievous! We had a lot of fun as kids."

THE PRANKSTER

Dad was known as a prankster from the start. Some of his mischievous behavior may or may not have gotten him kicked out of a couple of high schools, but it did get us through some tough times. "When I think of your father, I think of his laugh and his smile," more than one friend told me. Dad LOVED to laugh and make other people laugh.

On one family boat outing, my dad caught a small fish and surprised my Uncle Sonny by putting the live fish down his bathing suit. Everyone was in hysterics, and my uncle was laughing while trying to get the flopping fish under control and out of his pants. He had no help from the rest of us because we were all doubled over with laughter.

Growing up, I distinctly remember Dad standing over me with a glass of cold water—the threat of an icy bath if I didn't get up with my alarm. I'm not a morning person, so he delighted in this (not me, ahem). Another one of his shenanigans involved my brother and cousins; he would tell them he had left a little something in their shoes, insinuating that it was something gross. He never did, but they'd always fall for it; he was just that convincing.

My dad had a signature way of writing letters backwards, so I'd need a mirror to read the words. And it wasn't just to me. When I was cleaning out the house, I found a box of cards and letters with the same backwards writing that my dad had sent to my mom when they were dating.

Once, while we were visiting family, my cousin Julie, a nurse, decided it was time to get revenge on Dad for all his pranks over the years. So, late one night, she took a little saline packet, popped it so it squirted my dad while he was asleep, and ran back to her room. She did it again and again and again. Dad finally realized what was happening and a water war was declared! My dad fought to win. He actually took water from the toilet and tossed it at us! Back and forth, it went throughout the night till we called a truce. But in the morning, the garden hose was brought into the house, and he "accidentally" pushed my cousin into the pool in her nightgown. War over, white flag waved.

Julie told me, "We have a lifetime of memories, but this one always sticks with me."

Even in his darkest moments, like the days after my mom passed away, he was pranking. Family members came down for the funeral, and my cousin Matt left some things at the house. Dad said to me, "We should put some of those plastic roaches into the package so when he puts his hand in it, he'll jump." I, of course, was on board. We bought the most real-looking fake bugs we could find and sent them along with his items. We made sure to be on FaceTime when he opened the package, threw it to the ground, and walked out of the house, both laughing and shuddering.

THE LIFE OF THE PARTY

Dad wasn't just about pranks. He lived life to have *fun*. One year, while at a steakhouse in New York City for his birthday, he told jokes and made sure we were all smiling and having a good time. In fact, our fun and laughter was so infectious that it compelled people at the surrounding tables to join in when we sang "Happy Birthday" to him. It was the cherry on top of a great night. I can't tell you how many times we'd be out, and the surrounding tables would want to join in our fun, with my dad as the fearless leader.

Dad was the man of the hour at his best friend's son's bachelor party in Las Vegas. He helped the young guys meet girls at the pool, and they were all calling him "Uncle Frank" by the end of the trip. He was even the star of a kid's party. Lynn Gelinas, a family friend, remembered this story: "Your parents and Joey came by our house. It was my son Parker's birthday, and we rented a bouncy house. All of a sudden, we saw your dad kick off his shoes and jump right into the bouncy house with Parker! He was young at heart and that's one of the many things we loved about him."

People never believed Frank was in his 80s. Shawn Steele, a friend of my dad's, told me, "We could talk for hours about cars, boats, and fishing, and it was like talking to a brother, not someone who was twice my age."

Frank was the uncle and cousin and friend everyone gravitated toward. My cousin Donna Gonnella Francis remembers, "We'd come up to your house for the weekend, and I always wanted to get dropped off at the shop so I could watch Frank work on the cars. That was the most fun for me."

THE THRILL SEEKER

Dad's business was racing. He and his brother John started building engines at a young age and made a name for themselves as some of the best in the biz. If you were a local racer in the northeast or Florida, if you were NASCAR's finest, or if you had a car or boat that needed to go FAST, Frank Sirico was your guy. It was a fantastic sense of pride for Mom, my brother Joe, and me to go to the races and watch his cars leave everyone in the dust.

When I was young, we took family excursions to Six Flags Great Adventure. Dad was a big kid at heart and loved to ride the roller coasters. I won't lie, I'm a chicken, but I joined him a few times. I remember one time he got my brother Joe to go with him on a roller coaster that went upside down, and poor Joe was quite green when he walked off that ride. Dad was all smiles, though. He loved every minute of that adrenaline rush. Once, after I'd moved to Los Angeles, we went to Disney's California Adventure with a group of my friends. Dad headed straight for the roller coaster and wanted to know about all the fun rides.

Frank always dreamed of flying a plane. For his 80th birthday, we set up a trip to Atlantic City to see Sebastian Maniscalco. My cousin's friend had a connection to get us a private jet from Long Island to AC. Dad sat up front with the pilot and even got to fly the jet for a bit. I'm thankful he was able to live out that dream.

THE FISHERMAN

Dad's other love was boating. The sea was his happy place, his center, his zen. The guys at his marina became his brothers, sharing his passion for the salt life. When I was cleaning out his car, I found little slips of paper with coordinates of good fishing spots from South Florida to the Bahamas.

Fishing trips were a regular part of our weekends growing up and continued until his last days. His friend Cathy Passey told me this story: "One time we were coming back from a weekend in Bimini, and we hadn't caught anything. We had a little bait, a small bag of ice, and a small cooler left on the boat. On the way home, we came across a school of mahi-mahi. We threw in lines and caught more than we thought possible! In the middle of it, a shark jumped out of the water and grabbed one of the fish from the line. Your mom and my husband jumped back in disbelief, but we kept catching till we couldn't put any more in the cooler. We brought up 'the big catch' for years after that and always laughed about it."

Although my dad was a thrill seeker, there was no one calmer in the face of an unruly sea. I remember a trip to the islands in the early 90s and facing 10-plus foot waves. My stomach was not convinced we'd come out of it OK, but Dad knew exactly how to navigate through it and got us home safely.

Dad had in his repertoire what we affectionately call the "fish dance." When things weren't going his way on the water, he'd put on some music and dance it out. Sure enough, shortly after, the fish would hit. It never failed, even after he left this world. Not long after Dad's death, his friend Joe went on a fishing trip, a trip my dad had hoped to go on with him. Joe wasn't having any luck, so he took out his phone, showed some guys on the charter boat a video of my dad's fish dance, and told them the story. On the next drop, Joe caught a 356-pound swordfish. Never underestimate the power of some bad dance moves and an angel watching over you.

THE FAMILY MAN

Yes, my dad is an angel now, reunited with the love of his life, my mom, Barbara. Their love story is one for the ages. They met thanks to their best friends, who were married to each other. Dad and his best friend Michael were at Dad's shop in New Jersey when Barbara Jean Fontana walked in with Michael's wife, Nancy. Sparks flew, and that was that. My mom was dating someone else at the time (oops), but when she met my dad, she knew she'd found her soulmate. Anyone who saw them felt the love. They married 18 months after they met and had 52 years together.

My dad was never one to talk about his feelings. He had that old-school Italian hide-your-emotions mentality, but after my mom passed away, he told me he'd always known it was love at first sight and that he had to take care of her forever. Mom had health problems from the start, and in fact, she ended up in the hospital on their honeymoon. But Dad was always there to take care of her, to keep her going and help her through the pain.

Mom and Dad both wanted a big family, but because of her health issues, I was the only biological child they could have. They adopted a son, Joe, when he was two years old. We were a close-knit family from the start. The fab four.

Dad was never the right choice for my mom's parents. They preferred her former boyfriend, who was some sort of executive, not the "mechanic with the bad-boy streak." Her father, ON THEIR WEDDING DAY, encouraged her to walk away and never look back. She instead walked straight down the aisle to the man of her dreams.

When I was a teenager, they again tried to get her to walk away from my father and from our family, but she would not. Dad stood by her, comforted her when she cried, made her laugh to cheer her up, and told her he loved her constantly. Like I said, their bond was unbreakable.

People often wonder why I've been so picky about boyfriends and relationships. It's because of my parents (they hated when I said that, but it's true). I witnessed what they had, and I wanted THAT. I watched the little things they did for each other. The surprise parties my mom would throw for my dad, and the meals my dad would cook for my mom. The knowing glances, their inside jokes, and their infectious laughter. The family gatherings they loved hosting. Little bits of advice they both gave to anyone who asked. Their never-ending love for each other. The way they helped each other after my brother's death at 32, and the way my mom nursed my dad back to health after his heart attack in 1987. The way my dad took care of my mom through all of her health issues… the kidney transplant, the strokes, the seizures… the way he fought for her, as her advocate, when he thought a doctor wasn't telling us the whole truth. The way they'd hold hands and sit silently at the beach, watching the waves crash. Dad lost a part of himself when my mom passed away in 2018. He knew what he had; a partnership in the truest sense of the word and the gold standard in the love department.

THE FRIEND AND MENTOR

Dad was also the gold standard in friendship. His circle was huge, consisting of people from his childhood and people he had met in the last months of his life. I can't tell you how many people I talked to who told me how much of an impact he had made on their lives.

"He was always straight-up. No pretense about him."

"The world needs more people like him in it."

"He was a joy to be around at the marina, always in the action."

"He was the best neighbor and friend and human."

"I spent an entire day offshore fishing with him, just him and me. The fishing was slow, but the time went quickly because of the company."

"I owe a lot of my success to him. He taught me more than I can remember!"

"He was always willing to help anytime I had a question, and we'd always have a wonderful talk, catching up on life."

"He was a great fella and a stand-up guy."

"When I get depressed, I think of your dad and the memories, and I smile. He was a second father to me," said Michael Artiglere, the son of my dad's best friend. "When I was a kid, my dad and my brother and your dad went to Pennsylvania to go snowmobiling. The lake was frozen, and we were having a blast just doing our thing. Suddenly, we heard the ice crackle, and your dad said, 'OH SH*T!' As the ice was breaking, he made sure we all got off the lake before any of us took a freezing cold dip. He saved us. But that's just typical for your dad. He was always there for me. Always."

THE FIGHT

Dad's tribe was there for him when he began the biggest fight of his life, the fight against COVID-19. His doctor admitted him to the hospital on July 13, 2020 and started him on preventative treatments. He felt fine, his oxygen saturation was good, and his X-rays were clear. We talked and texted a lot because he was bored in isolation. I tried to get him to watch the TV show I was producing, but it wasn't his thing. He could never understand my love for celebrity and entertainment news, but he loved bragging to the nurses and doctors that I worked for E!. It warmed my heart when they told me that.

On the fourth day, after his chest X-ray remained clear, the doctor sent him home to rest and quarantine for the next 10 days. Dad tried to relax, but when you're diagnosed with a potentially deadly virus, calm doesn't come easy. He woke up the next morning, short of breath. His doctor ordered him back to the ER where they took a chest X-ray, which showed the virus had reached his lungs. They admitted him to the ICU, and he was put on oxygen. He would never leave the hospital.

Dad's friends and our family rallied to do what we could to keep his spirits up. "Hopefully, we can help—we can't let anything happen to our brain trust!" one friend texted. Dad did everything he could to keep his lungs working; breathing exercises, walking around when possible. He literally tried anything and everything.

"Forward motion. Let's keep up that positive thinking and do what you're doing, and we're going to get you through it," I told him.

"I love you," he said.

We decided that I would come to Florida just so I could be close in case he needed me. The hope was that he would come out of the hospital, and I could be there to help him out for as long as necessary. I arrived in Florida on August 3rd.

"You got this. I'm close by, so I hope you can feel the strength I'm sending you," I said.

"I do. It feels so good to have you here. I love you," he replied.

"Love you too, Dad."

On August 4th, his breathing got worse. "Don't know where this is going or the outcome yet. Sorry, Gina."

Dad was always apologizing, and I always told him not to. It wasn't his fault this happened. Trying not to let him know how scared I was, I reassured him. "We are gonna get through this, Dad. We are."

Little did I know that, on this same day, he was writing a list in his phone: what the house should be sold for, what the boat should be sold for, who to give certain things to, like his fishing stuff and tools that belonged to him and his brother. He knew he would not make it, and he left me a roadmap of what I would need to do when he was gone. I can only imagine how daunting that must have been for him.

Just before 6am on August 6th, Dad's doctor called me. "Gina, his oxygenation dropped significantly last night, and as much as I don't want to do this, we need to put him on a ventilator."

I shot out of bed and started pacing while he gave me more details. "Is he awake? Can I talk to him?" I asked.

He said, "Not right now, but I talked to him and told him the situation. He asked if it would help him fight the virus and I told him 'Yes,' so he agreed. He is cognizant and aware that this is necessary. I promise I will keep you posted once it's done to let you know what we can expect from here."

I hung up and immediately contacted my bosses to let them know I was calling out for the day. No way could I concentrate on celebrity news when my father was being intubated. As they had been all along, my bosses were super supportive and told me to take whatever time I needed.

I called family members and close friends to let them know what was going on. Once again, I dropped to my knees and sobbed. "Please don't take him from me. PLEASE don't take him from me. Please… please…"

His doctor called me that night. "Gina, I know this is difficult, and the thing is, we just don't know how long he will be intubated, or which way things will go. Nothing is guaranteed, but this gives him the best chance. We don't take it day-by-day – we take things hour-by-hour now."

And that's what we did. I spoke to the nurses several times a day, keeping close tabs on his blood gases, his X-rays, and his ventilator settings, which they would adjust to try to wean him off of it. It was an up-and-down roller coaster of emotions, as every rise, or fall, of a number would set off a hundred questions. What does this mean? Is he getting better? Will he be able to breathe on his own again? But the virus was new to everyone. It affected people so differently, and it was difficult to say what was or was not going to work.

One of his nurses told me the room my dad was in, so I drove to the hospital every night and sat under his window, just to be a little closer, to let him feel my strength. The doctors told me that Dad could hear, even though he was sedated, so I would FaceTime and play island music, and tell him he was my hero. I lovingly told him he had people praying for him and sending him love and strength from across the country, literally from around the world.

Twice, doctors told me to call hospice because he would not make it, and twice, he defied the odds. The second time, as he became more responsive, his nurse, Bill, shared with him what was going on. "You're still very sick, and we can do things one of two ways: you can go with God or continue to fight. Frank, do you want to continue to fight?"

Dad nodded his head vigorously. And he fought… so very, very hard. But the virus was stronger than the strongest man I knew. And after the most valiant battle, I held my dad's hand as he took his last breath. I was grateful that I was allowed to be with him for a couple short visits once they knew he wasn't going to make it, and as he passed. Most family members of Covid patients were never even allowed to say goodbye to their loved ones in person.

His death hit me like a gut punch I couldn't quite recover from. Despite the strong exterior, I am an emotional mess, and as the pandemic continues, I wonder if I will ever recover. I miss our phone calls on my way home from work, when he would make fun of my Los Angeles traffic hassles. I miss the pictures of the concoctions he'd make in his air fryer. I miss the boat rides, the laughs, and the quiet moments. I miss his epic side-eye that no one else would catch but me. I miss my dad.

At his funeral mass, the priest encouraged everyone to not take life for granted. That's how my dad lived *his* life. He made every moment count. As I try to navigate this new life without him and the rest of my family, I am attempting to do the same. The road in front of me is uncharted, but I know I have a guardian watching over me. I love you, Dad. And I will work till my last breath to make you proud.

ABOUT GINA

Gina Sirico was born in New Jersey and grew up in Florida with her loving family; her dad, Frank, her mom, Barbara, and her brother, Joe. She misses them all immensely.

Gina is a writer, producer, and content creator, and she currently resides in Los Angeles, California. She is a pop culture enthusiast and enjoys spending quality time with the ones she loves.

You can connect with Gina on Instagram and Twitter:
@GinaS1116

Mom and Dad's wedding. Those properly-posed and styled wedding photos are nice and all, but I love their genuine smiles in this one.

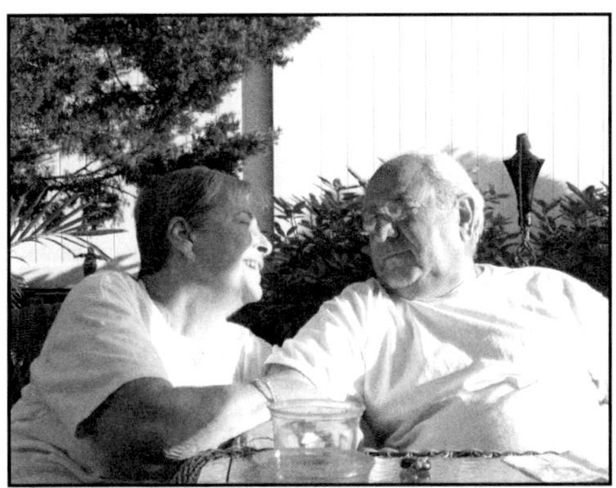

The look of love. This is one of my favorite photos of my parents. Fifty-plus years of connection, love and understanding encapsulated in one glance between two people.

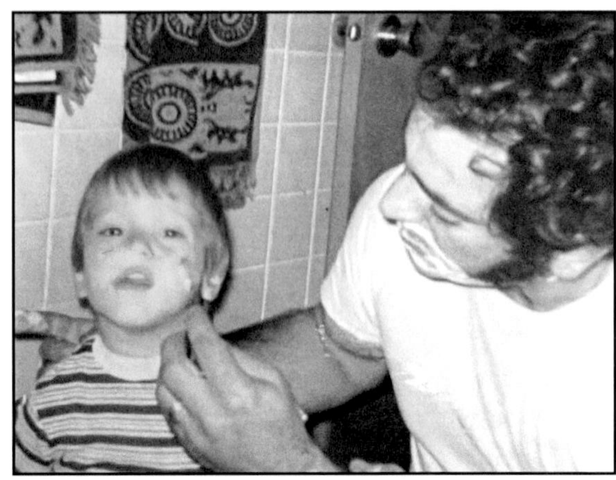

Like father, like son!
A sweet moment between Dad and my brother, Joe.

New Jersey, mid-1970s. Joe and me are all smiles hanging out with Dad.

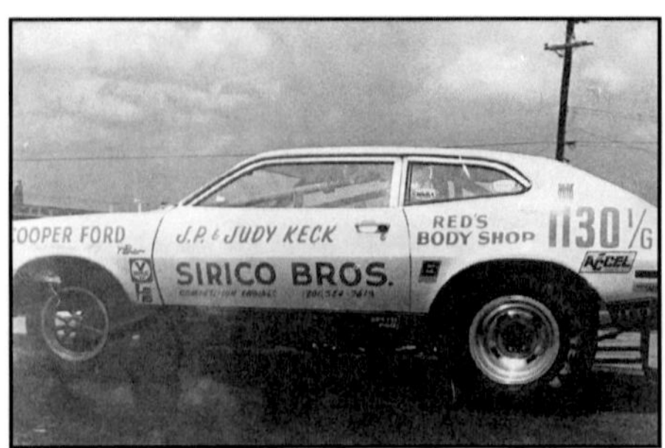

Need for speed!
One of the many race cars featuring an engine built by my dad and his brother.

What a catch! Dad loved spending time at the marina. His fellow fishermen were like another family. They still tell me how much he is missed around the docks.

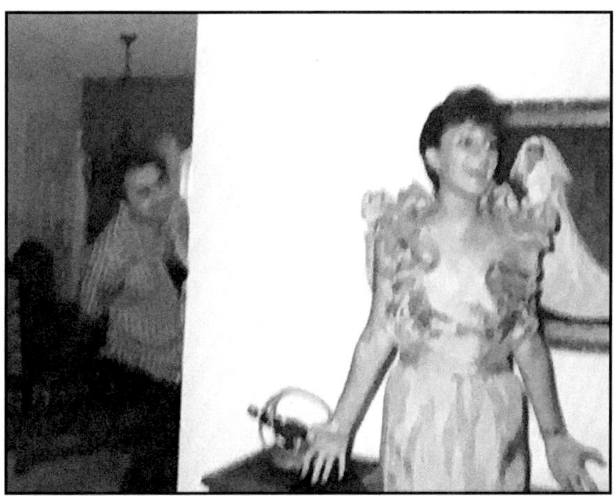

Frank in a nutshell. I was trying to be serious and take a picture before my prom. He was being silly and trying to make me laugh.

Three peas in a pod. I am usually a bad selfie taker, but this one turned out pretty well! They weren't just my parents, they were my best friends.

After my mom's death, we took my dad on a special trip to Atlantic City to see comedian Sebastian Maniscalco. Pictured: Dad's sister Josephine, nephew Matt, niece Julie, Julie's husband Frank, their son, Michael, Dad and me.

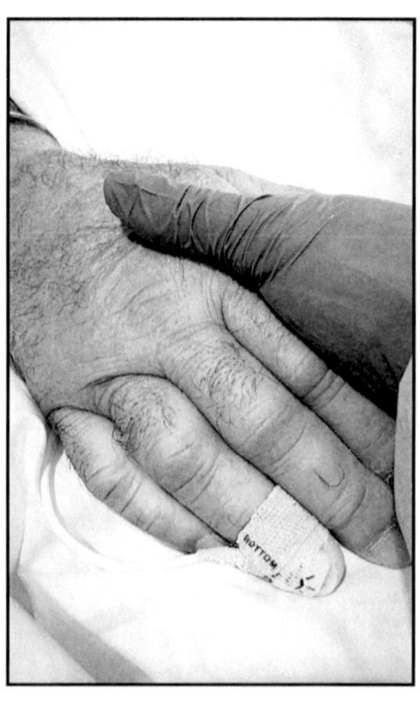

Unlike so many during this pandemic, I was able to visit my father in the hospital a couple of times, and to be there when he took his last breath. I hope he felt my love and strength in that room.

Anastasia's Story

FOREVER MISSED, FOREVER LOVED

By Konstantina Dina Kess

On May 29, 2020, I did a FaceTime call with my mom and my brother at 3:18 PM for five minutes. We told her that her COVID-19 test had come back negative. She was smiling and mouthing words but could not speak because of the tracheostomy. It thrilled her to see us, and she grabbed the iPad from the technician to blow us kisses. This was the last time we saw her alive.

My mom, Anastasia Koiveroglou, was born August 15, 1952, in Greece. She was the oldest of two daughters, and everyone affectionately called her Soula. My grandparents owned a convenience store, a little cafe shop, and were also tobacco farmers. My mom was very active, productive, and hard working from a very young age. She enjoyed cooking, cleaning, and keeping everything tidy and in order. My mom married my dad, Kleovoulos (Voulis) on November 28, 1976, and they had my brother Pantelis (Pat) on September 5, 1977, and me on January 23, 1983. My father brought us to America in the late 1980s, and we settled in West Orange, New Jersey. It was an exciting yet intimidating time. We boarded a plane in Greece and came to a completely different country. My parents desired a better life for their children. We did our best to adjust to this new, foreign place with an unfamiliar language and cultures. We had no other family, but we were happy.

My mom was a homemaker and stayed home to take care of us. She made the best meals and our house was always spotless. Mom adjusted very well to life in America and loved being here. She often told us this was one of the greatest countries. To keep us connected to our heritage and family, she made sure we went to Greece every summer when we were young. My maternal grandparents were great people. Sadly, my grandma was very young when she passed away in 1991. My mom was only 39 when she lost her mom. Her father passed in 1996, and it devastated my mom to have both of her parents gone at such a young age.

My brother and I attended Greek school in addition to regular school. My mom helped us with our homework and went over all of our work. She wanted to make sure we spoke and wrote both languages. Greek school was school we attended for a few hours after regular school, three times a week. We learned how to write and read Greek, Greek history, and some mythology. It was sometimes difficult to juggle both schools, but our mom was a tremendous help with our homework. She took the time to expand on topics we had a hard time with.

My mom loved to cook for guests, and she cooked up some amazing dishes. Everyone who enjoyed a meal at our house raved about how delicious her food was. I don't know how she could use only five ingredients and turn them into a delicious feast. Like magic, she made amazing dishes out of nothing! My mom made traditional Greek dishes like moussaka, pastitsio, and kokkinisto, and amazing desserts like baklava, kataifi, and melomakarona. The rich aromas filled our kitchen and left us waiting for the moment we would dive in! Since she was always cooking, our house always smelled delicious!

My mom made wonderful friends here, and she treated them with the utmost kindness. It was important to her that she spent time with them. A social butterfly in every sense! She had friends and cousins here in America and in Germany and Greece, and she checked in on them often to be sure everyone was all right. If someone was sick or had a problem, she worried and stressed about it. That's who my mom was—a woman with a big heart who worried and cared about everyone. It made her day to hear good news about anyone. I never even heard my mom yell at anyone or use bad words. She instilled kindness in us as we grew up. "Be kind to other people," she would say, "because we don't know what struggles they are going through in life." My mom discouraged us from raising our voices or using profanity. She really believed we could resolve everything by talking it out.

My brother and I couldn't have asked for better parents. They filled our home with love and provided us with everything we could want or need. Sadly, my dad was diagnosed with cancer in January 2016 and passed away March 25, 2016. Prior to that, my dad had heart issues for many years. My mom spent many years taking him to doctor appointments, cooking healthier dishes just for him, and staying on top of his medications. She selflessly took care of my dad for many years while taking care of our daily needs as well. If we were sick, her mama bear instinct kicked in and there were no boundaries to the things she would do to make sure we felt better.

At the beginning of 2020, I read some articles online about a virus in China that was killing people mercilessly. I didn't have a good feeling about what I was reading and shared my findings with my mom, brother, and husband. March 2020 came around, and we were told, at my job, that starting the following week, we would transition to working from home. With a sigh of relief, I counted the days to be working safely from home. On April 11, 2020, my mom woke up in the middle of the night with stomach pains, and the next day the pain had not subsided, so I offered to take her to the emergency room. She declined in fear of catching Covid. On April 13th, we donned masks and headed to CityMD because her pain had become unbearable. The doctor said my mom most likely had a stomach virus, or possibly an ulcer, and advised her to take some over-the-counter medication. At that point, my throat was hurting, so I knew it was best to get tested to see if I had the virus. I dropped off my mom and headed straight to Summit Medical Group. They called me the next day and gave me the startling results: I was positive! My heart sank, and I panicked in fear for my mom. We were told to quarantine. My brother, mom, and I were all sick. My brother was very sick but recovered without any issues. I had mild symptoms. My mom was getting sicker and sicker by the day.

My mom continued to fight the pains at home like a warrior, refusing to go to the hospital. Her main symptom was abdominal pain. In the middle of the night, April 15th, she couldn't bear the horrible pain anymore and knew she needed to go to the hospital. I got her up out of bed, but she immediately slipped out of my arms and fell. I called 911, and by the time the ambulance arrived, she was alert again. She did not want to go in the ambulance, and the paramedics said that, since she was alert, we could drive her to the hospital. So, after they left, I drove her there. They discharged her the next day on April 17th. However, on April 18th, she was in agonizing pain again, so I took her back to the hospital. The next day they called and, again, told me to pick her up, but I felt in my gut that she still needed medical care. I called my friend, who is a nurse at a different hospital, and she told me to bring my mom there. We jumped in the car with my brother at 10:00 p.m., on April 19th, and drove her straight to the other hospital. This would be the last time I would see my mom alive, in person. Our hearts broke knowing we had to leave her there, all alone, to fight an unknown virus. She was scared, gasping for air, and fighting for her life. The doctor called me a couple of hours later and gave me the dreadful news—Mom had pneumonia, COVID-19, and the flu. The doctor said her lungs looked terrible, and they didn't know if she would make it. My heart sunk, and I felt the earth beneath me disappear. How could this be happening? Where did she get the virus? Why my mom? Many questions plagued me, but I had to fight for my mom. I had to remain strong and do everything in my power to make sure she had the best outcome.

A few days after we checked her in, we got the dreaded call. On April 23rd, they intubated her at 11:56 a.m. Until that point, she called me often, saying she wanted to come home. She was scared and didn't know what was happening. With each phone call, all I could do was fight my tears and tell her everything will be all right. The last time I heard her voice through the phone was April 23rd, at 10:59 a.m. It was the last phone call I would ever receive from my mom, and I will never forget it.

After intubation, she had many ups and downs. I documented every phone call with the hospital, her stats, and who I spoke with. I called multiple times a day, asking for updates. Most days she was 40% dependent on the ventilator and was doing very well. Her lungs were improving, and she was always alert. The nurses taking care of her said she followed all commands when they lowered sedation, and she had no signs of brain damage. I remained hopeful, yet very anxious. This was a new virus, and no one knew what could happen.

They gave my mom plasma, at my request, at 4:00 a.m. on April 29th. We were so hopeful the treatment was the magic cure-all. Plasma was thought to help Covid patients at the time. I think the plasma helped her because her vitals were improving after she received it. They tried to extubate her two times but were unsuccessful. Each time, my mom panicked as they attempted to extubate her, so they would re-intubate her immediately. Eventually, they did a successful tracheostomy on May 14th. I think the tracheostomy was important because she was not panicking after getting extubated. The tube down her throat was really scaring her and causing her to panic. The tracheostomy allowed her to be extubated more efficiently.

The hospital called me on May 19th and shared they were moving my mom to a rehabilitation center. I did not approve of this because the reviews of the center were terrible, and it was in a part of the state I did not feel comfortable with. Despite my asserted efforts, they informed me I had no choice, and they were moving her that night. My mom passed eleven days later, and I have no doubt it was because of their neglect. She flourished in the hospital and was making strides with recovery. In her short, but devastating stay at the rehab center, she developed bed sores, fell from her bed twice, and her tracheostomy tube was left to clog. It makes me sick just thinking of what she endured. We tried on multiple occasions to have my mom transferred to different locations. A family friend even helped us, and he tried with all his being to get my mom moved to a safer location. He sent letters and faxes and reached out to people he thought could help, but no one helped us. No one! My mom was trapped there.

On May 31st, at 9:06 p.m., I received a call that they found my mom not breathing in her room. I called them back at 9:27 p.m., begging to know what was going on, and they told me they pronounced my mom dead at 9:20 p.m. My brother and I fell apart. I fell to the ground. It was the most painful call of my life. My mom, my best friend, my entire world, was gone from my life. The rollercoaster of ups and downs had ended, and just like that, my mom's life did too. Life, as I had known it, no longer existed. How would I continue to exist in a world without my mom?

It seems so unfair to me that my mom passed away from this virus. A woman, who was the kindest soul on the planet, died alone and scared, in an unknown place. How can life be so cruel? There are so many horrible people walking this earth, but an angel like my mom was taken from us. Every day I wake up and feel like it's a battle…a battle to stay sane and a battle to make sense of all of this. This invisible killer came out of the blue and took my mom away, along with so many others.

I hope whoever reads this chapter knows what an extraordinary person my mom was. Her kindness, her warmth, her humanity, and her love will live on forever in me. I will always cherish her for the rest of my life. There isn't a day that my brother and I don't talk about her and all the fond memories we have. To say we miss her is the biggest understatement. Our hearts ache like no other pain I've ever known. She had a heart full of compassion for both humans and animals. My mom adored all animals and found joy when feeding stray cats, the birds and even the squirrels. She would have gone out of her way to help you, or anyone, or anything. It didn't matter if she knew you or not, she would help you if you needed the help. Anastasia Koiveroglou was truly a one-of-a-kind human being.

Her love had no boundaries, and this awful virus took it all away. It hurts so much knowing her death could have been prevented. As long as I live, I will honor her memory and make her proud. I know she would want my brother and me to be happy and move on, but how do you move on when the pain is so strong? Every time I see a memorial, I submit something in memory of my mom. She deserves to be honored and remembered in as many memorials as possible. However, I feel the most important memorial is in the hearts of the ones who love her and miss her.

"We miss you and love you forever, MOM!"

ABOUT KONSTANTINA

Konstantina Dina Kess was born in Greece in 1983. She has one brother, Pantelis. Her family came to the United States from Greece in the late 1980s and settled in New Jersey. They kept close ties with their family in Greece. Konstantina lost her dad, Kleovoulos, to cancer in 2016, and she lost her mom, Anastasia, to COVID-19 in 2020.

Konstantina and her husband, William, live in the New Jersey–New York area. They have a little Maltese/Shih Tzu dog named Rhea who is the apple of their eye. Konstantina loves animals, and she supports various animal rescues and the ASPCA. Besides animals, she loves poker, hiking, game night with friends, and traveling. Traveling to Greece is especially important to Konstantina because most of her relatives still live there, and she loves and misses all her nieces and nephews very much. Due to Covid, she and her husband have not been to Greece in a few years. They are planning on a trip in the future.

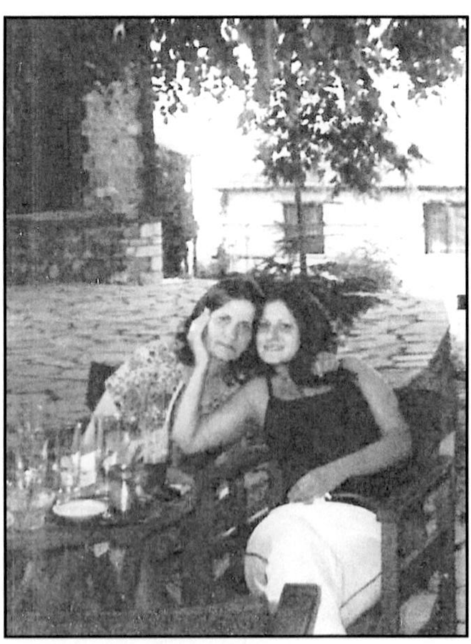

Anastasia Koiveroglou with daughter Konstantina Dina Kess.

Anastasia Koiveroglou landing in Greece.

Anastasia Koiveroglou with (from left to right): son Pantelis, nephew Niko, daughter Konstantina, and niece Stefania.

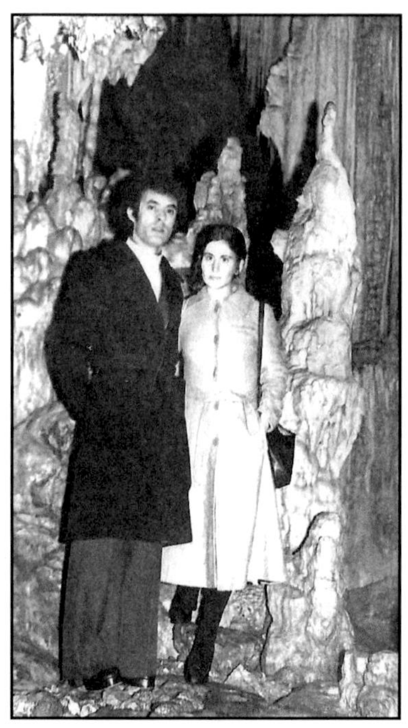

Anastasia with her husband, Kleovoulos, on honeymoon in 1976, in Greece.

With her sister, Violeta, in Greece in the 1970s.

With her son, Pantelis.

With her mom, Kiriaki, and husband, Kleovoulos, in the late 1970s.

In 1973 with her parents, Kiriaki and Kosta, tending to tobacco leaves.

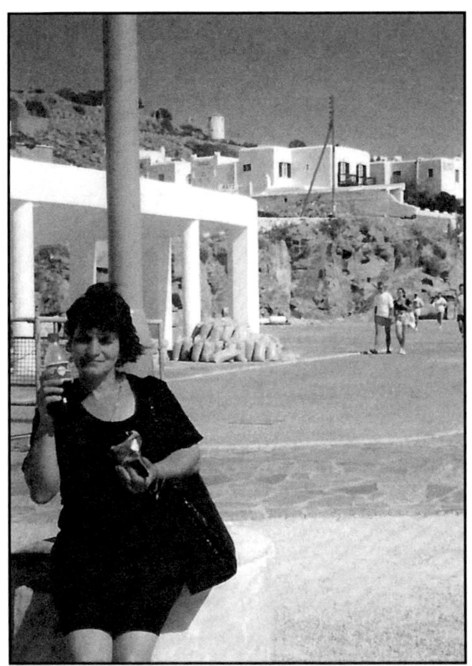

Anastasia Koiveroglou in Mykonos, early 2000s.

At the acropolis with her sister Violeta, in 2019.

Hosea's Story

FAREWELL 1ST SERGEANT

By Ira Richardson

In late spring, just after the close of the Great Depression in the United States (the recession of 1937), Ora Richardson, along with her husband, Ambus, welcomed their sixth son, Hosea Lawrence Richardson. He was my dad, or as I called him, simply "Pops." Born on May 24th, 1937, he was the last of their 13 children. It is difficult enough to imagine life without today's technological marvels, like video games, cell phones, smart watches, flat TVs, and electric cars, but can you imagine having no air conditioning, using an outhouse, or gathering your daily water from a well? Think for a second what it must've been like for things to have changed so drastically and quickly; one year, you're giving your livestock feed corn, and the next year that very corn is now on your dinner plate!

This big and beautiful family lived only a two-hour drive from Galveston, the home of Juneteenth, where the government literally had to step in and announce to the last slaves in America that they were indeed free. What was it like raising a black family in San Jacinto County, Texas in those days? I cannot imagine what it must've been like growing up in those dusty dirt fields of Point Blank, a city that, when counted in 2010, had a population of just under 700 people. Things could turn bleak quickly, and there were very limited government resources, so certainly raising 13 children during the Great Depression was not on anybody's wish list.

I asked Pop once, "What did you all have for breakfast?"

He told me one time he asked Mama Ora what they were going to have for breakfast, and she reached into the closet, handed him a shotgun, reached back into the cupboard, handed him a single shell, and said, "Whatever you bring back, Son."

A few years later, when Pop was 14, while attending a summer Christian conference in Houston, he met the beautiful Myrtle Jean Kelly. She was a light-skinned beauty of African and Irish descent, with long, flowing hair falling down beyond her shoulders, and a face full of freckles. He thought she was the most amazing girl he'd ever seen and was instantly smitten. She did NOT feel the same, however; she thought he was an obnoxious hayseed from the boondocks. Keep in mind, this was still during the time of segregation in the Deep South. They forced my parents to ride in the back of the bus and did not permit them to use "White Only" water fountains.

With few entertainment options available, Pop always worked hard on the farm, and when he actually focused on athletics, he became an almost instant star in both football and basketball at tiny Lincoln High. Anyone who knows anything about Texas knows that, to this day, there are few things more sacred than high school football. Unfortunately, his athleticism and education didn't quite align, and he ended up repeating his senior year. Without the multiple scholarships that are available today to student athletes, he followed his best option, which was the armed forces. So, at 19, my dad began his career in the United States Marine Corps and never looked back.

By this time, my pop had grown into his own. He returned to his hometown, a strapping six-foot-tall, 170-pound rock of a man, to look up his dream girl, Myrtle, who was now in college at Sam Houston University. Allegedly, he pestered her more than he wooed her, but WHATEVER he did… it worked! He eventually won her heart, and they were married on August 22nd, 1959. Their firstborn son soon followed, but he didn't survive. Two years later, on November 4th, 1962, the birth of my brother, Derek, made them parents. Almost immediately, they moved, on orders, to Hawaii, where my mother became one of the first full-time teachers of color and helped to integrate the state. I arrived nearly five years later, while we were stationed at Camp Lejeune, North Carolina, and our little family was complete.

This was all during the Vietnam War, in which my father served three tours as a sergeant and earned two Purple Heart accommodations after surviving a grenade blast and returning home with 22 holes in his flesh. As a small child, I still recall my old man returning home bandaged up more than once, on crutches or his arm in a sling.

After growing tired of base housing in Quantico, Virginia, my parents finally purchased a townhouse in nearby Woodbridge in 1972. My mom was content with a career in education at Quantico Senior High, and they decided it would be best if my father followed his orders solo instead of constantly uprooting his family every year.

By the end of the Vietnam War, things were certainly different. The soldiers returning home were different. Things occurred, which they witnessed or took part in on the fields of battle, that humans simply are not designed to process. My dad was not the same wide-eyed young man. You cannot experience the things that our servicemen and women experience in battle, and then return home to just flip the switch back to normalcy. That's not how our brains are wired.

My pop sought solace in bottled things. They helped calm the nightmares and ease the mental load, but everything comes with a cost. After nearly losing his beloved family, Pop put the bottle down in 1977. He continued to smoke cigarettes and gamble, but he was down a vice.

In 1982, when I began to show my own signs of rebellion, Pop finally retired after 27 years in his beloved Marine Corps. After retirement, he went to work as a sales associate at a local car dealership owned by a former serviceman. At Cowles Ford, he used his years of networking with both the local community and the military to become one of the most successful and well-respected car sales associates in the area.

By this time, my brother Derek had pursued his passion for race cars and was a master mechanic. My mom had continued to pursue her education, earning her master's degree. I had attended Longwood University, but in my last year of college, I found that the lure of crack cocaine was stronger than my quest for knowledge. I walked away at the beginning of my fifth and final year.

For the next 20 years, my life was an upside-down battle with me mostly down. Rehab after rehab, incarceration after incarceration, homelessness and hopelessness, my addiction controlled nearly every aspect of my life. Although there were moments where I could grasp enough of life for a temporary hold, these were short, fleeting, and few and far between.

One of these moments was in 1992. I met a beautiful, young lady named Lori, while attending cosmetology school and working as an apprenticed barber in a hair salon. She was my friend Keith's and Afia's cousin, and she had an adorable little girl named Terra. Lori saw enough in me to give it a go. We eventually had a daughter together, Skye, but I still had ME in the way. The relationship soured after my repeated failures at sobriety, and me being incarcerated more than I was at home. She eventually moved on with her life with another gentleman but blessed my family by allowing Skye to remain with my parents (where she spent much of the time already).

I began having bouts of sobriety. A few months here, a few months there, but I could never sustain any real clean time. This became an absolute point of contention for my parents. For an addict, every time you pick back up, you pull the scab back off of the healing that had already taken place. At some point, people just get numb. They get so tired of the lies, the hurt, and the disappointment that they have to turn you away for their own mental health. They may show tough love after they've enabled you for years.

Skye remained in my parents' care while I continued on my wayward path, breaking heart after heart, ruining relationship after relationship, and burning bridge after bridge. When it was all said and done, when I had nothing left but the smoldering ash and timbers of my once-so-promising life, I was broken and at rock bottom.

I was in my fourth and final long-term rehabilitation stint at the Salvation Army Washington Adult Rehabilitation Center, when I met a tall, gorgeous, light-skinned young lady named Karen. She was a local who had grown up her entire life in the District of Columbia. Her career was in law enforcement, and oddly enough, she seemed to run from what I had been running to. An unlikely fit, BUT we had an awesome time together, and I had finally found somebody as crazy as me! She had a teenage son, Christopher, one year older than Skye who, by then, was 13. At this point, I wasn't very confident in my choices, as I had now dated everyone from prostitutes to police, and crackheads to crime fighters. Yet, it was almost a natural progression as I tried to assimilate back into normal society after being on the other side for so very long.

On September 18th, 2009, Karen and I were married by a justice of the peace in Alexandria, Virginia, and guess who was there? My dad, her dad, and her sister. During that entire time, that awful journey, my mom and dad had been steadfast in my corner, helping me rebuild my life with the few remaining pieces I had. We found out Karen was pregnant with a girl but were given the gut-wrenching news that the child had a slew of very serious, life-threatening medical issues and was not expected to make it. We were both absolutely devastated. Karen had already miscarried before and lost a set of twins. We prayed on it and realized that any child deserved the best chance of survival. They told us they suspected the baby had Trisomy 18 and that she would most likely not make it to term. If she did, she certainly wouldn't make it through delivery. If by some small miracle she did make it, few babies make it to three months. Less than ten percent ever survive to ten years of age.

On February 22nd, 2010, we welcomed our amazing daughter, KalaRose, at Holy Cross Hospital. She was the tiniest little baby, with a head full of straight, dark brown hair. They transferred her to Children's Hospital in DC, where she remained for three months before we finally took her home. Amazingly, KalaRose not only survived, but she has THRIVED, blasting past all of our expectations! She was born with cleft lip and palate, clubbed feet, fused wrists and elbows, and one kidney vertical and one horizontal. Our daughter remained on a G-tube (feeding tube) for the first three years of her life and underwent a dozen surgical procedures before she was five. During the entire process, my parents were totally committed to my growing family, and less than a year later, we discovered we were expecting again. Eighteen months later, we welcomed another daughter, AriJean. Four years later, we welcomed Chauncey, our only son together.

Over the course of all of this time, we relocated nearly every year, moving all over Southern Maryland. We simply lacked consistency, as Karen could no longer work because of health-related problems, and KalaRose needed a watchful eye over her. The one constant we had was my parents.

August 2019, Mom and Pop celebrated 60 years of marital bliss (okay, they survived each other without causing bodily injury to one another!). In all truth, their story was beautiful to witness. I got to see my dad gather himself and mature as a dad, a husband, and a human. He got to see the same of me. I'm proud Pop got to see me finally get (and STAY) sober after nearly ten years removed from active addiction. I look back at all the lessons he taught me about life, about people, and about me. I am not sure he realized how incredible his journey actually was, and how he affected all that loved him. His wit and charm, his humor, insight, and wisdom were unparalleled.

While Pop's physical health had begun to wane in his last years, because of injuries sustained in war and sports, his mind was still amazingly sharp. He had everybody in his vicinity in stitches with his antics! As children growing up, Derek and I wanted to be just like our dad, because he wasn't just our dad, he was our hero. Our dad pushed us to be the best version of ourselves by challenging us to challenge ourselves. He helped me reset my moral compass after having spiraled so low. At every nook, crook and turn, he helped usher me through doors that were closed in my face. Pop helped me rebuild the countless bridges I had burned to soot. He was thoughtful and generous with his time and his resources. He wasn't perfect. He was flawed, and that's why he was so loved and adored by everybody, not just us. My parents were the oldest residents in our community, living in the same house they had purchased during Vietnam. That little house felt a lot emptier after we lost Pop.

On May 21st, 2018, we lost Derek suddenly to sepsis. We had all gathered around his hospital bed as he took his last breaths, and they unplugged him from the life support machines. It was the saddest thing I had ever seen. While it shattered our hearts into a thousand pieces, it was my parents' love and our amazing family that helped pull us all together again.

Forgoing DC area VA hospitals, Pop thought he would receive better treatment at Hunter Holmes McGuire VA Medical Center in Richmond, so we began taking him there. From their home in Woodbridge, the trip is usually one-and-a-half hours, depending on traffic. With traffic, it could easily become a three-hour trek or more. It was during these trips that we grew closer, and I could gather a much more profound respect and admiration for this man that God had blessed me with. We traveled up and down the highway, listening to old school blues or spirituals, or better yet, 60s and 70s falsetto music. He was an entire show I had all to myself. Without question, my dad is the funniest person I've ever met. Through all he had been through, he still found a positive spin and never sat miserably upon anybody's pity pot.

On Thursday, March 19th, 2020, Pop was released from a veteran-referred, Richmond, Virginia, area rehabilitation center while they were in quarantine. When I picked him up, he had a slight cough, which I assumed was a remnant of his former battle with bronchitis. While they did have plastic sheeting up and were not allowing people to enter the residential part of the facility, nobody was wearing PPE, and the social worker actually gave him a big hug upon his departure. When I asked him about the folks in the hazmat suits in the opposite hallway, he simply said, "Those are the people they believe have that Coronavirus stuff."

The entire ride home, he had the nagging cough. Not a loud choking cough, but an annoying, "give me a Ricola" type of cough. We talked, we laughed, and we even stopped at a barbeque joint to grab some grub. When I got him home and settled in bed, I took his bags to the basement. When I opened his bags of clothing, I discovered them to be soaked full of urine. We were furious! They had not been monitoring him at all, simply changing him once he was soaked. Over the next 24 hours, I laundered all of his clothes and my mom bathed him and changed his leg wraps, while Karen sat with him for hours to keep him company.

That weekend, things seemed fairly normal. Outside of his lingering cough and somewhat weakened state, it seemed the worst was behind us, considering everything he had been through. Then Monday came and our nightmare began. March 23rd, 2020, Pop was weak and belligerent. He quickly declined and spiked a fever. I told him I had no choice but to take him to the hospital, but he was so weak I couldn't even help get him to his feet. Eventually, I, along with an EMT, got him downstairs on his chair lift, and the ambulance took him to our local Sentara Hospital. We didn't know it would be the last time we saw him.

I grabbed his file and release paperwork from the rehab center and traveled to the hospital directly after the ambulance. They, however, would not allow me in. I told them he had been exposed to Covid while at Canterbury Rehabilitation and Healthcare Center in Richmond, but they said they had to wait for the test results to return. To err on the side of caution, Skye went to stay with her boyfriend, Jamaal. We talked daily, but it was all a lot for a 20-something to take in.

We talked with Pop on the phone several times a day. Two days later, March 25th, I was sauteing onions and bacon in a skillet, when my five-year-old son commented on how good it smelled, and I realized I couldn't smell. It was simply gone! No congestion, or runny nose, just POOF, gone! Two days later, I lost my taste the same way. Just gone in an instant, as if stolen while I slept. By this time, Pop had been in the hospital for a couple of days, and the nurse said he was laboring with oxygen a bit. They were going to give him a little help by placing him on a ventilator. Remember, this was March 2020, and it was all new. They didn't have rapid tests or the technology they have now, so test results took several days to return.

By the time the positive test results returned, eight days later, it was almost a foregone conclusion. I had lost my taste and sense of smell and was facing overwhelming fatigue and headaches. Karen collapsed one day while walking up the steps and was so weak she just lay there until I could come help her up. Mom began getting weak and had lost her appetite. I took her to Dumfries Health Center, and they did a swab for a Covid test.

Karen and I were also in the process of moving, and she got a call that our new home had been approved and to come pick up the keys. I asked her not to, stating we stood a better chance with all of us fighting together, but she just wanted to be away from it all and in our new place. I helped her load the minivan and hugged her and our three children (5, 8, and 10) goodbye, not knowing if we would see each other again.

After they placed Pop on the ventilator, we did not have any direct contact with him. We only received updates from the nursing staff via cellphone. There was no FaceTime, skyping, pics, or anything else available to us. Three days later, I received a call at 4:00 am from Karen, saying that she couldn't breathe, followed by a call from Prince George's Fire and Rescue telling me if she were to have any chance at all, she would have to go RIGHT THEN. I jumped in the truck and headed the hour north to Clinton, Maryland, to get the kids. By the time we got back to my parents' house, Mom's doctor had called and confirmed what we already suspected. She too was positive with Covid pneumonia and needed to get medical treatment immediately.

I've seen some pretty bad days in this life, but having your mom, dad, and wife all in the hospital battling Covid at the same time really makes you question a lot. By God's grace, they felt my mom might have a better chance convalescing at home, so at almost midnight, I shot back up to Sentara Hospital and picked her up. Karen wasn't so lucky. She was placed, almost immediately, on a ventilator, and both she and Pop hung on life support at the same time.

Over the next few days, Karen improved while Pop gradually declined. Then, one awful night, it was as if he had "stepped off of a ledge." At about 9:00 pm on April 13th, 2020, I received the call that my dad, my pop, my hero, and my friend, had passed. And just like that, he was gone.

"Yes, he's gone," I heard the nurse on the other end say in a thick African accent.

"Excuse me?" I questioned, not really understanding what was happening or unable to process the words I'd just heard.

"He's gone. He's passed," she said again, very matter of fact.

I was stunned. "Dumbfounded" is probably a better word.

"Well, umm, what do I do? What am I supposed to do?" I asked. She may have thought I meant about his body, but in my heart, I was asking how do we go on as a family without this man?

"Somebody will be in touch," she said and then simply hung up.

My mom, who was fighting Covid pneumonia herself when he passed, has never been the same. Physically, she recovered most of her health, but we came extremely close to losing her. My wife was on a ventilator for over a week and had to have her foot amputated due to complications from Covid. I, myself, am a long-hauler, with battle fatigue, joint pain, and headaches. I haven't been able to taste or smell since March 2020. I eat from memory, with only base flavors such as salty or sweet. I cannot smell a thing. Not cigarette smoke, not any aroma… good or bad. I can't smell the stinky guy at the grocery store, or even a skunk next to me in my own backyard.

Covid has turned our entire lives upside down, but nothing has damaged us more than having lost such an amazing man. There are times I wonder if Pop was just unlucky. I mean, how many parents bury two of their three children? How many people are born during the worst economic crash in American history, and then die during one of the worst pandemics of the last 100 years? A man who goes clear across the other side of the world to fight for a country that ten years prior wouldn't even allow him to share their restrooms or water fountains. A place where a soldier can get blown to bits in the service of their country, but yet honored with trinkets and trophies and then, years later, denied reasonable medical treatment and financial compensation. A country where a man is a pillar of society, a hero in his community, and a legend amongst his peers and comrades, but left dying in a hospital bed for eight days while they await results to return from the lab. A place where our most historically treasured resource, our amazing senior citizens, have died in record numbers, and many of us still selfishly refuse to inconvenience ourselves just a little because we feel our rights are being violated. As if the right to LIVE is nonexistent. Sadly, nearly one million American families have experienced the same gut-wrenching loss. The empty chair during the holidays, or that rocker or recliner that was his or her favorite spot, reminds us of our tragic loss.

Per Pop's wishes, we cremated his body, and his remains were stored until we got the go-ahead from Quantico National Cemetery. Eight months later, on December 11th, 2020, we held a small, 35-person maximum (including staff), Covid-restricted memorial service in the chapel of our beloved Star of Bethlehem Missionary Baptist Church, in Triangle, Virginia. The service was livestreamed so the rest of our family and friends could be a part of it. Following the service, we laid him to final rest at Quantico with a 21-gun salute, and the full military honors so deserving of the hero he was. Had it been "normal" times, the chapel would've been standing room only at its 300-person max, and the procession would've stretched for miles! Let there be no mistake about it… Marine Corps First Sergeant Hosea Lawrence Richardson was larger than life itself.

During their 60 years of marriage, Mom and Pop grew an amazing extended family of godchildren, and others that simply fell into our fold because of the love my parents gave. When Pop passed away, it crushed so many hearts. I'm not claiming him as saint; he was flawed like all of us, but my pop had a conviction within him that rose up from those dusty fields of Point Blank, Texas, and he carried it with him everywhere he traveled around the world.

Today, I'm a part of some amazing groups whose members have shared some similar tragedies. We choose to keep Pop's memory alive by carrying on some of his favorite traditions. The biggest is just gathering. He LIVED for it! Nothing on this planet meant more to him than gathering together and breaking bread. While I've vacated the traditions of cornbread and buttermilk, chitterlins, and pig's feet, I do live for Mom's sweet potato pies and casseroles, vanilla pound cake, and chicken and dumplings, just to name a few of his favorites. Sometimes when I'm sitting, enjoying these things, I can almost feel him beside me, shaking his head in approval. He's smiling from ear to ear, saying, "Mmm, mmm, mmm, I KNEW I picked the right woman!"

Pop, not seeing you is hard. It took me a very long time to come to terms with the fact that you are really gone. Throughout much of my youth, you were away on deployment, and your final couple of years were spent at a long-term rehabilitation, so for a long time I guess I expected you to walk back in the door, or to get that call to come pick you up. That call never came.

ABOUT IRA

Ira Richardson was born in Camp Lejeune, North Carolina, to a Marine and an educator. On both his mom's and his dad's side, he was the only child out of an entire generation born outside of Texas. He grew up in Woodbridge, Virginia, where he graduated from Potomac Senior High School, followed by four years of undergraduate studies at Longwood University (formerly Longwood College) in Farmville, Virginia, where he majored in social work with a minor in journalism.

Today, Ira splits his time between Woodbridge with his mom, and a home in Glenn Dale, Maryland that he shares with his wife and three grade-school children. He also has a 29-year-old stepson and daughter-in-law who reside nearby as well. Sadly, he lost his eldest daughter, Skye Elizabeth, in an automobile accident on March 11th, 2021, exactly three months after laying his father to rest. While he has admittedly faced his fair share of strife and tribulation (much of it self-imposed), battling everything from food and drug addictions to homelessness, dereliction, and incarceration, nothing was worse than that day.

"Easily the single worst day of my life," he declares, "and I've seen some pretty bad lows. My greatest lessons in life have been my most painful. What have recent years taught me, you might ask? Well, let the people in your life that you love know that you love them because they can be gone in an instant!"

He tries his best to wring the most out of each and every day with the realization that yesterday is gone, and one day, tomorrow won't arrive. Staying in the moment seems to work, at least for now…

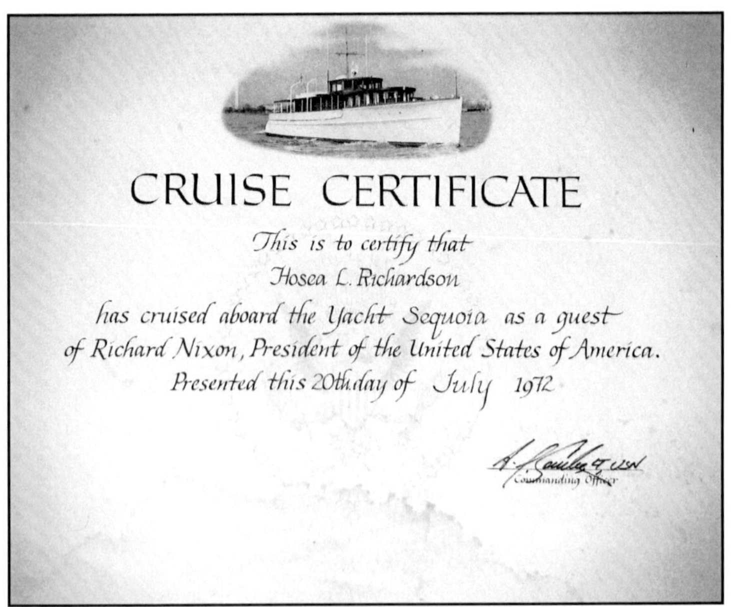

CRUISE CERTIFICATE

This is to certify that

Hosea L. Richardson

has cruised aboard the Yacht Sequoia as a guest of Richard Nixon, President of the United States of America.

Presented this 20th day of July 1972

Commanding Officer

My dad was a war hero and honorary guest aboard the yacht of then President Richard M. Nixon.

It wasn't very often that we were blessed with visitors from Texas, but we absolutely loved it. Auntie Fannie Mae, Pop's oldest sister, and his nephew, (my cousin) Rickie.

Holidays were everything to my old man.

Nothing mattered more to Pop than family.

All grown up at our Houston homecoming, circa 1987.

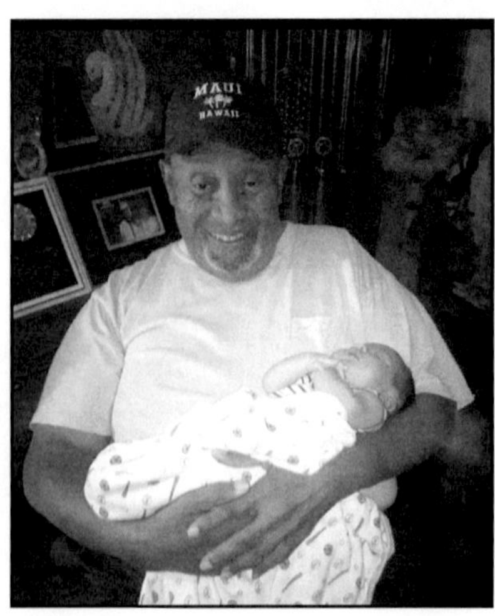

The first day he met his grandson Chauncey. One of the happiest days of his life

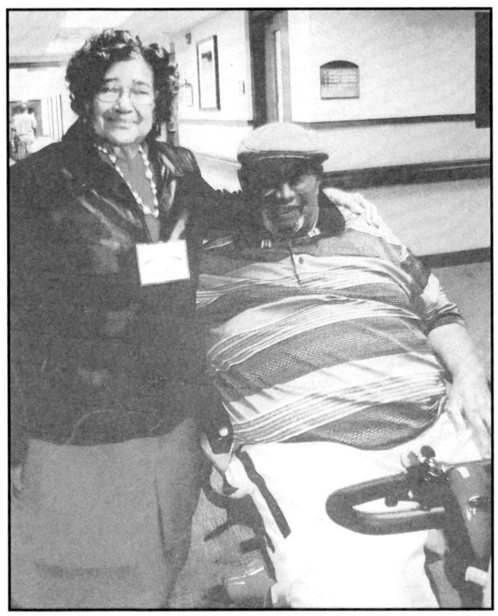

The last pic that we have of Pop. Mom went to visit him at the rehab center where he would eventually be exposed to Covid.

The jungles of Vietnam.

Pop had his "own lane" when it came to fashion.
He loved to dress, but he loved family even more.

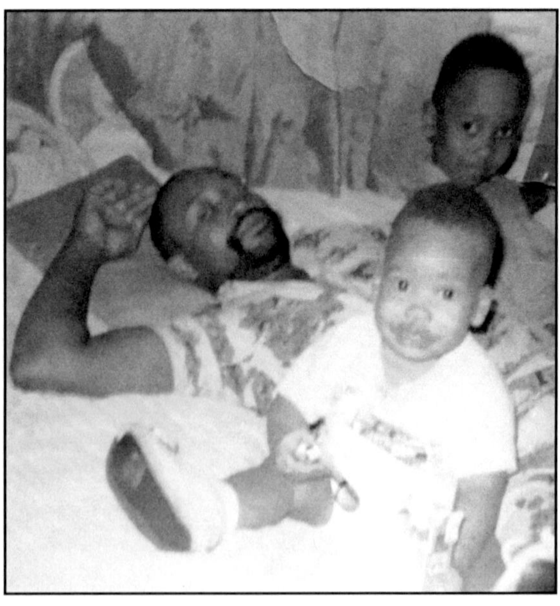

The king with his princes while home on leave from Vietnam.

CAL'S STORY

By Hannah Ernst

INTRODUCTION

It's hard to grasp the concept that inside one person lives thousands of versions; a husband, a father, a grandfather, a brother, a son, an uncle, an artist, etc. Who my grandpa was to my grandma is a different version of who he was to my sister, and the memories he created with my mom differ from the ones he created with me. Sitting down to write this, I quickly realized that telling my grandpa's story from my perspective alone wouldn't do him justice. While I've known my grandpa my entire life, he's only known me a fraction of his. Before I knew him, he spent decades living a life in Brooklyn, New York, and New Jersey with a beautiful woman by his side. Hoping to portray my grandpa as best I can, I've collected a series of stories from his wife of 60 years, Sheila; from his daughter, Karen (my mom); and from me and my sister Abbey. This is Cal Schoenfeld's story, a tribute to a man with a large nose, a pair of glasses, a slight waddle, a distinctively infectious laugh, and a trademark crooked grin.

A BLIND DATE

It was a joke at first between her and her friends, a bunch of 16-year-old girls talking about boys in the mid-1950s, throwing ideas around, and my grandma initially had no intention of truly seeing it through. He was 21, said to be handsome, and supposedly had a charm and humor unlike anyone else. After a couple of minutes thinking it over, my grandma finally agreed. What could go wrong?

That night, he came to her home, and the first thing that struck her was how polite he was. He'd planned out the date. First, they would go to the movies, and then they would grab some ice cream afterwards, a last-minute switch-up, he later told my sister and I, after he couldn't get a table at a fancy restaurant. The entire time he made her laugh and smile, complimenting her bright red curls, which he absolutely adored, and teasing her about the periwinkle sweater and skirt set she was wearing. He never forgot that outfit, and in later years, he would remind her of how eye-catching she looked in it, of how the color contrasted with her blue eyes. I asked my grandma what she remembered about that night, and her eyes lit up as she explained the simple jokes he would tell. "He was just fun." A grin slipped across her face when she added, "And he called me 'freckle face.' He loved joking about me." My grandpa wasn't one for showing off or acting more than he was, and I realized from the way she smiled, remembering the jokes he had told her that night, that it was his simple, quick-witted self that got her to agree to a second date.

The neighborhood in Brooklyn where my grandma grew up was primarily of strict Jewish faith and Italian heritage, and so as a practicing orthodox Jew, she fit in. My grandpa, however, grew up as a reformed Jew, which meant that he did not follow as many rules or practice to the extent that her family did. This posed an ever so slight issue when he called the next day, which was a Saturday; Shabbat. Shabbat is a Jewish holiday that takes place every week, starting at sunset on Friday and ending the following sunset on Saturday. During this time, people observe it by resting. Businesses close for the day, no chores are done, and for stricter households like my grandma's, no electricity or technology is used. Needless to say, my grandpa did not get a very kind answer when my grandma's father demanded he call back later in the night and abruptly hung up.

My grandpa never made that mistake again. Every time he wished to talk to her on a Friday, it was through a call before sunset, and if it was a Saturday, he waited until sunset. He abided by these rules so much so that he would wait outside her home until the sun went down on Saturday nights, when most of their dates tended to be. Just as the sun set under the horizon, he'd head up to her apartment for whatever was planned; one of her favorite ways to enjoy an evening was to take a train ride to Coney Island to ride bumper cars.

When I asked her what was most memorable about their dates, and if there was some ritual for them, she chuckled and nodded. "Our goodbyes." I won't lie. That struck me as odd for a moment, but she happily elaborated. The home my grandma grew up in was small; her mother, herself, and her two younger sisters all lived there. There was a long hallway with doors on either side, and she explained that he would walk her up into the apartment before they'd quietly find her door and whisper soft goodbyes. My grandma smiled when telling the story. "My family would be snoring in their rooms to the left and right of us, and we'd try our best not to laugh as we said goodbye. Cal never forgot that, and neither have I."

RAISING A FAMILY

Their wedding was on December 20th, 1959. My grandpa proposed to my grandma on her 18th birthday, and they were engaged a little over a year. When I brought up their wedding, she immediately joked that he danced with two left feet. "Oh, but he was so good at thinking fast," she told me, holding back another laugh. "We thought somebody had paid the photographer, but it turned out nobody had. Apparently, no one could afford him, yet someone hired him anyway. So, when the guests' backs were turned, Cal snuck into the wedding presents and took out the cash to pay the photographer. He subtly mentioned his stealthy moves throughout the night."

My grandparents were married for 60 years, and they were the epitome of yin and yang. It's what kept them together all those years, my grandma told me. For as long as I can remember, and anybody who knows my grandma can attest to this, she has been hyper. My grandpa, on the other hand, was relaxed. The two defined the concept that opposites attract, and they balanced each other out in a way nobody else could. Despite having different interests and liking to do different things, they always found a way to include the other. A perfect example of this: my grandma loves shopping, and my grandpa adored art. Neither one cared much for the other's pursuit, but my grandma always bought him his favorite type of shirt, or abnormally large shoes, while he always adjusted his paintings, just slightly, to add a few more modern elements to his contemporary style. Or he'd go all out and paint her a picture solely for her, such as the redwood tree forest he painted for her as a birthday present one year that has forever stood as her favorite. "He was my soulmate," she said, then added, "and if I could talk to him right now, I'd look at him and say 'I wish you were here by my side.'"

My grandma and grandpa had two children; Erik, my uncle, and Karen, my mom. I asked my mom about her memories of him, and almost instantly, she replied, "The Singing Chicken." What that initially meant, I hadn't the slightest idea, but she then explained that it was a song he would break into when she was little and in his art studio. They would be together, each working on their own projects (she, doing some type of homework or drawing and he, working; he was a freelance commercial artist and worked in the basement of their home). It was random, and he'd just suddenly start singing, but it always made them laugh.

Just as he used to bring my sister and me into the city, he also took my mom there when she was a child. Their favorite spots were Coney Island, where they'd grab hotdogs at Nathan's Famous restaurant and visit the aquarium; the Bronx Zoo, where he would adore the otters and seals; and the National Museum of Natural History, where she'd admire the dinosaur fossils, and he would make funny animal noises while looking at the stuffed animals. He also loved the Hope Diamond, which is exhibited there, and would joke about someone stealing it; he would laugh about how stupid someone would have to be to steal such a precious but iconic jewel, and then attempt to sell it back to the museum. Afterwards, they would walk to the Strawberry Fields memorial for John Lennon and sit by the Imagine mosaic. Then they would finish their trip by driving by the Dakota where he lived.

Lastly, there were the emails. Every day, he greeted her with a "Good Morning" email that he would send when she first got into work. It was a small part of her day, but now its absence is heartbreakingly prominent.

COUNTLESS MEMORIES

I was born on November 7th, 2004, a day that was surprisingly warm, and something my grandpa would tell me over and over. He joked about the fact that my delivery was way too fast and that he hadn't even had time to read the Sunday New York Times he had bought that morning. Some of the earliest memories I have with my grandpa are stepping on the black squares in the black-

and-white checkered floors of stores at local shopping centers and having an absolute blast doing so. He was always so happy to be a part of anything I did, so when I asked him to read to my class in preschool, he eagerly agreed. Even as a little kid, I'd tell people my grandpa was a "joker," but then I'd immediately back up and explain that he wasn't the bad DC villain "Joker," that he was, instead, just a buffoon with too many jokes for his own good.

My grandpa was everything. He was the guy in the crowd at every school musical, and he was the guy that sat next to me during Friday night dinners. With a Brooklyn accent I made fun of and a slight waddle I copied teasingly, he was my number one supporter. No matter what I was doing, be it a test, an arts-and-crafts project, or an art business venture, he was always the first to compliment me, or provide tools and ideas that I wouldn't have had otherwise. He was a genuine artist and had a talent unlike anyone else in creating abstractly unique pieces that either left people confused or entranced. He always joked that if he could elicit any kind of reaction, whether it was love or hate, he'd done his job right. I like to think I got my artistic perspective from him. Some of the best memories I have with him are in his basement, the same one my mom and he used to work in, each of us working on our own projects, but listening to stories of his childhood growing up in Brooklyn.

That was the thing about my grandpa. He could talk for what seemed like hours, cracking himself up with his own jokes, and oh, how he loved telling stories. And he always told the same tales too, like the time when he visited an art museum and somebody placed their glasses on the floor, and people thought the glasses were themselves an art display. He was in New York City every week, going by himself via bus, or having my sister and I sleep over when we were younger, and then the four of us would all go together. That is another memory I have, my sister and me in our beds at my grandparents' while he set up movies on the TV like "Princess

Frog" and "Gnomeo & Juliet." "Brother Bear" was my favorite too, a movie he accidentally bought but gave to me anyway, and we both ended up loving. When my sister and I were little, we went into the city at least twice a month. Something he loved teasing me about was Irving and Seymour, two pigeons he claimed were always around us. Whether we were at Zabar's getting frozen yogurt or at the Children's Museum, he'd randomly point at two pigeons and say, "There's Irving and Seymour!!" I was little, so of course I believed him.

There are so many things that made him special. Between the mints he'd have imported from Europe (which he'd sneak to me on trips to the city), to his love for otters, his habit of cutting little articles he'd think I'd like out of the newspaper, and the pause he'd give, no matter what the situation was, followed by hysterical laughter whenever someone farted, he was so uniquely him. Being married to my grandma, who made sure he was nothing but the picture of health, he had to sneak goodies and sweets. He prided himself over a secret stash of dark chocolate that's still hidden somewhere in his art studio. To this day, we don't know where it is, but knowing how neat he was, whenever we find it, I'm sure it'll be all stacked and labeled to perfection.

My sister shares a lot of memories of him, too. When I asked her what she wanted to include, she laughed and mentioned Mallomars. They were popular in his day, and after he brought them up in conversation when we were younger, we asked to try them. After that, they were an essential part of being at my grandparents' house. Even more essential was my grandpa's need to sneak one of the two cookies my sister and I were each given for himself, which is how he earned the infamous title "the Mallomar thief." Granted, he always replaced whatever he'd taken from us, but it was the fact that each time he'd have to find some elaborate way of taking them rather than just asking. Abbey also mentioned his scandalous habit of cheating at cards, to which he would claim he never *intended* to do so, and she ended with how he always greeted us with, "Hello, beautiful."

THE VIRUS

The beginning of the end began around the end of March 2020, when my grandpa started coughing. It was really nothing at first, something that was simply brushed under the rug as seasonal allergies, considering he always experienced horrific symptoms around springtime. But there was something off as his cough progressed. COVID-19 was still considered the novel virus and, at the time, was plaguing Italy, so it still hadn't really affected New Jersey; there wasn't any mask wearing or social distancing. My grandma took no illness lightly, though. Even a headache was sometimes treated with a trip to their doctor. Considering how easy of a cough it had been initially, and seeing as it was the beginning of spring, the usual time of an allergy flare-up, he had an online telemedicine-call with his allergist, which resulted in a Z-pack. It didn't work.

About a week after his initial symptoms, my family decided it would be best to stop our weekly Friday night dinners. Instead, my grandparents brought food to our house, and we'd greet them from inside of our garage while they stood near the middle of the driveway. The second Friday they came over with food, we heard my grandpa let out this cough. It was just one cough, but it wasn't normal. It was a deep, throaty cough that made us all glance over at him, but he brushed it off as nothing. He always did, stating it was his allergies, and we believed him.

On April 9th, he wrote my mom an email, as per their daily morning emails. However, this one was alarming. "I'm going to quarantine," he wrote. "It's better than the alternative." What did that mean? Almost instantly, my mom responded, asking if he thought he had COVID-19. Then she ended up calling him. My grandma answered, and in the background, my mom could hear my grandpa coughing. It was a sickening cough, one that instantly raised red flags. But, again, they brushed it off; this time it was my grandma who said he had taken his allergy medication and had just swallowed the wrong way.

Earlier the next day, something possessed my mom and my sister to drive over to my grandparents' house. My grandpa was sitting on the bench in the foyer while my mom and Abbey stood outside. He told his jokes and gave out smiles, making conversation like normal, but it was when he made the subtle quip of "I get out of breath just tying my shoes" that set my mom on edge once more. But, at the moment, he seemed fine, and that was enough to send my mom and sister back home. It was later, around 6 o'clock that night, that my grandma called my mom in a panic. Although it was a call to my mom, and she had answered it on her phone, I still heard loud and clear: "He can't breathe."

There wasn't any hesitation. My mom and I got in the car more quickly than I can ever remember moving. She was trembling as she drove, mumbling, "That's my dad. He can't die." The distance between our house and theirs is about a 10-minute drive, and in the thousands of times we've driven to their house, I don't think we've ever gotten there that fast. Paramedics were already there when we arrived. They were inside the house, except for two others who were scattered outside, and all dressed in hazmat suits. And eventually, through tears in my eyes, I watched as they wheeled my grandpa out of the house on a gurney, an oxygen mask over his face. He was wheezing, making this awful sound while trying to breathe. His back was turned to us, and as the paramedics spoke to the surrounding emergency responders, the gurney clashed and rolled. I couldn't help but notice that my grandpa was laughing. Even as he fought for air, he was choking out jokes and making the paramedics smile.

I'd never considered my grandpa old before. Sure, he was 83, which, yeah, is old, but he never *looked* old to me. He had such a youthful soul and was always so active in everything he did that he never seemed old. But at that moment, when the paramedics rolled him down the driveway and for the first time, when he faced us, he looked so frail. He didn't have his glasses on, so maybe that was why, but with disheveled hair and an oxygen mask, he looked so old and weak. When he saw my mom and me, his face noticeably dropped. "What are you doing here?" He didn't say it, but he might as well have. His eyes said it, and the way he sunk back a little into the gurney said it. With a slight wave goodbye, he disappeared into the ambulance.

My grandpa was in the hospital for four weeks. The first week he was on nothing but supplemental oxygen, complaining about having to lie on his stomach (a position the doctors said would help him), and cracking jokes about how the socks were too thin to ever really warm his feet. The machines they connected him to were far too loud for him to ever really hear us, so we lost quite a few conversations to expelled oxygen. One thing he never let up on, though, was how awful the food was. He absolutely hated it. Fortunately, a week into being in the hospital, we got the doctors to agree to let my grandma make a cheese sandwich. It was a simple meal, and one that was probably wrapped in the insane amount of wax paper layers my grandma uses with every meal she makes, but she made it.

It was also the last meal he ever ate.

April 17th, 2020 was the last day any of us got to have a genuine conversation with him. The last words he said to me were to make a joke: "I'm breaking out of here." It was then followed by, "Love to all." While fighting the oxygen, it was all he really could say, and it's how he always ended conversations. "Love to all."

He spent three weeks after that on a ventilator. We spoke to him over the phone, and my mom went through hell getting his stats every morning, evening, and night. COVID-19 has a phenomenal way of getting your hopes up just enough and then causing them to suddenly plummet again. There were days he was doing so well that we thought they might take him off the ventilator, but other days, it just got worse and worse. With a viral plea and much persistence, my mom managed to get him convalescent plasma, a novel treatment at the time that had the potential to work. He was the first to get this new treatment in the hospital he was at. We had such high hopes it would work.

I spoke to him over the phone; we all did, but it wasn't like he could respond. And then we were told we could speak to him over FaceTime. I'm the one who volunteered to do that. I got to FaceTime him a few times, but the first time I saw him, I couldn't really get any words out. It wasn't him. It was, but it wasn't. His beard had grown out (he was always clean shaven), his hair was a little longer and unkempt, and he was sunken in. I was looking at the shell of a guy I'd known my entire life, and seeing him like that has got to be the worst thing I've ever known. He fought beyond anything against the virus, but eventually passed on May 8th, 2020, solely because of COVID-19.

As I write this, COVID-19 still rages on a year and a half after my grandpa's death. There is no resting at peace for him, at least not yet, as people still joke about the mortality of this virus and demean its existence. Upon his passing, I created an international art project that memorializes and tells the story of those lost to COVID-19, named "Faces of Covid Victims." Each portrait represents a loved one lost to Covid within a yellow heart. The yellow heart symbolizes support and remembrance. Through it, I've told the story of thousands of individuals who have all suffered the same fate as my grandpa, and through their stories, there is one thing in common: there's no pattern. There's no stereotypical group of people who will die more than another. This virus does not just select the immunocompromised and the elderly. People of all ages, children and the old alike, of all ethnicities, races, religions, from different locations around the world, have passed. COVID-19 is not a joke; our loved ones are not just a statistic or a number. This project has helped me in ways I never could have quite envisioned. I have learned the stories of thousands of people and families who went through the same exact thing my grandpa and my family endured. Through art, the means through which "Faces of Covid Victims" operates, I feel as though I pay tribute to my grandpa with every memorial. He was my everything, as the loved ones I commemorate are everything to their families, and in combining my grandpa's love for telling/learning stories, and our shared passion for art, I feel like each portrait, at least a small part of it, is dedicated to him.

Grandpa, I love you. I'll always love you. And I miss you more than words can describe. I hope you're safe, I hope you're happy, and I hope you know that every day and night I'm thinking of you. I miss you, and I love you.

Hannah Ernst

ABOUT HANNAH

Hannah Ernst is 17 years old and grew up in Parsippany, New Jersey. She is currently a junior in high school. Hannah is an artist, and has channeled her grief of losing her grandpa to Covid by creating the Facebook page *Faces of Covid Victims*. To date, she has drawn over 2500 silhouettes and vows to continue drawing loved ones lost as long as she can.

Facebook: https://www.facebook.com/facesofcovidvictims

Instagram: @covid.victims

*Brooklyn, New York,
Approximately six years-old.*

*High School Graduation from
Erasmus High School, 1954.*

*Wedding Day. Married Sheila
Schiff on December 20, 1959.*

Cal and Sheila Schoenfeld, 1960s.

Family Photo with daughter, Karen, and son in law, Steven Ernst, and grandchildren, Hannah and Abbey.

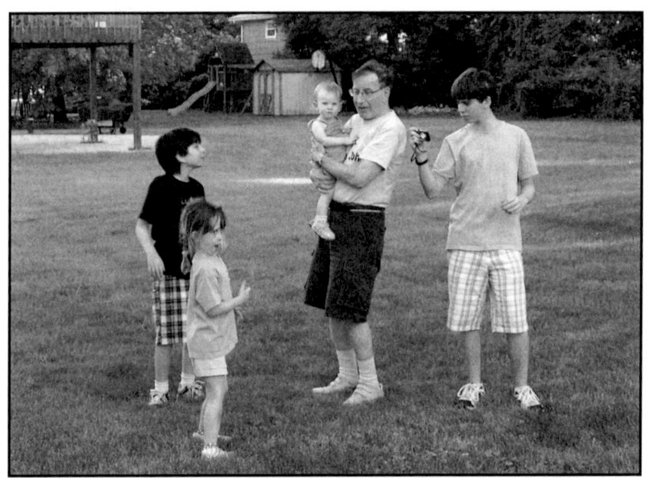

Cal playing outside with his grandchildren, Avi and Max Schoenfeld, and Hannah and Abbey Ernst.

Cal at the park with his two children, Erik Schoenfeld and Karen Ernst.

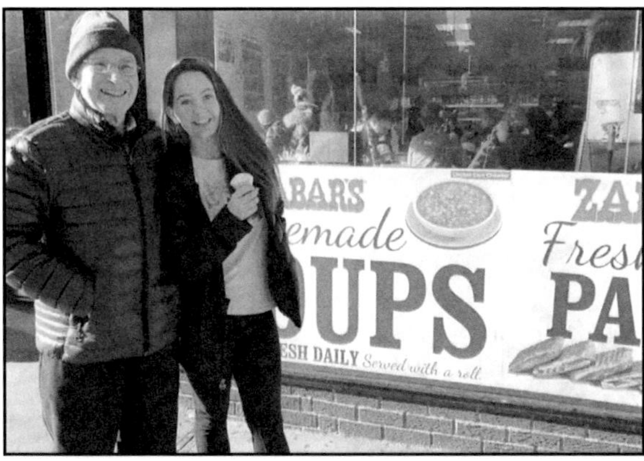

Cal and his granddaughter, Hannah Ernst, at their favorite spot in New York; Zabars.

Cal and Abbey Ernst at the Bubble Show in New York.

Cal at the World Trade Center with his favorite bridge behind him, the Brooklyn Bridge.

Anna's Story

By Amber Carter

Anna entered this world on November 2nd, 2006. Her delivery was the sweetest and easiest out of all five of my children. She immediately captured the hearts of not only me and her father, but of her big sister, Sophia, right away. Her big brother, Johnson, asked me to "put her back" since he had been convinced, even though I said she would be a girl, that she was supposed to be the best little brother ever made. Soon after, he realized that he too loved her more than anything, and they became best friends.

Anna barely cried, always smiled, and slept well enough. As she grew, it was apparent that if she wanted to do something, she was going to do it. Anna also always seemed to avoid chores and stay out of trouble, which drove her siblings crazy. Looking back, I am certain they were right, but it was so hard to punish her. She just had a funny way about her, which made it hard to follow through with discipline. For instance, anytime I asked her to do the dishes, she "had to go to the bathroom" and then would conveniently forget.

Anna's interests grew to include drama, theatrics, and a lot of dancing. She was fearless, hysterical, creative, and emotional, while still content with her life. Anna could go into the middle of a crowd of 10,000 people and do something most would consider embarrassing and not think twice. She had so much confidence; it gleamed from her smile and stride. Though she never got to perform professional theater, she certainly did her fair share of school plays and choir concerts. In second grade, Anna took part in a math musical version of Sherlock Holmes. My little budding performer was so cute, and she remembered all her lines. She also played a pilgrim in kindergarten and a flower in her fourth-grade play, *Nuts*. Anna enjoyed singing in the choir, so we attended many concerts at school. She was a good student, but school was second to her socializing. Eventually, we enrolled her in dance class at one of our local dance studios, and she wanted to take everything they offered. I had to scale her back because our wallet couldn't afford it.

My husband is a United States Marine. As a young military family, we have endured more than our fair share of difficulty. Military life for dependent children is difficult. Along with moving every few years, military children are expected to behave a certain way. Though I know my husband and I were doing the best with what we had in our parenting toolbox, we failed time and time again to truly provide the loving home our children deserved. They had stability, and we provided them with everything they needed, and most of what they wanted; however, they carried the emotional weight of both of our expectations. We were hard on them, expecting too much, and though it had changed each of our children over the years, somehow Anna managed to grin and bear all of it.

Despite all of this, we did fun things as a family at least once a year, even if it was just going to visit our families. We went to Washington, D.C., when Anna was almost five, and walked what seemed to be 30 miles in a day. We visited science museums, aquariums, and beaches, and even rode horses. In 2012, we moved to Okinawa, Japan, for what turned out to be Anna's favorite duty station. How could it not be? It is a tropical island with friendly locals and very safe for kids. Our children thrived there. School was great, they had good friends, and our family had a great support system. We lived in Japan for five years, until Anna was ten, and enjoyed so much together in our time there. We climbed Mt. Fuji, went whale watching, enjoyed traditional Okinawan and Japanese culture and food, and we did so many other amazing things other kids only dream of. Leaving Okinawa was the hardest move for most of us, as we left what really felt like home. We didn't leave Okinawa without a surprise, though. I found out I was pregnant with our fifth child after a long, eight-and-a-half-year break. It was an unexpected, but welcome blessing!

Before we departed Okinawa, Anna's face developed some spots with hyper and hypo pigmentation, which I thought little of as we had spent a lot of time in the sun. We assumed it was that. However, once we arrived at our next duty station in Fort Sill, Oklahoma, my husband realized Anna could not make a fist, and her facial features were thinning out. I made a doctor's appointment, and they referred us to a rheumatologist because her physician suspected juvenile arthritis. We traveled to the Oklahoma Children's Hospital an hour and a half away. We didn't know it then, but these would be the times Anna and I would talk and get to really know each other over the next three years. Most times, we went to these appointments alone or with her baby brother, David. We always visited the Asian market after Anna's appointments so we could enjoy our favorite Japanese treats.

They quickly diagnosed Anna with Juvenile Limited Systemic Scleroderma, otherwise known as CREST syndrome and Raynaud's phenomenon. It is an incurable and rare autoimmune disease that causes overproduction of collagen in the body. Raynaud's is a common side effect of scleroderma, causing poor circulation in the tiny blood vessels, usually in fingers and toes. The doctor sent us home with steroids, another medication for her poor circulation, and some pamphlets. They assured us Anna could live an average life with this incurable disease. I then did what any parent would do; I went home and started researching. The information I found was awful, scary, and left me already grieving the lost alternate life my daughter had dreamed of. Research showed that not only would this affect her skin and facial features, but it could also affect her heart, lungs, and joints. Anna was already experiencing muscle aches and chronic fatigue, which she didn't want to mention to us. I also learned the Raynaud's was causing her fingers and toes to turn blue. Worst-case scenario, she could lose her digits if the circulation loss got too bad. It terrified me, and I learned quickly that "Doctor Google" sucked.

The medications Anna took caused a fast heart rate and upset her stomach. Once again, I did tons of research, but this time on adult scleroderma because there was nothing much on the rare juvenile form. It was so overwhelming. I suggested to her rheumatologist that she start every medication at the lowest dose and monitor her from there. Thankfully, she agreed, and though we had to add other meds over the next three years, she was thriving and doing great on those doses. We kept her extremities warm and her stress level down. Anna joined dance class, could almost make a fist again, and was close to doing a split! She was living her best pre-teen life and doing great.

In February 2020, Anna had her annual pulmonary function test, in addition to some other maintenance things, to make sure there was no further progression of her disease. They said she was in tip-top shape. While we had heard about what was going on in Washington State with this new virus they were calling COVID-19, we had thought little about it since it hadn't spread as far as we knew. We had planned a trip to Dallas for spring break because it was close to home, and Anna and her sister Corinne wanted to go to Legoland. The prior year, we had gone to the Grand Canyon. Spring break was our time to schedule family stuff. My husband was planning to go back to Okinawa for an unaccompanied, one-year tour in July without us, so this would have been our last big trip before he would leave for the year. Then Covid started spreading.

There were 35 known cases in Dallas and talk of schools shutting down for a couple of weeks to monitor this new threat. We still planned to go on the trip; however, our oldest daughter, Sophia, was monitoring the news closely and was very concerned for Anna's safety. She voiced her concerns, and though we ignored her initially, we canceled our plans and stayed home. School did not return after March 23rd, and we were now in a new era of virtual schooling. Truthfully, the end of the year didn't matter. If you had good grades at the end of spring break, your child didn't have to do much to stay afloat.

We lingered at home, doing everything virtually as cases were rising everywhere. Dance class was now over Zoom, my husband's work was over Zoom, and church was over Zoom. We only left the house to pick up school lunches and for the occasional grocery run. At this point, in Oklahoma, masks were optional but required on the military installation. We wore them mostly everywhere. Even though I can't say we took it too seriously, we still followed any rules that were in place.

In May, our oldest daughter graduated high school at a socially distanced outdoor graduation. It was such a beautiful day, and we were so thankful for what so many students didn't get to have. The next month, we puttered around as Anna prepared for her dance recital in June. Her dance studio had worked out a brilliant plan so they could still have the recital, and her level performed on June 17th. They awarded Anna with "Best Hip-Hop Dancer" for the year! This small, but beautiful, award meant everything to her. We were so proud of her, and it was so great to see her face beaming with accomplishment and pride because she was finally in her element.

Anna made me promise I would force her to try out for the next youth theater play offered by our local playhouse. They only offered one children's play a year, and it was coming up in August. She was afraid to sing in front of people, but she knew she had to do if they were going to accept her. They put auditions on hold and then we missed them. We planned on trying again for the adult play later in the year. That time never came for Anna.

On Father's Day, we decided it was safe enough to drive to Texas to a remote dinosaur museum for our toddler. We knew there would be a limited amount of people there; in fact, we were the first of the day and the only people there the entire time. It was a great Father's Day for my husband. We stopped for ice cream on the way home, and the day ended without incident. We were happy. A couple of weeks later, I came down with what I thought was a sinus infection. I was treated at an urgent care. They said they were not testing me for Covid because I had not been in contact with any known cases, and they sent me home, something I will always live to regret. On July 4th, we had a small dinner and a few fireworks with one other family and enjoyed our last family gathering.

July 5th, after attending church on television, Anna asked me to take her to get a pair of jazz shoes because she had already plotted to add yet another dance class into the mix for her upcoming year. So off we went. The next day, Anna started dance camp and attended on Monday and Tuesday. On Tuesday, her dad picked her up, and she wasn't feeling well. We advised her to just take it easy for the week, and she could start back up the following week. She was sad but understood. With an autoimmune disease, fatigue and body aches are nothing new. She relaxed for the next couple of days, and on Thursday, she felt better. On Friday, she wanted to take a nap, so her dad carried her upstairs. When she awoke, she called for me, and I had to help her downstairs. My husband and I knew she had to go to the hospital. She was lethargic and unable to carry her own weight. Her skin color was off and very pale. He carried Anna to our car, and I took her. She walked into the hospital next to me, and two hours later, we left without her.

When we got there, the nurse put her in a wheelchair to be triaged. They did a sepsis screening on her. All vitals were normal, but she was very cold. It seemed like her Reynaud's was going haywire. Once they put her in a room and placed a warming blanket on her, they then put in an order for a Medi-flight to the nearest children's hospital. But before the doctor could get back into the room and have an IV started, Anna went into cardiac arrest. I screamed for help, and they rushed her to another, bigger room where an incredible amount of hospital staff attempted to save her life. I called our church deacon and my husband and told them to come right away. When our priest and deacon came, they were allowed in to give her last rites. My husband arrived, and we waited in a room close by. Eventually, the doctor found a very faint heartbeat, and we had a tiny glimmer of hope. They asked us to come to the room to hold her hand and talk to her, but they lost her heartbeat again. At 7:52 pm, July 10th, 2020, the doctor pronounced her deceased. Anna lived for 13 years, 8 months, and 8 days.

After we left the hospital and returned home to give our other children the worst news they'd ever heard, the hospital called to tell us they had tested Anna for Covid, and she was positive. The following day, the rest of our family got tested, and all our results came back positive. We do not know where we had contracted it, and as far as we know, we did not give it to anyone else. Our family had to grieve in isolation for three weeks. We couldn't have visitors besides the people who dropped food and flowers at our door. Because we could not have a normal funeral, the funeral home arranged for a private viewing for me, my husband, and our four remaining children before they cremated Anna. We were fortunate to have a limited funeral at our church once we were out of isolation. It was livestreamed and over 2,500 people viewed it. So many things about a Covid death are much more difficult than other deaths.

There are two timelines now for my family; one in our imaginations has Anna in it, growing, becoming the actress she always wanted to be, having a big family like ours, celebrating her siblings' accomplishments, conquering her illness, and setting an example for other youth like her. The other is our reality, the one where we wake up, and she is not there. Anna is no longer here to be a big or little sister to her siblings. She isn't here to support them, and they can no longer do the same for her. Anna is not here to act silly with her friends, or grow up, learn to drive, go to prom, graduate, have a family of her own, or pursue her dreams of being an actress. Our world has lost the brilliance it once had with Anna in it.

We continue our regular family traditions, mainly for our toddler, David, because he deserves to know the same family that Anna knew. However, we have added a few new traditions to make it through the tough days, like her date of passing and her birthday. We eat Chinese food from Anna's favorite restaurant, visit her grave, and leave some sort of treat there. We reminisce about all of our fond memories with her. On her birthday, November 2nd, which is also All Souls Day in the Catholic faith, we attend Mass and celebrate, not just her, but all the souls who have gone before us. After church, we go home to eat and sing "Happy Birthday." Then we release balloons, and we each take a moment to say something we are thankful for that Anna taught us.

Our family created a nonprofit in Anna's name to give youth with scleroderma, and their siblings, help when starting or continuing secondary schooling. The Anna Belle Carter Memorial Foundation will keep Anna's memory alive and help change lives, which she cannot do here on Earth anymore. It is our mission to offer three scholarships per year. To learn more information about Anna's foundation, please search us on the internet or Facebook.

One of Anna's sixth-grade journal entries had this quote from Mother Teresa: "I alone cannot change the world, but I can cast a stone across the waters to create many ripples." I knew in my heart Anna would change the world. I just never fathomed this would be how. Her ripples will go far and wide. I have heard it said that grief is the true price of love. I can now testify from the depths of my soul that this is true.

If Anna were still here, she would want to help people who are immunocompromised, like she was. She would wonder why so many people are hesitant to protect each other by wearing a simple face mask. At her tender age, Anna would ask, *Why not just do it if it can save another person's life?* My sweet Anna would encourage others to be kind and compassionate to each other because everyone is struggling with something. In honor of Anna, I ask you to please think of others and just be kind.

I will leave you with one of Anna's creative works. She wrote this poem when she was in third grade at Bechtel Elementary School, and they published it in the *Sun Art Magazine* when we lived in Okinawa.

I Am Special

When I'm by myself and I close my eyes,
I'm a superhero flying off a building,
I'm a baby near computers,
I'm a president in the White House,
I'm a teacher sitting during a lesson,
I'm a powerful woman outside a school,
I'm whatever I want to be,
And anything I care to be,
And when I open my eyes,
What I care to be
Is me!

~

ABOUT AMBER

Amber Carter grew up in Binghamton, New York. She is the mother of five children and a military spouse to a U.S. Marine. Amber loves being a mother and always strives to help others. She currently lives in Lawton, Oklahoma, with her husband and their family.

Amber is the Pastoral Life Coordinator and Coordinator of Religious Education for her local Catholic military community. In her free time, she enjoys watching her children play sports, working outside in their yard, creating arts and crafts, and spending time with the family doing recreational things.

You can connect with Amber via social media and through email at acartermomof5@gmail.com. If you are interested in finding out more about her daughter Anna's memorial foundation, please visit @AnnaBelleCarterScholarship on Facebook or scan this QR code to visit the ABCMF web site:

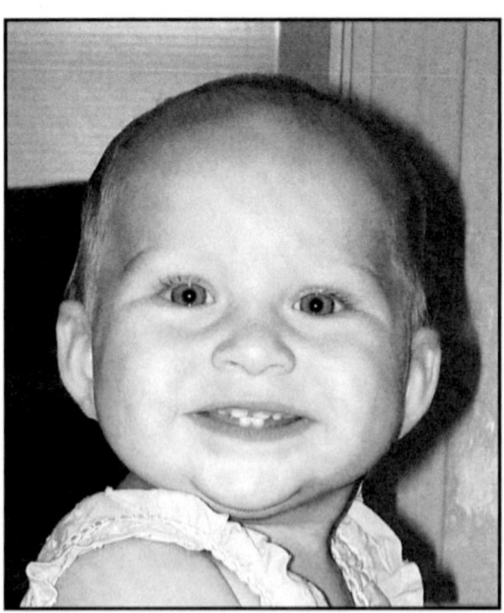

Anna at 11 months old.

Our family at station 8 on Mt Fuji.

Anna and her siblings at the Painted Forest in New Mexico, on the way to the Grand Canyon.

Anna's first day of her last year of school (7th grade).

Anna and her brother practicing for the Daddy-Daughter dance (he stood in for her Dad).

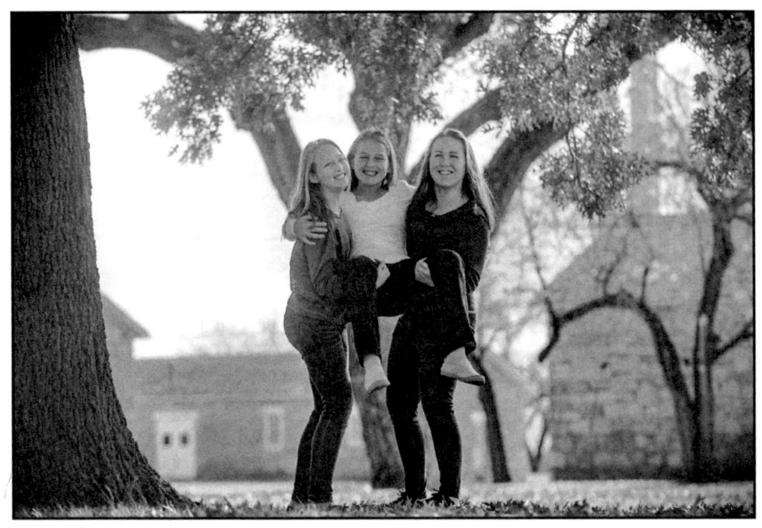

Fall family photo, 2019, Anna with her sisters.

Anna at her last recital 2020.

Anna and her siblings in Washington DC.

Anna and her Hip Hop trophy.

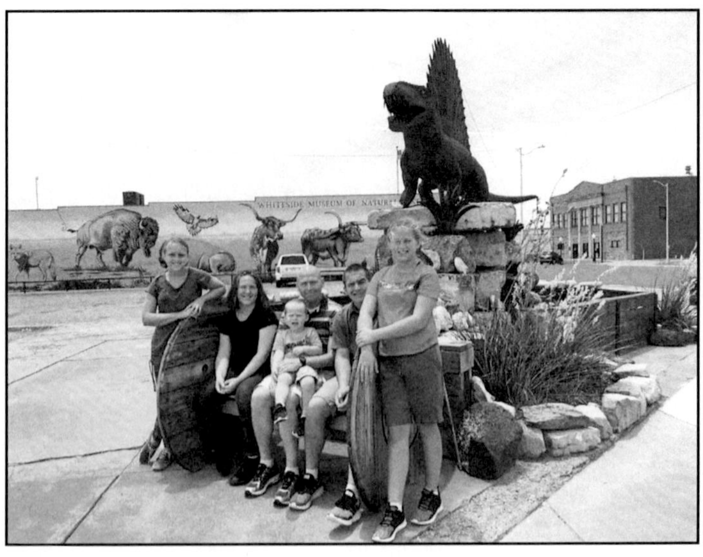

Our last trip anywhere as a family. Fathers Day 2020.

FACES OF COVID VICTIMS

PUTTING A FACE TO THE NUMBER

Images Drawn by Hannah Ernst, Artist & Chapter Author

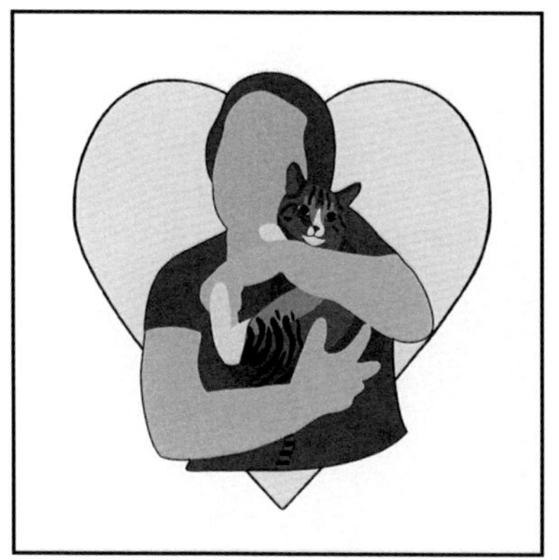

Vivian Meitzler

Rose Phillips

Hal Stein

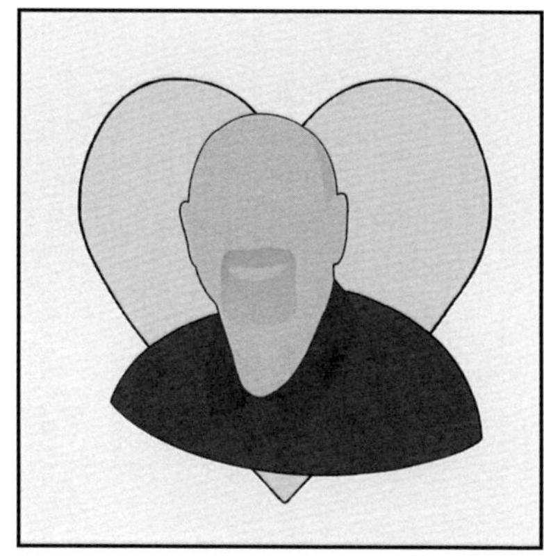

Paul Letizi

Mary Castro

Antoine (Tony) M. Nixon

Cheryl Stedman

Angelo Mazzola

Isabelle Garza

Vince Foreman

Joni Lancos

Ray Maskell

Carmelina Cabanillas

Louis Sarrel

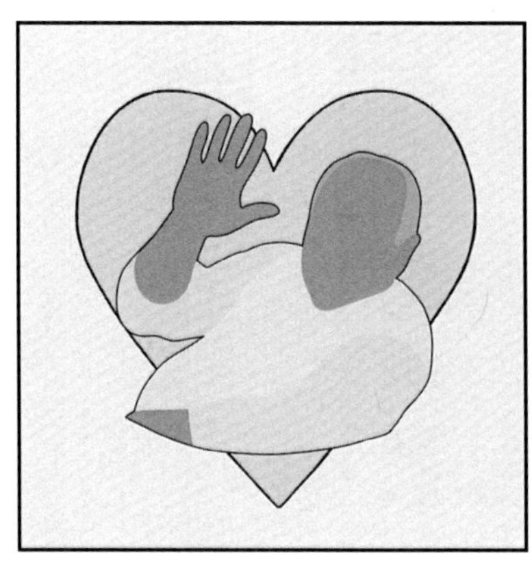
Frank Sirico

Anastasia Koiveroglou

Hosea Richardson

Cal Schoenfeld

Anna Carter

SURVIVING GRIEF

As you can see through the collection of stories bravely shared in the pages prior, the process of grieving a loved one is just too complex to streamline. The five stages of grief, denial, anger, bargaining, depression and acceptance represent the framework of healing from loss, and it is by no means a linear path. Walking yourself through the path to recovery will most likely be one of the hardest roads you will have to learn from. It is important that you do so with love. A self-love that is patient and does not shame or guilt us when we feel a bit more comfortable sitting in sorrow than in acceptance of moving forward. It may be comforting to give yourself permission to feel both, the version of you that wants to recover and feel ok, and also the piece of you that couldn't bear to think of moving beyond a particular stage of the grieving process. Grieving is messy and there is no one right way of doing it. Respect the limitations and needs of your mind, body, and spirit, and reach out to loved ones who can help hold space when overwhelming emotions arise. As the mind tries to make sense of loss and the drastic changes that follow, we can support the process by reflecting on comforting memories and honoring our loved ones with memorials. We can often process traumatic losses more comfortably through creative mediums like painting, poetry, collage making and music making. The expression of grief through art goes beyond words and allows the creator to present pain in a way that can be profoundly healing.

Remember to prioritize your mental health daily. Seek support from friends, family, support groups, or professional grief counselors. Grieving the loss of a loved one while managing the fears and anxieties associated with the COVID-19 pandemic can be extremely overwhelming. It is common for our minds to cluster fears together, especially when it is reinforced with loss. Pay attention to your own anxieties and how you are using your inner dialogue to work through big emotions that may be from a cluster of fears.

Healing from loss in a healthy way is to experience overwhelming emotions as they come, instead of denying the body the ability to process and store it for future protection. Healthy healing is by no means meant to look good or be experienced silently. There is no right or wrong way for healthy grieving, and any loss is significant. If you are having a particularly hard time understanding and coping with the loss of a loved one, please reach out to a professional for help right away. You do not have to do this alone.

Rachelle Coffey, LPC-IT

www.opticresources.org